William Black is the autho~~r~~ *Land That Thyme Forgot*, a~~nd~~ Sophie Grigson of several be~~stselling travel books~~. *Fish, Organic* and *Travels à la Carte*. He has sourced ingredients (fish in particular) for many of the UK's finest restaurants and he lives in Oxfordshire.

PLATS DU JOUR

A Journey to the Heart of French Food

WILLIAM BLACK

CORGI BOOKS

TRANSWORLD PUBLISHERS
61–63 Uxbridge Road, London W5 5SA
a division of The Random House Group Ltd
www.rbooks.co.uk

PLATS DU JOUR
A CORGI BOOK: 9780552154604

First published in Great Britain in 2007 by Bantam Press
a division of Transworld Publishers
Corgi edition published 2008

Map drawn by Joy Gosney

This book is a work of non-fiction based on the experiences and
recollections of the author. The author has stated to the publishers that,
except in such minor respects not affecting the substantial accuracy of
the work, the contents of this book are true.

Every effort has been made to obtain the necessary permissions with
reference to copyright material. We apologize for any omissions in this
respect and will be pleased to make the appropriate acknowledgements in
any future edition.

A CIP catalogue record for this book is available from the British Library.

Addresses for Random House Group Ltd companies outside the UK
can be found at: www.randomhouse.co.uk
The Random House Group Ltd Reg. No. 954009

The Random House Group Limited supports The Forest Stewardship
Council (FSC), the leading international forest certification organisation.
All our titles that are printed on Greenpeace approved FSC certified paper
carry the FSC logo. Our paper procurement policy can be found at
www.rbooks.co.uk/environment

Typeset in 12/14.5pt Sabon by
Falcon Oast Graphic Art Ltd.

Printed and bound in Great Britain by
Printed in the UK by CPI Cox & Wyman, Reading, RG1 8EX.

2 4 6 8 10 9 7 5 3 1

To Claire,
with love.

CONTENTS

RECIPES

ACKNOWLEDGEMENTS

To all the Vérys, the Carrés, the Thibaults, and to everyone I met along the way, a *grand merci*.

To Doug Young, Linda Evans and Emma Musgrave, and all behind the scenes at Transworld, thank you, too.

To the editing skills of Kate Samano, thank you for all your skilful snipping.

And to Heather Holden Brown, thanks for your energetic support.

There is an earlier book called *Plats du Jour* that some of you may know, first published in 1957 and written by the estimable Patience Gray and Primrose Boyd. It was called 'a design for action in the kitchen'. This is more a design for reflection in the kitchen.

My biggest thanks are to Claire for her love and support, and to Lola, Floflo, Dee, Chacha and Georgie for loving France and speaking French with such devotion.

Bon appétit!

Ile de Batz Roscoff

Aber-Wrac'h

Mont St Michel

Binic

Pleumeur-Bodou

Vannes

Quiberon

Pyla

Bayonne

Tarbes

Espelette Pau

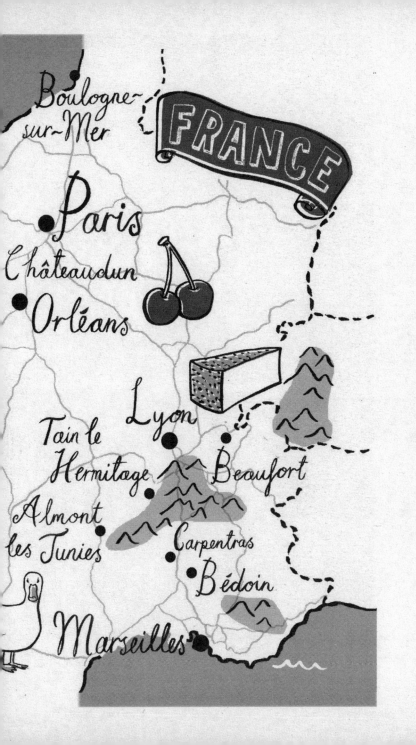

Introduction

EACH YEAR, AS SUMMER ARRIVES AND THE GOAT'S cheese supplies are getting dangerously low, people begin to plan their annual migration. Two-for-one ferry offers tumble into the inbox, and thoughts turn almost ritualistically to fun, to good food, to holidays. To France, the sacred hexagon. To the first time. The last time. And those glorious markets.

This migration has a global feel to it. In the Netherlands, people load caravans with enough food to see them through their week away in France. Meanwhile in America, enthusiastic citizens set off for the country they know better as Paris, while in the Far East tour groups polish their camera lenses and dutifully collect as requested at the right time and the right place for their long journey westwards, dreaming of what might be in store for them.

Many set off from the UK, too, stuffed improbably into a car, and arrive dehydrated, storm tossed or sun roasted. They exhale, relax and unwind. A warm smile envelops the jaded soul. Oh, how we all love France!

If my love for France has moved beyond the hopeless infatuation it once was, it still holds true. Years spent working and living there have brought a sense of familiarity, but now, well into middle age, I am about to set out on a new journey around France, a sort of guided fugue, to revisit a country that some people said had lost its sense of superiority, and was riddled with malaise and self-doubt.

To make this journey more familiar, more personal, much of it is made in the company of my French family, for as the pages turn and summer approaches, so does my second marriage. My fiancée Claire is French. So is our little daughter, Lola, who could say Camembert at two. And it is due to them that I have France in my bones once more.

But food is my forte; another passion, anthropology, my distant training. Wherever I am, I love to tease out the story of the why and the what we eat, to try and provide a glimpse into a people's very soul. My formative years were spent lugging food back from France to London in an Aladdin's cave of a truck, to supply some of the city's most exigent chefs. By the time I gave all that up, I had been travelling to and fro between France and the UK for about fifteen years. It felt like a hundred. Every week I crossed a now-distant frontier that divided a people who loved to talk about food, to eat and celebrate the glories of taste, and one that tended to glorify excess, and that mainly of drink, rather than food; one where talking about the brilliance of a chef was almost seen as perverse.

My my, things have indeed changed. The chef has now become a media superstar in Britain, his success often depending more on his ability to entertain than to cook. But then chefs always were complex beasts.

Among them is an old friend of mine – my culinary mentor, if you like – the French-born but proudly Gascon chef Pierre Koffmann, who sought and found his fortune in London. He is in a way a chef's chef. Wary of the camera lens, his dedication to his métier has always been total, his working hours behind the stove, and his knowledge, prodigious. He achieved the golden accolade of three Michelin stars in 1993, back in the days when they really mattered. And it was from him that I learnt that good cooking is nothing without the finest produce. He encouraged me to bring back the best that I could find. And that meant from France, naturally. I travelled high and low, and gradually established a network of the most fabulous food suppliers. But that all seems rather distant now. I moved on, and dabbled elsewhere, and lost contact with this particular and very personal foodweb.

Twenty years ago, French cuisine really did rule the world. It was the benchmark, much as Italian courtly food was in the Renaissance, a truly global and aspirational model.

Or rather it ruled *a* world, one that was essentially urban, technical and élitist. One that revolved around *un* restaurant, *le* chef, terms which, of course, together with the word 'cuisine', indicate that this dominance was long established and highly successful.

The language of a working kitchen was almost always French, echoing with cries of *Ça marche!* and *Oui, chef!* and *chaud*, particularly during *service*. The *mise en place* was part of the pre-service routine, the essential business of preparation. The kitchens were divided up into sections, each ruled by a *chef de partie*.

So how then, I wondered, was French food culture faring today?

New food movements have appeared world-wide to replace the *roi absolu*, haute cuisine. A revolution? Perhaps. Almost all of them have come from outside France, and have in turn encouraged a deal of navel-gazing within. The unashamedly cosmopolitan cultures of Australia, the USA and to some extent Great Britain have created a food culture that reflects the decline of the national, or perhaps the dominance of the global. Molecular gastronomy (even if no one is too sure what it actually is) seems to be thriving, and is often seen to be an energizing, radical attempt to break the traditional model that was once called haute cuisine. French haute cuisine, that is.

Even the business of producing food has begun to change over the past two decades. Organic and biodynamic methods of production are gaining wider acceptance, and are fast becoming almost mainstream. We much-abused consumers are rather fond of the idea of protecting the environment, once seen as the domain of well-meaning sandal-toting do-gooders. But it now concerns us all.

And what was happening to the rich regional food culture of France? And to those rootsy dishes that reflect their *terroir* and food culture so deeply?

Terroir. It's a key word, and one that is hard to translate, into English at least. *Terroiristes* are thick on the ground in France, and the visceral closeness that French produce has to its physical earthy roots gives French food a primacy over all others, according to many.

The idea of returning once more to France was intriguing. It seemed there was much to see, and much to reflect upon. And so off I set one autumn day to criss-cross the country, taking trains of big speed and planes of little legroom. At times I drove, and walked, covering some, but far from all, of the country's regions. Some were places I knew well. Others I had never seen before.

1

Pâté de Campagne

ONE WINDY APRIL DAY WAY BACK IN THE 1970S I SAILED across the English Channel in a solid wooden ketch, a spotty seventeen-year-old who had never been abroad. We sipped warming chicken stock to keep our hearts from stopping altogether, and leapt up and down checking the compass and the radio to make sure we weren't heading for disaster. It was all fabulously exciting.

As the night wore on, we scraped past vast supertankers and were inundated with salty brine as their wash swooped us up and down like toytown boats. But slowly, oh so slowly, the lights of France came closer and closer still. The orange glow of Le Havre began to fill the sky, and the stars twinkled above magnificently. We arrived late into the night, weighed anchor and slept a little.

And in the morning I climbed up into the

dew-spattered cockpit that smelt of varnish and *bouillon*, and saw the guts of a vast techno bridge that swooped from one side of the estuary to the other, a veritable paean to modernity. This was and is le Pont de Tancarville, a magnificent, awe-inspiring icon of the creative industrial French spirit that still lives on. You see it in the TGV, *les trains à grande vitesse* that criss and cross the country so emphatically, so rapidly and so efficiently. You see it in the Pyramide at Le Louvre in Paris; in the Eiffel tower; in the breathtakingly beautiful bridge at Millau that looms magically through the clouds. It is the French state at work, mustering the finest talent from all over the world to give the country its unique identity.

But at that time in the morning – and this was many years ago – le Pont de Tancarville was quite empty save for one lone figure tramping across from south to north, silhouetted by the morning sun.

I looked at him closely. I remember him well because it was all so laughable. He was pushing a bicycle, had a beret on his head and a baguette under his arm, and was dressed from tip to toe in *bleu de travail*, those blue overalls so beloved of French working men. You could almost hear the accordion wheeze and whine as he walked across. He should have been playing *pétanque*, I suppose, to remove any shred of doubt that this was indeed France. It seemed quite remarkable to me that at last I was abroad.

And then on we went to Paris. Down the River Seine, cluttered with dead fish and muddy spume that spewed from the weirs and dams as the water tumbled over. On through Rouen, and then eventually, as the serpentine Seine passed Argenteuil, we came across the vast Renault factory, the centre then of much radical thought and revolutionary practice. It was still churning out cars at the time – Renault 8s, I think – that all, without exception, had yellow eyes. France loved to be different.

That night we moored in the shadow of the Place de la Concorde, right in the heart of Paris. I went and watched the mad rush of yellow headlights and listened to the strange-sounding klaxons. Duh duh duh, they went. In the morning, I joined the modest crowds in the Louvre and gawped at the Mona Lisa, still pre Code, unsullied and innocent somehow. And then a few days later, off we set down the River Seine towards the South, the sun and the Mediterranean. After Paris, France became even more entrancing.

When we arrived at Joigny, a local family fêted us, and drove us around in an open-topped Deux Chevaux that wobbled and bounced to its own fluid rhythm. The father was an ex-maquisard who had a traditional sense of hospitality, and plied us with wine and food. He liked the British.

In Burgundy, the river turned to a canal, and France became more remote. I loved wandering off to the local store and bringing back some lunch for us all. Big bottles of red wine, *vin* that was very *ordinaire*, emblazoned with stars around the top and a finger-cutting tin cap that covered one of those plastic capsules that once littered the countryside like chewing gum in modern cities. They were everywhere. The wine glugged coarsely from the bottle into our Duralex glasses, frothing lightly and almost glowing in the sun.

Then to the baker for a baguette. *Bien cuite*, crusty and still warm. It was impossible not to nibble the end on the way back to the boat. To the *pâtisserie* for a cake or three. And whenever I could, I queued awkwardly in the local *boucherie* for a thick chunk of *pâté de campagne*, wrapped in waxed white paper peppered with red checks and pictures of smiling pigs saying, Eat me. Kill me. Chop me up!

Moist and unctuous, the pâté could be scooped or cut, and just eaten oh so simply with a cornichon or two and a torn chunk of baguette. It was full of subtle flavours, of pork and pepper, and a little hint of cloves here and nutmeg there. It spoke of warmth and red wine and sleepy afternoons.

So *pâté de campagne* brings me right back to the past and my very own private France, the country that I fell so much in love with all those years ago.

Twenty years later, I moved to France, to live and work in the blustery north, in the country's biggest fishing port, Boulogne sur Mer. Oh, the hours we spent arguing! My workmates were a disparate bunch of Boulonais. They had no doubts that French was the best language. That the French were the best lovers. That French food was the best in the world. These were the days when restaurants were wallowing in Francophilia, imitating and reproducing the classics and newer versions of the classics, and that curious thing called nouvelle cuisine, which was the first time in a very long while that the French actually admitted to being influenced by, or even interested in, food from elsewhere – the Far East in this case.

Before that, you have to look way back into the early nineteenth century, when Anglomania took France by storm, and restaurants – still then a relatively new phenomenon there – modelled themselves on English taverns.

Pâté de campagne is now part of the supermarket repertoire, stuffed into plastic and peppered with preservatives. But then, every town and every village had its butchers. Usually a whole cooperative array, each with their own specialities. Pâté was a glorious mix of cuts and flavours, a thick meaty slice that was moist and inviting.

It was beyond the regional then, as it is now. Its roots were wide and far-reaching, as were the baguettes. At every stop, we bought some more pâté, and became expertly critical. Too dry here. Too spiced there. *Pâté de campagne* is not impossible to re-create, thankfully, and every now and again I troop off to my local butcher to stock up on some fatty slices of pork, clean off the mincer, and watch the flesh disappear into tubes and nozzles, and become something that is, for me at least, truly evocative.

Pâté de campagne

Serves 8

Ingredients
2 onions
1 soupspoon lard
200g pork back fat, thinly sliced
500g fresh belly of pork
500g pork chine
150g shoulder of veal
150g pork liver
1 clove garlic, crushed
3 eggs, beaten
100ml eau de vie
1 tsp quatre épices (a mixture of pepper, cloves, nutmeg and ginger)
½ tsp chopped thyme
2 bay leaves
15g sea salt
6g ground black pepper

PÂTÉ DE CAMPAGNE

Method

Peel and finely chop the onions, then fry them in the lard over a low heat for 5 minutes.

Line a terrine with fresh back fat, leaving some spare hanging over the edges.

Cut the meat into large dice and mince into a bowl on a medium setting. Add the eggs and garlic and mix thoroughly, then add the onions, eau de vie, quatre épices, thyme, salt and pepper. Mix by hand.

Prepare a bain marie that is large enough to hold the terrine and bring it to the boil. Add the mixture to the terrine, pressing down to make sure there are no air spaces left. Cover with the spare back fat, and put the bay leaves on the surface. Cook for 2½ hours in the oven at 180°C.

When the cooking is finished, remove the terrine and leave it to rest for 15 minutes. Then put a weighted wooden board (or similar) on the surface, and allow to cool completely. Place in the fridge for 24 hours before serving.

Translated from *Recettes d'Autrefois*, Reader's Digest, France, 1995.

2

Cotignac

ANY TRIP TO FRANCE SHOULD START WITH A VISIT TO a market. This is the best way, perhaps the only way, to enter into the gastronomic spirit of the country. In Italy it tends to be the beauty of the towns, the cities, the people that teases the eye so readily. But in France, for me at least, it is the markets. From the Ardennes right down to the southern tip of Corsica, all bombard the senses with their perfumes and their colours, which evolve in a slow, eternal rhythm, changing with a seasonal regularity that most of us crave.

Well, it's market day in Vannes, a wind-blown Breton city on the ravishingly beautiful Morbihan coast. It has its own rather subdued prettiness, its tall angular houses dripping with tacky red pelargoniums. This is where Claire's family live, and where we have begun to establish our French roots.

I walk down the streets where only weeks before we had lingered in holiday mode. The shop that was full of buttons and lurid trinkets in summer is still just as full of buttons and just as empty in October. I wish 'bonjour' to Madame, who so courteously mended my glasses for no charge.

I glance at the *boulangerie*, where they make such a delicious *kouign amann*, a defining Breton gateau of monumental richness that oozes butter from its very soul. I find it almost irresistible and make a note to make my own one day. But I resist. This is the sort of thing that is better left to the expert, to the artisan. Better by far simply to rely on local lore and reputation, and buy the best.

The merchants arrive, and unravel their clanking stalls. The man from the *mairie* wanders around and asks for his rent. Café-owners sweep the pavement and set out their chairs, and wait for the tables to fill.

If the summer rush of tourists has now gone, the smoking Celtic travellers with their rasta locks, pierced noses and dogs on leashes have not. Every town, every city, every village in France seems to have its hardcore market-goers, the essence of the place, those who know the stalls with practised intimacy. I begin to do the rounds with Claire's parents, Dany and Jean-Paul. Jean-Paul scurries off to do the things he always does. He prefers to do them alone. That's fine by me. Dany and I look at baby clothes.

I know how Vannes works, its nooks and crannies, where to find the best beaches, who sells the best cheese. The fundamentals, in other words. It is the sea that I love so down here. It scintillates. The light is brilliant. When I lived in the far north of France, all seemed grey, windy and watery.

So, first a coffee, my habitual *pain au raisin* and a copy of the local paper, *Ouest-France*. I get the feeling that in the provinces you might just miss reports of global holocaust, tucked into a middle section of the paper after the main news about tragic motorcycle accidents and forest fires, local grievances, meetings of ancient combatants and bagpipe concerts. All the French nationals, with the exception of *Le Figaro*, seem to be hard pressed these days. They are a Parisian thing. The regionals, however, thrive.

So I thumb through the paper and read of weird food festivals, of local life, and begin to feel as parochial as everyone else. Local papers encourage a sense of place, of region, and a provincial spirit. For years, I couldn't work out why French Sunday newspapers were so awful. Elsewhere, Sundays seemed to be about absorbing endless reams of newsprint, and the minute analysis of everything and nothing. But now I understand. In France, on Sunday everyone joins the queue for the local *pâtisserie*. There's no time for papers at all. And it's the best day to eat *kouign amann*.

Come Sunday and France erupts with heaving

lines of patient punters waiting their turn to delve into the litany of familiar, lovingly crafted creamy *pâtisseries*, of Paris Brests and Religieuses au Café, of glazed and purple *tartes* and *tourtes*. I hesitate to use the English word 'cake'; it has neither the finesse nor the subtlety of *pâtisserie*. I am reminded of a word of advice often offered in France: you'll rarely get a *pâtissier* who is a good *boulanger*, and vice versa. So that's another shop you need to discover. Then there's the butcher, the fishmonger, the cheese shop. And to top it all, there's the market. Heavenly? Almost.

So if you're staying long, then you'll need to find a good *pâtissier*. Join that queue. Savour the shop's openness. Almost everything else will be shut, for the French still believe that shopping hours should be strictly controlled, and that families should sit down and eat together at *midi*. The idea is that you take the pastries back to Mémé and Pépé, or visit some ancient aunt whom you don't really like, bearing these creamy, heart-stopping gifts.

When I arrived at the café with my *pain au raisin* tucked into a little paper bag, I gripped the chair tightly and asked for what I knew I would not get: a coffee Italian style. Coffee lore is still resolutely pre-Starbucks, away from Paris at least.

'Ah! Non, monsieur! We don't do that here,' café-owners will emphatically tell you.

So a cappuccino can be a dangerous thing to ask for in France. You may well get a squirt of cream from a *bombe*. Eruptive. Unpleasant. I stick to *'un café très serré, s'il vous plaît'*, 'a very strong coffee, please'. It usually does the job. Requests for a macchiato are met with utter incomprehension. A café noisette with warm milk almost approximates.

The fish stall beckons. Off we go to the covered market, where earlier I had seen piles of bright-eyed, dazzling silver sardines. *'Il ne manque pas une écaille!'* they said. Not a scale missing, a blessing of perfection. We'll eat them raw for lunch, delicately filleted, sprinkled with lemon juice and olive oil, and pick the scales from our teeth. We muse over the *bars*, sea bass, caught hours before in a wide-eyed gasp, beautiful and glamorous fish. They now have to be labelled and segregated from the proletarian farmed sea bass that have become almost ubiquitous.

Then we pass the cheese-seller, who has noticed us in the distance.

'Ah! Your friend from England!' she says to Dany and Jean-Paul. 'Bonjour, monsieur! Welcome!' I shake her hand, and thank her for her contribution to my cholesterol level. 'I didn't get any Beaufort this week, it wasn't good enough,' she tells me. My love for this cheese is constant and irrepressible. Any visit must include a ritual purchase of Beaufort.

Beaufort is made high up in the French Savoie, right on the Swiss border. It is a cheese to savour, subtle and intricate. It is my perfect cheese, the cheese of my dreams, and I had long dreamed of visiting the village where it is made. I have problems with those stinking cheeses like Munster and Vacherin. I have to be in the right mood for that sort of gastronomic blast, although a smelly cheese can be a remarkably subtle thing.

Here in France, so famous for its extraordinary range of *fromages*, cheese is just one way to savour the changes, the variations of this complex, vast, maddening country. The variations of taste, the whys and the wherefores. What makes this cheese so perfect and this one so dull? Why the difference? Wherefore the difference? And how on earth do you know what to look for?

We move down to the organic section. Past the carrots with dirty faces, beetroot with rough and tough scars. Even celery, usually so anodyne and wrapped in plastic, seems to have a little life to it here. Why do people buy these *produits bios*? Is it a health or taste thing?

Bio means organic in French. It is short for *biologique*. Then there is the fascinating system called biodynamics, which is in a way organic plus, and uses the force of the moon and the stars to guide planting and sowing times. It calls for odd potions of rotted cow's horn to be sprinkled over growing crops in the most minuscule amounts, but shares with organic farming a firm and verifiable belief that feeding the soil should be the focus for food production, rather than the tinkering of 'conventional' agriculture that relies on artificial chemicals, and does so, as we shall see, at a price.

The *bios* stick together, surrounded by the cheaper stalls around the edges of the market. It's a mesmerizing time of year, perhaps the best month of all. The wet autumn has begun to tease wild mushrooms from the ground, and the orchard fruits cluster in huge wooden boxes. There are tempting piles of glorious Reinettes d'Orléans, the perfect apple for a Tarte Tatin, luscious and lively. Even the odd quince has arrived, which excites me deeply and makes me dream of the days I will soon spend making *cotignac* (quince paste, a.k.a. membrillo) back home.

Cotignac

An autumnal treat. You may know this better as membrillo. It goes as well with an old Manchego as with a mature Basque ewe's cheese, an Ossau-Iraty. Cotignac is now said to be a speciality of Orléans where it is made in moulds resembling the face of Joan of Arc.

Method

Get as many quinces as you can. Make sure they are ripe: they should smell strongly of quince. Wash off the fluffy down, and cut into quarters.

Don't worry about the pips. Put them all in a large pan – a preserving pan is ideal – and add half as much water as you have quinces. Cook briskly for at least 30 minutes.

Pass them through a mouli légumes. If there is one thing any good French cook has, it's a mouli légumes. They are indispensable. Weigh the quince mixture, then add the same weight in sugar. Return to a clean pan, and cook on top of the stove until when you drag a wooden spoon across the bottom of the pan it remains clear to view. This can be a matter of hours. Be patient and think of France.

Pour into baking trays to cool, or a Joan of Arc mould if you have one, and allow to dry for a few days. Cut into diamond shapes, and roll lightly in granulated sugar. They will keep for at least a year. Delicious dipped in good chocolate.

One man has a table dotted with mounds of *bolets*, the poor man's cep, and *bleuets*, or blewits, with a gorgeous purple tinge to their flesh. You can inhale their earthiness. He has a damp handful of *girolles*, or chanterelles, their ribs flecked with pine needles, and even a few dark and doomy *trompettes de la mort*, trumpets of death – or, as they were once called in English, Horns of Plenty.

We stop and chat to a man who is rather shyly offering edible seaweed on little toasts, with anchovies and tomatoes. He looks remarkably like a penguin, and is so nervous he can hardly look us in the eye, but we smile sweetly, listen to his patter, and patter on.

While the woman who specializes in the delectable strawberries from Plougastel is winding down, her season nearly over, her neighbour, *la dame aux framboises*, is positively inundated with richly perfumed autumn raspberries. But just a few weeks ago, things were entirely different.

It is odd how a pile of strawberries always seems to bring a smile to the face. The universal appeal of sweetness, perhaps. Strawberries just seem to have that unique ability to soothe and titillate the senses. Unless, that is, your path crosses, as it surely will, a soulless strawberry that has been pummelled into life by artificial this and that to give retailers their supposed holy grail: strawberries for sale 365 days of the year. We are in the midst of a revolution, a backlash against this affront to our senses, the supposition of our desires.

For many, this is part of the appeal of France. The idea that it is somehow in a purer, unsullied state of being, where the evil world of global capitalism is being held in check. The truth is not quite so glib. Supermarkets in France are playing the global game with skill and great success.

In Vannes market, however, the ebb and flow of the seasons is still reflected in the stalls. A few weeks after the strawberries are at their peak, the redcurrants and *cassis* begin; high summer arrives with the tourists, and the market moves from soft fruit to orchard fruit, then back again, with a final flourish, to the autumn raspberry.

We pass another *fromagerie*. Dany tells me, 'I never go in there, it's far too expensive.'

But I am drawn once more by the siren call of good Beaufort. 'Dany, he has some,' I say excitedly, and tug her into the cool, ripe air of the cheese shop.

I ask for something obscure, some Laguiole, not a local cheese at all but from down in Auvergne, and watch and inspect while the proprietor talks to me. His cheese looks magnificent. And so does he. The shop is elegant, clean, neatly laid out, and yes, a little more expensive than its competitors. But in a part of France more famous for butter than cheese, it is lovely to come across someone fired with enthusiasm about his métier, a man who can be passionate about a handsome bunch of *crottins* (goat's cheese). It is still, thankfully, a defining quality of France that the repertoire of indigenous food knowledge, despite everything, survives.

We move outside, attracted by piles of perfect Reines Claudes and Mirabelles, still covered with a virginal bloom and oozing freshness from their unblemished plummy bodies. There were still a few exquisite *pêches blanches*, white peaches, deliciously scented in the morning sun. And sanguine *pêches de vignes*, and peculiar disc-shaped *pêches plates*.

How do *you* use a market? Do you wander, observe and pounce? Do you stay with the regulars and trust in familiarity? I tend to cruise, to watch from afar, and judge at the end of round one. And then return and finish the deal.

I need some Reines Claudes to see me through the hours of driving ahead, so I can suck on the stones and lap up the kilometres without going mad. One stall is notably cheaper, so we queue and wait and watch.

'Ha! Only one kilo,' the stall-holder says mockingly to Madame at the front, who looks far from delighted to be addressed at all. 'Buy some more. Make some jam. I'm sure you've got nothing else to do this weekend!'

'Monsieur, it's just the fruit I want, not a lecture.' And she huffs off.

'Parisienne!' he mutters darkly under his breath.

The next morning, I am due to set off for the distant south-west of France. I say goodbye to Dany and Jean-Paul, and climb into the car for my bum-numbing trek. I have enough Reines Claudes for a very long drive.

3

Salmis de Palombes

TAKE THE D ROADS, EVERYONE TOLD ME. TAKE THE D roads. Which is all very fine and dandy, but when you begin to clock up quadruple digits on the odometer, you start to yearn for the relaxing monotony of the *péages*, the network of fast toll roads that gets you from A to B in relative comfort. But at a price.

So I began to meander down south from Brittany through the Vendée, and stopped at a little market in a town called Michel Chef Chef, attracted by its peculiarly weird name. The market was minuscule, and dead. Chef chef was gone gone. I D'd onwards towards Bordeaux.

A day in this most elegant city had to be finished by eating its great speciality, a *côte de boeuf* grilled over the cinders of an open fire, with blood oozing from its very pores, in one of Bordeaux's finest restaurants, La Tupina. It was, let me say, exquisitely perfect, tender and full of taste, served with *pommes frites* cooked in goose fat. I dare not call them chips. This was meat at its best. Matured, not hustled to the table. Sourced from the country's finest beef herds. Not far from Bordeaux is the town of Bazas, which is renowned for its beef. *Boeufs de Bazas* are cosseted and mollycoddled through their privileged lives, and their meat finds its way into gastronomic glory holes such as La Tupina.

But I was actually headed seawards, and had OD'd on D roads. Forgive me, Bazas. A hotel beckoned in Arcachon, where I collapsed into a suite of nylon pinkness and slept the sleep of the dead.

Just below this trendy little port, down on the coast of Les Landes, with its casino and seafood restaurants, its oysters and outlandish prices, are the dunes of Pyla.

I set off by the light of the early morning to see them, just as the owls were beginning to yawn and the eastern sky was beginning to smile a little. Stars shone with a reddish glow, and the air was delicious and morning fresh. Past the villas and holiday homes, now dead and shuttered, the road runs southwards along the coast, turns inland a little, then loops back. And as it does, you may just glimpse a colossal glowing mound of sand through the pine trees, impossibly high, it seems. Stepping out across the car park, past the kiosks and bars thankfully all quiet at this time of the morning, with birds criss-crossing the trees and happily chirruping, you are drawn towards the light. And the sand.

And there they are. One of the most spectacularly beautiful things I have seen in France. One dune, and then others running off into the distance, vast mountains of sand. It is almost impossible to imagine quite how they stay there, unmolested by the elements, luminous in the morning sun, ochre, warm and so dramatic. But there they stay.

Even if the dunes have been thoroughly appropriated by man, they still retain a feeling of savage power. Fibreglass steps aid the not-so-intrepid to the top, and what a spectacular view! The dunes lie along sea that is green-cusped and silent from this height, and are washed and swished along their outer edges.

The sun slowly rose, warming the darker shadows a little. But there was no calm. Far from it. First there were *les sportifs*, a dozen or so, lovely in brilliant-scarlet figure-hugging Lurex, who were running up the dune en masse. How I longed to tell them there were stairs. How I longed for them to pause and reflect and listen to the birdsong. But no. They yelled and shouted at each other to *allez allez*, their feet sinking into the sand as they ran to the top. The noise shattered the calm of this awesome place. They screamed as one group attempted to out-do the other, driven by a mad and pointless combat.

And that wasn't all. Oh no! As I sat and watched them, gripping my thighs and wondering just how many centimetres of dune I could have managed, a flock of pigeons flew by in their anxious way. And Crack! Crack! It was, remember, early autumn, a time of year that is indescribably precious to many in south-west France, the season of *la chasse aux palombes*, the pigeon hunt.

And didn't I know it. Only days before I had left home, our neighbour, a man of considerable and varied talents, spied a pair of fat canoodling pigeons with their crops stuffed full of grain, and, to the horror of the kids, shot them clean and true through the head. Brilliant, I thought. And remembering a previous plea from me, he brought a brace round, perfectly clean and dry-plucked without a blemish on the skin. Into the pot they went to make a fine *salmis*. Which was exactly, I suspect, where the two I saw end their feathered lives at Pyla were destined. Small world, eh?

But this is more than just food for the pot we are talking about here. It is a highly significant sport for Frenchmen of a certain age, fiercely defensive of their rights, protective of tradition, and reluctant to accept not only that hunting might be up for a moral challenge, but that changes in the environment are said to be altering migratory patterns, presenting some pretty fundamental problems for *la chasse aux palombes*.

Pigeons have always been opportunistic birds, which is part of the reason for their evolutionary success. Quick to colonize towns and cities, they are almost overly familiar, and most of us have no idea that there is a migratory population at all. But just as their ancestors settled down and became urban, so the remaining migrants are becoming increasingly drawn to a more sedentary life. We are seeing, if you like, evolution in action.

Another problem is that this migration starts ever later, stretching far beyond the traditional peak of mid-October when, given a favourable – southerly – wind, thousands of pigeons still take to the air and attempt to reach the warmer climes of the Spanish Extremadura to overwinter.

But, reason these highly Cartesian pigeons, why fly so far south if it is almost as warm in the north, where they can happily gorge themselves among the pine forests of Les Landes, or the beech and oak forests of Gascony, le Béarn, le Gers and the Pays Basque. These birds are brilliantly plumed migrators, whose characteristic aura of blue excites the autumnal *chasseur* so, particularly in Aquitaine. And despite not playing the migratory game according to plan, they are still highly sought after.

Palombes are also becoming increasingly tempted by the vast hectares of corn grown in the south-west to feed the geese and ducks that are so central to culinary life down here. So it all seems like very sensible evolutionary behaviour to me.

Creatures naturally reacting to global warming. Why risk your very existence when food is so readily to hand?

Two distinct populations are evolving. Those birds that overwinter in the forest, and those that do so in the agricultural zone. They both feed off corn, but forest birds tend to move to the fields in the day and return to the trees by night, while the others stay put. The pine forests around Pyla and in the coastal zone of Les Landes host the majority of the forest-dwelling pigeons, hence the eruption of guns that morning.

But what's of particular concern to the inland *palombières* is that the birds appear increasingly to favour this coastal route, flying close to the Pyla dunes, for reasons that are not as yet completely understood. Thus you will see shocking tales of diminishing pigeon counts splashed across the headlines of the local press, plotting a depressing decline, and provoking much tut-tutting.

For once, the committed hunter and the scientist have come together to count the birds that fly by throughout the region and plot their path. Birds are ringed and observed with clinical precision, so we now know that these athletic creatures fly from as far north as Finland, travelling over four thousand kilometres right to the tip of southern Europe, no doubt sickened by the awful food up north, having read President Chirac's embarrassing piece of gastronomic xenophobia. (Perhaps I should remind you, he categorized the Finns and the British as offering the worst food in the EU.)

But there is, inevitably, disagreement as to how many birds are left. It is a question, as ever, of quite how you interpret the figures. The Groupe d'Investigation de la Faune Sauvage (GIFS) currently estimates the migratory pigeon population to range between three and four million, so *la chasse aux palombes* should have a future, rather than merely a much-lamented past. So the pro-hunting lobby argue, anyway.

But talk to environmentalists and the interpretation is different.

In the Pays Basque, there is an organization called Organbidexka Col Libre that has managed to survive for over twenty years in direct opposition to the 'arrogant and incompetent' hunters. They really put the cat among the pigeons by renting one of the hunting stations high up in the Pyrenees, which had long been one of the hunting lobby's traditional and most-treasured sites, and have been collecting data for their own purposes. Both lobbies use science to prove various points, but here the birds are greeted by long lenses and ornithologists rather than the barrel of a gun. Wise birds fly Basquewards.

The Organbidexka Col Libre's conclusions are more stark than those of the GIFS. Around eight hundred thousand pigeons are shot every year, they say, an unjustifiably large amount which is causing a serious decline in the migratory population. Yet in 2005, according to the current tally, the pigeon population seemed to be at its highest for years.

2005 also saw the world become increasingly nervous about the possible eruption of bird flu.

Chickens may have taken heart when they noticed that sales were plummeting, but they would have been wrong to do so: the production machine ineluctably rolled on and on, and all that happened was that the most privileged birds – those chickens that were '*élevés en plein air*', free-range, and could actually move their legs – were confined indoors. All birds became suspect, pigeons included, and stories of doom and gloom, both human and avian, were luridly splashed about the media.

But what of the 'hunt' itself? To the onlooker, it seems an almost ludicrously complicated business for very little reward. But to judge it on the catch alone completely misses the point. The majority of people in the south-west seem to passionately love spending time in a *palombière* each year, eating and drinking, gossiping and bitching. It is a social event, where the young begin to learn from the old, a time away from stress and strain.

Throughout the area there are quite a few variations on the 'let's kill a pigeon' theme. Inland, decoys are used, live birds that are cosseted and hand-fed, and placed in the trees to send out a comforting signal to the others that it is OK to land. Yes, all you have to do is to wear a stupid helmet, open your mouth, flap your wings a little and they come and feed you.

This was pretty much what was happening at the *palombière* I visited in the shadow (almost) of the Gascon joke town of Condom. To enter, you must first whistle and wait for the signal to proceed – by invitation, of course, for this is all highly ritualized. Rules and hierarchy must be respected. So, out comes the *chef de cabane*, opening a door carefully camouflaged by moss. 'Bonjour! Ah, the writer from England! These are lean times up here, not too many *palombes* around this year. But come inside, we'll have something to eat . . .'

And *palombes* were indeed few and far between.

You quickly begin to sense the bonhomie, and knuckle down to a spiel of endless mirth and hearty jokes: 'What on earth does an Englishman want to know about pigeons for, you just have to go to Trafalgar Square. Ha ha ha! Have some more armagnac.' And so on. To keep me focused, they had kindly brought a few pigeons from the market, and while these stewed quietly in the pot, we all reflected on the appeal of the *palombière*.

'Well, it's good to be with friends, and most of us have the most terrible jobs. I mean, look at Pierre here. He's a structural engineer! Imagine how boring that must be.' This from a scion of the local pharmaceutical company.

Coffee, talk, lunch.

'Where have all the pigeons gone, then?' I asked. 'I saw quite a few this morning over by the coast.'

'That's what's been happening for years. They all seem to be flying over the coast and they hardly ever come over here at all.'

Meanwhile, on a branch a few metres away sat their pride and joy, a rather disconsolate pigeon with a casque on its head, a siren call, it was assumed, to passers-by. A quick jiggle on a pulley and its wings flapped a little, a sign that all was well at this particular spot, and that no bird should fear a short, possibly very short, sojourn.

The system, like that in all *palombières*, was a mix of the ingenious and the rudimentary. But the hut was blissfully domesticated, with a little gas cooker in the corner, glasses, wine in copious amounts, and a table covered with one of those plastic tablecloths decorated with dead fruit so beloved of the French.

But in the sun, slightly lubricated by alcohol, all seemed genuinely sweet and harmonious. A few glances at the sky were all that was needed. The wind was blowing in completely the wrong direction and it was beginning to cloud over. So we talked of the *salmis* that was cooking.

'Ah, now that's the sort of dish that makes the day here so wonderful, *salmis*!'

If the *palombière* of my Gascon buddies was on the lower level of sophistication, it was thoroughly enjoyable. But over the departmental border in Les

Landes, things were different. There they used a more complicated network of decoys, that could be moved along caged runs at the pull of a rope, and it was also the habit to net the birds rather than blast them with a gun, and then either wring their necks and eat them, or keep some of the more beautiful specimens as decoys.

The mortal enemy of the migrating pigeon is either a hunter or a falcon. It was long ago noted that pigeons tend to fly closer to the ground as soon as they sense the presence of a bird of prey. The hunter, being a canny subspecies, has dreamt up subtle ways to imitate the falcon, here dropping a huge net over any pigeons seeking shelter. And so we have our wicked way with them. Place a few relaxed decoys in the vicinity and flocks of passing pigeons will feel sufficiently at ease to fly to a neat clearing on the ground, stretch their legs a little, and hey! A fine net drops from the trees and covers them.

Perhaps the most bizarre method of all is practised high in the mountain passes of the Pays Basque, where the locals throw curiously chalked white wooden paddles high into the air, which somehow forces the pigeons to land.

However, *la chasse* has become increasingly controversial. There are those who find the idea of leisure appealing, but rail at the deliberate destruction of life. Respect for the environment is a duty, a sign of good citizenship, if you like. It is no longer easy for the hunters to dismiss the protectionists as incomers, foreigners and fools. Yet both camps can find beauty in the flocks of birds, the trees, the silence and direct communion with Nature. Where do rights and tradition now lie? Is it perhaps no longer acceptable, on a global level, to cause suffering to animals in the name of leisure? These thorny issues are yet to be resolved in France, as elsewhere.

Detractors may well tell you about the grim lot of the *ortolan*, the sweet, delicate and entirely blameless bunting that has had the misfortune to become one of gastronomy's most sought-after specialities. Particularly here in the south-west of France. Yes, I admit to having eaten one once, and was gravely disappointed. These days their capture is forbidden, but in a restaurant that must remain anonymous, I was regally entertained to this rarest of dishes, *ortolan rôti*. I am told they serve them still.

Ortolans are caught in a net and fattened in the dark to such a level of obesity that they positively explode with fat in the mouth when cooked, so much so that tradition has it you must wear a bib, which of course I did, and which of course made me look a fool. The bird was brought lovingly to the table and I was encouraged to eat it quickly, to press it firmly against the roof of my mouth to savour the delicate aroma in the fat.

I did as bid, and the sensation of pain as the burning fat seared through my upper palate led me to think that perhaps this was a gastronomic blast too far. Let the poor creatures live a little before they are treated so. Times move on.

Salmis de palombes

Serves 4

Ingredients
4 wood pigeons
Salt
Pepper
100g butter
100ml goose or duck fat
2 carrots, finely chopped
1 large onion, finely chopped
3 shallots, finely chopped
A bouquet garni
60g white flour
1 bottle good red wine (the original recipe calls for two, but that seems a little excessive)
½ litre chicken stock
100ml armagnac

Garnish
250g chopped Bayonne ham
10 small onions, chopped
300g wild mushrooms, chopped
2 slices of good-quality bread, fried in goose or duck fat and broken into croutons

Method

Lightly fry the livers and offal of the pigeons, if you have them, with the chopped vegetables in the fat. Sprinkle on the flour, and cook a little more. Cover with the wine and stock and cook gently for two hours on top of the stove, then pass through a chinois/sieve.

Butter the pigeons and roast them in the oven for twenty minutes at 180°C.

Pour the sauce over the pigeons to serve. Season to taste, then flambé the armagnac, and add. Serve with the garnish.

Adapted from *Cuisine et Vins de France* by Curnonsky,
Librairie Larousse, Paris, 1953.

4

Biperrada

DRIVING THROUGH LES LANDES CAN GET TO YOU AFTER a while. The pine trees and flatness help develop a sense of ennui, and despite the siren calls to nibble at foie gras, you begin to yearn for a contour or two. Fingers begin to tap out songs ominously on the steering wheel. 'Climb every mountain', 'Doe, a deer, a female deer . . .'

Luckily I was travelling Basque-wards, to the hilly south-western edge of France, as mysterious and sensitive a place as you will find in Europe these days. I was trying to catch the annual Fête d'Espelette, when a tiny town in the Pays Basque bigs it up and goes all rootsy with its prime crop, chillies, or *piments*, as they are called down there.

While many of us become quite excited by the idea of collapsing borders, the Basques under-standably have bitter memories and yearn for the one thing that has so long been denied them: nationhood. 3 + 4 = 1, they say. Three French provinces and four Spanish ones make the Basque homeland, Euskal Herria.

Basque cooking is diverse, a fascinating mix of land and sea, introverted yet worldly. While the three French provinces have their gastronomic heads mostly turned inland, famously to the red of their chillies, and the green of their valleys, to their exquisite ewe's cheese and, most famously, to Bayonne ham, in Spain their hearts turn more to the sea than the hills.

Basque cooking is earthy, and uses both olive oil and butter, the latter mainly to make cakes, particularly that iconic masterpiece, the Gâteau Basque. Nearer to the sea on the French side, around Hendaye and St Jean de Luz, there are specialities that sing the sea in a very Basque way, with tongue-twisting names and a shot of *piment*. The great fish stews of France have their soulmate in Basque *ttoro* and the tuna-based *marmitako*.

As a cultural warm-up to the fête, I had been whirled around the area by a local ham-producer, Pierre Accoceberry, whose hospitality knew no bounds, despite the fact that he was in the middle of arranging a huge feast for hundreds over the weekend and was up to his eyeballs in powdered *piment*.

The whole village was prettying itself for this annual event. Streets were swept, leaves bundled away. A nervous energy was in the air. Light bulbs swung from the trees, and yes, hundreds upon hundreds of chillies hung from the roofs and walls, which were all painted in their brilliant Basque colours, white and a characteristic maroon. It was all quite beautiful. The sun shone, indeed it was so warm that people were surfing not far away in Biarritz and there was much talk of the joys of an Indian summer.

Monsieur Accoceberry has ham in his blood, as well as a muscular handshake, bright eyes, and a refreshingly polite, almost old-worldly way about him. We sat down and talked ham and *piment* for a while, praising the joys of good food, moaning a little about the demise of things – well, this was France, after all – until he made a call, bundled me into his car, and off we set into the hills to see how a real Bayonne ham was made.

I was not sure that I had ever tasted a good Jambon de Bayonne, a shocking thing to admit, really. The problem is that this ham has become so ubiquitous, almost mundane, sliced and pre-sliced and boned and rolled. This seemed a classic case for an inquisitive gastronome to seek out the best.

And the secret is not just a well-fed pig, but the air and salt that cures the ham, and time that gives it character. In the mountain valley of Les Aldudes, not far from Espelette, Accoceberry and a few other producers have built a modern curing house that allows the hams to mature under the best conditions. But the curing house is not entirely open to the elements. These hams are too valuable to risk unforeseen variations in heat and humidity, which can easily ruin a year's production. A few dogged producers still try to make ham according to the old ways, but technology is, after all, a useful tool.

So temperature and humidity are carefully controlled, and the hams hung high to mature for as long as the producer wishes. And there in serried rows, dangling as casually as coats on a hook, were hundred upon hundred of true Bayonne hams, made from pigs that were raised locally and not transported all the way from Holland. The French long ago created a highly respected system of quality called the Appellation d'Origine Contrôlée, or AOC, that allows a specific product – be it edible or drinkable – to carry a name that includes a specific geographic origin so long as it respects certain rules. It is a system that should maintain quality, a protectionist ploy that suits the French agricultural model well. And crucially, it helps preserve the diversity of foods within their *terroir*.

For the most part the pigs that are made into Jambon de Bayonne are pretty bog-standard, fast-growing Duroc hybrids, but there were a few hams made from an older, leaner pig, the porc Basque, that gives a finer taste and texture than the Duroc crosses that Accoceberry generally uses. But they are few and far between.

Basque pigs are piebald, evidence of their cosmopolitan origin, having been mixed long ago with white pigs that were brought in from Britain to improve yields. On the other side, their genes are from the entirely black and now pretty rare porc Gascon, which in all likelihood came across the mountains from Spain long ago, a distant relation of the famous *cerdo Iberico*. Both Gascon and Basque pigs are noticeably calm and chilled, but – same old story – ham producers wanted bigger and faster-growing pigs, so these original breeds almost became genetic history. But we consumers like character in our food, and there is now a revival of these ancient breeds under way.

I stocked up on ham, and breathed the mountain air. This was a busy time for Pierre, and I appreciated his sense of hospitality.

'We Basques appreciate interest in our culture. You've come all this way, so this is the least I can do, to show you how things are here,' he told me as we sped off in his car, swerving expertly around the bends and through villages and hamlets, all of which he commented on. 'They are strongly Basque here', 'This village has a good sense of identity', and so on.

I asked whether we could follow up the story of the local Ossau-Iraty, a ewe's milk cheese that is sold in small two-kilogram rounds and is considered to be one of the finest of all. This, too, is protected from infamy by a blessed AOC. It is not just a Basque cheese, however. The area of production is remarkably extensive, and stretches right across into neighbouring Béarn. The Basques prefer a harder, drier cheese, which is often eaten with the exquisite black-cherry jam made nearby at Itxassou.

Or is it? Itxassou cannot begin to supply the demand for their jam. Their cherries may be delicious, but they are also fragile and need to be used quickly. Hence the tradition grew to make them into jam. The two main varieties, Peloa and Beltza, are fabulously black and juicy, but traditionally the trees are large and difficult to work, so modern varieties are being planted on to more manageable dwarf stock. You will, if you go there, no doubt notice dinky little pots of this *confiture de cerise noire*, but remember that much of it is only *made* in the Pays Basque, and not from Pays Basque cherries. An AOC would make things so much simpler.

We pulled up at his cheesemaker and breathed sheep for a while. The flock was from a unique Basque breed called Manech; they looked stark and tough, and gazed at you aggressively. Very Basque. Together with the Basco-Béarnais sheep, they are the only permitted source of milk used to make Ossau-Iraty, which is an AOC.

They had a subtle sales technique on this farm.

They sat their extremely ancient granny – well into her nineties, I was told, and who loved to sell – by the roadside. She happily chatted with the passers-by, telling them all about how life once was, and how good the cheese was that sat maturing gently in the back of the farm.

Back in Espelette, Accoceberry introduced me to an enormous, jovial man who ran one of the village bars, a famous ex-rugby player brimming with charisma who agreed to tell me how to make the famous Gateau Basque. In the back of the bar lay pile upon pile of Gateaux Basques waiting to be baked, some filled with crème patissière, others with that cherry jam again.

'Just make sure you get the oven at the right temperature!' he said as he rushed in and out, telling me snippets of the recipe and losing me completely. And off he dashed again, for tomorrow, after all, was the fête, the biggest day of the year for Espelette.

As a grand cultural finale, I was taken off by Accoceberry to watch the fearsome game played by Basques called *jai alai*.

'It means Happy Festival in Basque!' he told me.

The game was played at supersonic speed, and sweat poured off the two players, who each wore a strange wicker glove and proceeded to try and cause their opponent to die of apoplexy. It was magnificent. Everything about the Pays Basque seemed to say 'tough', from the sheep to *jai alai*.

Accoceberry kindly left me in a bar filled with big, tough-looking men and wished me well. Off he went back to his logistics and his *piments*.

Come the morning of the big day, the roads began to clog and the ditches filled with parked cars. People flocked in from far and wide, for this is a fête that has truly taken the world by storm. But Espelette is not New York. The streets were soon filled to bursting, as everyone stocked up on *piment* this and *piment* that. I tramped the streets and pushed through the crowds and nodded to the people I recognized from the day before. It was all very amicable, until I walked into a shop selling plates, and saw some terracotta dishes that I thought were particularly beautiful. I took out my camera and snapped a picture, and felt an arm grip me tightly.

'What are you doing?' I was asked by a perspiring hefty man in a Basque beret, his eyes livid with fury.

'I am taking some photos with my camera,' I told him helpfully. 'I thought your plates looked lovely.'

He looked at me murderously, and flew into a ludicrous hissy fit. I was not a dangerous spy, I assured him.

But why the notebook?

'It's OK, I am just here writing about food, and about the fête.' About hospitality, I thought, and that famous welcoming spirit.

'Huh! Did you see that? Someone was trying to take a photo of plates! Why, they should call the police!'

If there is one dish that represents the domesticity, the colour and the rich, fertile land of the French provinces of Euskal Herria, their uncertain roots and indomitable, almost paradoxical Basque view of the world, it has to be piperade. It's pretty easy to cook, familiar, but alas is much abused and misrepresented. Which all seems to be pretty Basque, too. Piperade in Basque becomes *biperrada*, and in honour of this tortuous language and its people, I will use the Basque term.

Biperrada is best eaten with a slice or two of thick, quickly cooked Bayonne ham and the freshest eggs you can get. Some say that the gastronomic roots of *biperrada* aren't in the Pays Basque at all, but over in the Soule valley, around Mauléon, in the Béarn, where farming families once put old bread to good use – waste being almost sinful – by making what is now called *piperade blanche*, white piperade. Crust and crumb are gently cooked over a low heat in pork or duck fat, with onions, a little garlic and locally grown peppers, but no egg. While the bread binds the peppers and onions together, this can just as well be done with eggs, which is how the Basque version of piperade has evolved. Too often dismissed as scrambled eggs with peppers, it is a better dish altogether when made carefully. It, too, is made from *poivrons*, sweet or bell peppers, as well as onions and tomatoes, all cooked slowly but separately in goose or duck fat. What else? Although it is one and the same plant as the *poivron* that goes into piperade, you would never use *piment d'Espelette*. Why not? Because it is a condiment, to be sprinkled with moderation, a sweet, only mildly *picante* version of the chilli.

Biperrada

Serves 6

Ingredients
500g tomatoes
500g onions
500g sweet red peppers
4 eggs
2 dessertspoons goose fat
25g butter
4 cloves garlic
A bunch of parsley, chopped

Method
Chop the peppers, onions and garlic and fry gently in the goose fat for 40 minutes. Add the tomatoes,

skinned if you prefer. Cook for a further 30 minutes over a gentle heat. Beat the eggs in the butter, then add to the vegetables. Season, add the chopped parsley and garnish with Bayonne ham. Excellent with a thick slice, lightly fried.

5

Confit

ESPELETTE TO TARBES IS A LOVELY ROLLOCKING journey, and I felt liberated to be driving only tens of kilometres for once. This was what I assumed to be deepest Gascony, but despite it having almost the clearest culinary identity of any part of France, and despite its name being synonymous with good food, big wine and the even bigger thighs of big-hearted rugby players, I still had to ask myself: where the hell was Gascony?

My confusion had all started over a conversation about *garbure*. My Gascon mentor, chef Pierre Koffmann, was looking at the protean plan for this book. He huffed at this and that, and saw that under the word 'Gascony' I had written *confit* and *garbure*, the two key regional dishes, or so I thought.

He told me about making *confit* with his grandmother, the busy preparations, the cleaning of great pans and glass jars, and the duck markets of the region. But '*Garbure* isn't from Gascony, you know. It's Béarnais,' he told me.

'Oh,' I replied apologetically.

You go to Brittany, and know where it is. Normandy, too. But Gascony? Yes, in France of course, and yes, down there in the south-west, but it has no clear boundaries, no roadside signs, nothing but a name that everyone seems to know. No one can define the region too clearly. Gascony is, you see, part of that ancestral pre-revolutionary France that was once even ruled by England, long ago, back in the thirteenth century. Old France still lives on beneath the surface.

Gascony had its own language, a dialect of Occitan, which sadly is now even deader than the great poetic Langue d'Oc itself. And we are told that Gascony is roughly equivalent to the modern-day republican region of Aquitaine, which has of course taken its name from another ancient pre-revolutionary kingdom: Aquitaine whence Eleanor came. Ah! Easy then? No. Because the ancient Aquitaine doesn't actually approximate to modern Aquitaine at all, whose capital was and is Bordeaux. This is a modern post-revolutionary construct, a region that includes the unwilling Basques, the Béarnais, the Landais, all people who feel themselves to be very different, and who are in a way lumbered with the revolutionary and oh-so-French passion for *égalité*.

It has been said that while the British invented industry, the French invented equality. And, in its honour, one of the great revolutionary ideas was to divide France into approximately equal *départements*, thus annihilating ancient boundaries at a stroke. If you look at a modern-day map of France, you can see the basic idea. There are no great differences in their size, unlike Britain, where the county of Rutland is tiny when compared to Yorkshire. Like Rhode Island compared to Texas.

I arrived in Tarbes only lightly frazzled after the glorious drive from Espelette and stretched and yawned and slept.

If you are lucky enough to find yourself in Gascony, and actually realize that you are there, then welcome. Unwind. Look to the south, where perhaps the snow on the Pyrenees is piled high and thick in the distance. Take advantage of the chill. On a clear day, the Pyrenees glow wondrously in the distance, looming rather ominously like a vast frozen tsunami.

Autumn in Gascony is a particularly magical time of year. This is, after all, when Gascons like to scuttle off rather secretively to the woods and forests and their *palombières*, when they dream of pigeons and exquisite ceps that rudely thrust their heads through the fallen leaves. Corn cobs take on the colour of bold sunshine and are stacked high in the fields to dry in the *séchoirs*, to be fed to the geese. And ducks.

This is the time when Gascon thoughts turn to fat and palmipeds, a time when cooks clean out their ancient pots and pans and begin to plan for Christmas, and more. It's time to make *confit*.

It is an ancient ritual for families to get together to make jar upon jar of thick duck and goose *confit*, when their meat is preserved by being cooked in lashings of softening fat. *Confit* is a marvellous food. It's what I would call genealogical. It begets. With a good stock of *confit*, you can make salads in summer, and soups – *tourains*, *garbures* – in winter. (Yes, *garbure* really does exist in Gascony.) You can use the fat for cooking potatoes or wild mushrooms. But *confit* isn't just duck. Or goose. The word comes from the French verb *confrire*, which simply means 'to cook with' – fat, in this case, but it is also used for making sweets with sugar, and also pickling with vinegar. It is why jam is called *confiture* in French.

You can make *confit* out of sausages, gizzards, onions or limes. All you need to master are the fundamental principles, and you are away. It is neither difficult to make nor to store, and provides a rich source of energy throughout the year. It is a food that matures and improves with age – if it lasts, that is, so addictive can it become. For despite the idea, the way it sounds, if you like, *confit* is much more than fat and grease. It is quite delicious, and just as remarkably, instead of hardening the arteries appears rather to lengthen life. It's all part of that mysterious, much-lauded French paradox, when two of the very best things in life, red wine and *confit*, seem, rather like that pill that once fortified the over-forties, to prolong active life. Not a bad claim for any food. Or drink.

However, to make *confit* you cannot use just any old bird. It calls for a bird that has been deliberately fattened, a web-footed, waddling wonder, a duck or goose stuffed with corn in the name of gastronomy – the origin, of course, of one of the world's finest and most controversial specialities, *foie gras*. But although *confit* is in a way a by-product, it has its own culture and is enduringly popular, and in the south-west as inevitable as a *crêpe* in Brittany.

However, the world is beginning to express doubts on this business of force-feeding – *le gavage*, as it is called in French. In this age of globe-trotting you can easily go and see for yourself what it entails, but don't be too easily led by the doom-and-gloom merchants who tell tales of monstrous cruelty. Judge for yourself. All I can say is this: from my point of view, there are crueller things carried out in the name of producing food.

I have seen birds being fed – force-fed makes it sound like Abu Ghraib – and the ducks I saw did not flap or fluster, but seemed quite content to have their heads lifted, throats stroked, and a funnel full of grain put down their gullets. *Foie gras* producers need to be delicate and gentle, or the birds become stressed and agitated and do not gain weight, which is not good for business.

Truly, I have been more repulsed by visiting intensive poultry farms, and seeing pigs enclosed in pens. By cows milked to buggery, and rabbits locked and fattened in tiny cages.

But if you do go and see with your own eyes, then try and visit one of the most evocative of all of the south-west's markets, the *marché au gras*, and perhaps even bid for your year's supply of duck carcasses, and make your very own *confit*.

I spent a happy Monday morning in the village of Samatan, almost overwhelmed by the bustle and bounce that the market gave to what seemed to me to be a perfectly unassuming little Gascon village, not far from Toulouse. It was as if the circus had come to town. The cafés were heaving, papers were being sold on the pavement due to the exceptional bustle of the day, and even the lousy *boulangerie* had sold out of croissants. And all because of those doughty *musqué* ducks. As I passed the stalls, everyone assured me: '*C'est un musqué, monsieur. Je ne triche pas!*' – 'It's a *musqué*, I'm not cheating you.' A *musqué* being a Muscovy duck, the preferred bird for its carcass and liver.

The *marché au gras* was only part of the whole, the heart and soul of the market, if you like. Around its perimeter lay a whole host of stalls selling everything from the traditional shell suit to *confit* itself. A couple of nuns were tempting all and sundry to taste their cheese, looking slightly incongruous, it has to be said, among the round and ruddy-faced Gascons. They were selling thick, heavy loaves of bread – bread to keep – made from *levain*, natural yeast, rural cousins to the fragile and rather urbane baguette. And everywhere, noise. Blasts from the village loudspeakers. Music from the man selling Charles Trenet CDs wafted around the *saucissons*.

Eventually, right at the far end, I found what I was looking for: the *marché au gras*. Walking past a bizarre collection of live birds that included not just the usual egg-layers and strutting cocks, but a gaggle of turkeys and the odd parakeet, I thought it all seemed healthily vibrant, considering the mounting hysteria about avian flu.

A little further on, I passed a man with a bowl brimming with this year's *haricots tarbais*, superb beans that can be dried and stored and are excellent in a cassoulet. I bought a kilo for my allotment, where they live on triumphantly, unfazed by their change in location. Then on I went into the hall of beige death. I hadn't been to a *marché au gras* for years. The last one I'd seen was to the north at Fleurance, a Tuesday market, and Samatan brought it all back. It had the same ordered trestle tables, laden with row upon row of ducks, the odd goose, and bags of hearts and wings and gizzards.

If you are lucky enough to have a home down

here, there is little excuse, apart from culinary nerves, to stay away from your local *marché au gras*. They usually begin with the sale of the carcasses at about ten in the morning, followed by the whole ducks, liver and all, a more expensive and specialized business altogether. For beginners and amateurs, and for making *confit*, a liverless carcass should do fine.

Now, a good Muscovy carcass weighs in at around five kilos. They are massive compared to regular ducks, and I should add that *confit* doesn't work too well with a mass-produced rubber duck. They are just too flabby and small, and not really worth the bother, which of course raises the question of how to make your own *confit* if you have neither a house in Gascony, a large pot, nor about thirty kilos of spare luggage allowance. Well, I have just the answer.

Cruising anonymously between the rows, I could begin to see the ducks that were selling well. At each transaction, the seller would yank the bird's head, which was listlessly hidden from view, to show the prospective buyer that this *musqué* had the tell-tale yellow crest, a sign of its breeding. All that remained was to see quite how fat the duck was.

The cleanliness of the bird is a good indicator. Some were carelessly tied with string, messy, and sold slowly. Others looked far more professionally prepared. And a quick look inside showed you more. Thick layers of hardened fat lined the body cavity.

I asked one of the producers if she wouldn't mind telling me what exactly made a good duck.

'What are you going to make?' she asked. '*Confit?* Well, you need fat, for a start. Look here.' And she prised open the cavity, loosening the string a little. 'It's clean. Smell it!'

I leant over and stuffed my nose up the duck's rear as politely as I could. It smelt clean, yet ducky.

She showed me all the little bits of fat around the carcass. 'You can use it all. The more, the better. How many are you looking for?'

She had four birds left.

Four times five. Twenty kilos. Tricky. I was due to fly back to England in a few days, and my luggage allowance was already in danger of being overwhelmed.

What was I to do? Jettisoning my socks would have been easy. My pants, less so. My laptop, improbable. But crucially, I had those beans, and a few more days when I was surely incapable of not buying anything else. And then there was the hotel to consider, who had kindly agreed to look after my purchases until I took a plane back home. I couldn't invade their space totally.

I told her my problem.

'Ah! You can't throw out the beans, monsieur.' She pointed to a couple of bags she had to one side. 'Why don't you take these? They are goose wings.

You'll get lots of fat from them, and they taste good too. They make good *confit*.' And they weighed in at barely a kilo.

I reached for my Euros, settled the deal, and flew home with the goose wings, two ducks and my beans nestling next to the laptop. Nearly twelve kilos of birdy bits. I was a happy bunny, as we gastronomes say. Or should I say a happy *lapin de garenne*. Maybe not. You'll only ask me where the hell is Garenne. Actually, where the hell *is* Garenne?

Making Confit

Despite my goose wings and good fortune, we are to all intents and purposes talking duck here rather than goose. Geese do not take kindly to being force-fed. They are more aggressive and greedier – hence costlier – than ducks, so you see them only rarely. As far as *foie gras* is concerned that's a shame, for goose liver is finer than duck liver, particularly when eaten cold as a terrine. The goose was the original bird whose liver was fattened and nourished – it is thought by Jews, who had in all probability learnt the skill from the ancient Egyptians. Geese travelled better, and were stronger and hardier than ducks.

If you can find a supply of whole *canards*

musqués you will need time, and a large pan, higher than it is wide, for the fat tends to dissipate. *Canards gras* (force-fed ducks) are quite easily come by; wherever there are good French restaurants, there should be a specialist supplier who will be able to source them for you. (See Appendix for list of suppliers.)

You first prepare the pieces by cutting up the carcass. Remove the legs and wings, and then begin to remove the breast, or *magret*. We need to talk *magret* here. The *magret* is the breast of a force-fed duck or goose, and *not* the breast of any old duck. Given that a good carcass of a *canard musqué* will weigh about five kilos, the *magret* is far bigger, thicker and tastier than a regular duck breast. Restaurant lore says that it was 'invented' by the highly respected Gascon chef André Daguin, but that seems a little ridiculous to me. The *magret* was always there. It can be made into *confit* just as well, but provides an initial reward for all the work you are about to carry out. Some French supermarkets sell cuts of duck for *confit*. Legs are particularly useful.

Assemble your bits, and rub them all in salt, then leave them in the fridge for forty-eight hours to suppurate quietly. Then take them out, carefully wipe the salt away and cook very slowly for at least three hours. Not at a rapid boil, just a gentle simmer. The French have a word for this: *mijoter*. It implies long, careful cooking, and is what you should do to make good *confit*.

When time is up, or you feel like stopping, allow the duck to cool, remove the pieces and put them in tall glass Kilner jars or ceramic pots, whose bottoms you have first covered with a little fat. Then cover the duck with more fat, until the pots are full.

And that is it. *Confit* will theoretically keep for months in a cool place, but better still, keep the jars in the fridge if you have enough space. And how best to eat it? Heat it till the skin becomes crisp, and serve with a salad. Use the fat to cook potatoes, mushrooms, anything that comes to mind. Enjoy what are called the *graisserons*, the little bits left in the cooking fat. Look for *gahuzagues*, or goose tripe, rare now but exquisite. And don't forget, if you feel that winter cold coming on, out with the goose fat and smear it thickly on your chest. Then you too will discover the inner joy of making good *confit*.

6

Poule au Pot

*Si Dieu me prête vie, je ferai qu'il n'y aura point de
laboureur en mon royaume qui n'ait les moyens
d'avoir le dimanche une poule dans son pot!*
So long as God gives me life, I will ensure that every
worker in my kingdom will be able to afford a hen
for the pot on Sunday.

Henri IV

MY DUCKS AND I PILED INTO THE CAR AND SET OFF FOR
a few days in Pau, before the flight back to England.
It was by now extremely blustery – and yes, there
seems to be a lot of bluster in this book, but off-
season travel is the stuff of this food writer's dreams.
Pau is the birthplace of France's most intriguing
monarch, Henri IV, and I became thoroughly
immersed in his story while cruising the city's sights,
worrying about my ducks in the hotel fridge.

It may seem terribly clichéd to all you devoted gastronomes and historians out there, but although this was a story I had heard many times, I actually knew little of the details.

Now, as a rule, dead kings don't talk. But Henri, unlike almost all other French monarchs, is constantly referred to, and appropriated by all and sundry. Most monarchs just die and decompose, but there are a select few who have managed to resonate, to become part of the bricks and mortar of culture and transcend all boundaries of time and place. Whether by sheer brutality, or achievement.

So, say Catherine the Great and we think horse, and Russia. In England, Henry VIII means girth, beards and marital harmony. George III? Lunacy or liberation, according to which side of the Atlantic you are based. Genghis Khan? Well, it's steak tartare and screaming hordes to me, but strictly speaking he wasn't a king. And who have we from France? The pampered absolutist Louis XIV? Wigs, public eating and Versailles. Marie Antoinette? Cakes. Or was it brioche? In any case, a slur, historians tell us. She never actually told the masses to depart en masse and eat cake at all. (It was *pain mollet*, I suspect.) And sugar was far too dear, my dear.

But if I write Henry IV, what do you think? To an English speaker, probably Shakespeare. And two parts. If you are French, or mildly francophile, I bet it's a hen, a *poule au pot*, for this remarkable

French king is one of the few to have survived the Revolution with his reputation intact, and is famously remembered for wanting each and every one of his subjects to have a *poule au pot*, a hen on the table every Sunday. It was a brilliantly populist gesture, made centuries before focus groups were even thought of. He was a monarch blessed with good sense and a clear vision of what he wanted his country to be.

Tolerant, for one. Born a Protestant, he controversially converted to Catholicism on ascending the throne. 'Paris is worth a Mass,' he allegedly said, but remained true to his wish for France to be a mature enough nation to tolerate difference, expressed in the signing of the Edict of Nantes in 1598.

On his death at the hands of an assassin in 1610, the country resumed the persecution of minorities and non-Catholics. Eighty-seven years later, the Edict was renounced by Louis XIV. The Protestant Huguenots left en masse, rightly fearful for their future. Many who remained were brutally massacred in the name of God. Henry IV's reputation has survived intact, about the only French king's to do so.

Henri was born on 14 December 1553 in the Château de Pau, where his mother, Jeanne d'Albret, was heiress to the Kingdom – a much-attenuated one at that – of Navarre. His father was a Bourbon, Antoine de Bourbon – Vendôme, a licentious man who liked to fight and fuck.

Now let's look at this story of the *poule au pot*.

Born in the Béarn, Henri would no doubt have been familiar with this dish, and known that it was far from being the everyday diet of his subjects. But wishing for a bowl of good *bouillon* for all and sundry would have had little impact. No, Henri recognized the value of achievement, of the yearning for the good life and for good, solid, homely food.

And inevitably, his native city celebrates both Henri IV and *poule au pot* at every opportunity. So it was hardly original, I admit, to be tempted into a restaurant that looked horribly empty on that particularly horrible autumnal day, to eat *poule au pot*. For the second time in my life.

Poule one was sublime. Old Madame Fouteau ruled the roost on a farm not far from Condom in Gascony (we are in the Béarn, remember) and had agreed to show me how to choose your *poule*. It was a matter of catching your chicken. She took me outside, and walked stealthily around the *poules* that were scratching the ground stupidly before us.

A *poule*, I should say, is not a young chicken, but an old bird that has lived and seen action, and been allowed the luxury of a life. Much like Madame Fouteau. Weighing in at a minimum of two kilos, they simply cannot be replaced by a large broiler fowl or giant chicken. But I have used a large free-range hen to make *poule au pot* and it worked brilliantly, so don't despair. We'll get you there.

'Ah, that one will do!' she whispered quietly. She

enticed it like a dog into her arms, and broke its neck. 'Yes, that one will do nicely!'

We plucked and pulled the sandy brown feathers from its limp body, and went and toured the farm. We tasted their armagnac, I seem to remember. Vaguely.

That evening, I sat around the table with Madame Fouteau's family and watched her serve this most exquisite bird, stuffed with – well, wait and see – and served with the clearest, sweetest chicken *bouillon* imaginable. It was wonderful. Truly delicious, with the chicken falling from the bone. The brown meat especially had a glorious texture and taste. Utterly yum.

Poule au pot

This recipe has been adapted and translated from a gorgeous book called Cuisines des Pays de France, *published in France by Éditions du Chêne, 2001. It is the closest I can find to the* poule au pot *I ate in Pau. There is a sort of culinary crescendo about the dish, so go with an appetite, and a good bed nearby.*

The bouillon is served first from a vast steaming tureen, then the bird with its stuffing, accompanied by one or both sauces. It truly is a fabulous dish. Henri IV had good sense.

Serves 6

Ingredients
1 large good-quality boiling hen,
with giblets
3 carrots
2 long turnips, locally called
navets chinois
1 leek
1 bouquet garni
3 litres chicken stock
Salt and pepper

For the stuffing
The giblets of the chicken
3 chicken livers
300g sausagemeat
3 slices of good-quality bread
100ml milk
2 eggs
1 shallot
4 cloves of garlic
1 sprig of thyme
1 bay leaf
Bunch of parsley

For the rice
400g white rice
1 onion

For the white sauce
50g butter
50g flour
2 egg yolks
2g piment d'Espelette powder, or paprika
750ml chicken stock

For the tomato sauce
4 tomatoes
3 shallots
2 green peppers
2 cloves of garlic
50ml olive oil

Method

First, prepare the stuffing. Soak the bread in the milk. Finely chop the chicken giblets and livers, garlic and shallot. Add the eggs, and the bread squeezed dry, season and mix thoroughly. Add the sausagemeat. Use French or Italian-type sausages with low levels of breadcrumbs and additives. The better the sausage, the better the stuffing. Mix together. Put the thyme, bay leaf and bunch of parsley into the gut cavity, then fill with the stuffing. Sew the cavity tightly shut so the stuffing doesn't escape.

Put the hen in the chicken stock, add the bouquet garni, season and cook for two hours in a large pot on the stove. Clean the turnips, leek and carrots, add them to the pot and cook for another hour. When the bird is ready, take it off the heat and leave it to cool in the stock.

While the hen is cooking, prepare the tomato sauce. Cut all the ingredients into little dice, seal them in a pan in the hot olive oil, season and cook for two hours at a low heat.

Now prepare the rice. Take a little of the fat off the surface of the stock pot with a ladle. Chop the onion and fry it gently for three minutes. Add the rice and fry that for a few minutes. Then add some stock from the pot. The process is the same as making a risotto. Add stock little by little, until it's absorbed and the rice is cooked.

Prepare the white sauce just before serving. Melt the butter, add the flour and mix together. Take off the heat and add the stock, then reheat, whisking vigorously to keep lumps from forming. When the sauce begins to thicken, season, take off the heat again, add the egg yolks and Piment d'Espelette powder, and whisk energetically.

Serve the hen cut into pieces, with the stuffing, rice and vegetables arranged on a serving dish, accompanied by both sauces.

So, while in Pau, I walked into a restaurant called O Gascon to eat *poule au pot* number two, and settled in front of the lavatory, where for some reason single middle-aged men are often placed.

Flipping through the menu in a rather desultory fashion, I wanted to say, 'Bring out your finest

food, good woman. Bring me my *poule, ma poule*.'
But I thought a little ritualistic glance at the menu
was in order. It was, after all, a restaurant. I
demurely ordered the inevitable.

First, they brought the broth, *le bouillon*, dark
and copious, steaming heartily from a vast tureen,
ladled it lovingly as if I was truly helpless, and left
me to slurp and sip away. The castle glistened in the
pouring rain. But all seemed well with the world. I
savoured the extraordinary revitalizing power that
you get from chicken stock. Jewish mothers are
never wrong. There was a spring in my heart, and
a warmth of spirit that I had thought long lost as
the rain tipped and tipped and tipped down.

Madame came and asked how it all was.

'Marvellous!' I said in French. Or '*Formidable!*'
Something brief and expressive.

'I imagine you sell a fair amount of *poules*,' I
remarked.

She eyed me closely. '*Ah, oui monsieur.* We are
very *terroir* here, you know. Everything we use
comes from the region.'

Terroir.

In France it is almost suicidal to be otherwise.
The word resonates and echoes through tracts and
labels, and is, perhaps conveniently, almost
untranslatable. It describes the physical attachment
that produce has to the land, that which gives it
character and, by assuming its mantle, assumed
excellence. *Terroir* incorporates culture and history

into food. And for the French it is *the* key word that expresses the firmly held belief that their produce is superior to anything that comes from beyond the borders of the enigmatic hexagon.

Everything, everywhere you go, is local. The word *terroir* began to terrify me, to haunt me. It began to make me awfully suspicious. It reminded me of the chefs who used to say, 'Ah, I do all the markets every night,' forgetting that they too needed to sleep once in a while. Or the shops that swear that everything they stock is sustainable and organic.

It annoyed me above all in the supermarkets, which have created a happily bucolic range of foods cleverly pitched to appeal to those who value taste, to ensnare them, so they can be happily enmeshed in the convenience that is being offered. And yet it is a poisoned chalice. You can now buy sausages from Savoie, or *andouillettes* from Vire; countrywide, you can sprinkle your food with Piment d'Espelette from Ajaccio to Metz. Foods that belonged once so clearly to a particular place have now gained a nationwide market; soon they will be seen in a store near you. And thus French regional food is slowly losing its very raison d'être. Now, I bleat not on account of progress and larger markets. Indeed, they secure the future of foods rather than endangering them. It is the loss of culture and the inevitable dumbing down of tastes that depresses me, as these poor unfortunate foods and dishes are lost in translation, irreparably damaged by sell-by dates and profit margins.

But here, in the shadow of Henri IV, somehow I believed Madame implicitly. I trusted her sense of professionalism. Another bowl of *bouillon* was served and then came the hen, with its magnificent *farce*, or stuffing.

Firm meat, from legs that had walked and run and lived, lay on the plate. Not anodyne muck with a hint of fish. You needed a knife to cut into the flesh. A French chef once told me that he thought Poulets de Bresse would never sell in Britain or the US, because you actually need teeth to eat them. There was resistance to the meat.

And this *poule* was mighty good. A huge solid bone, more archaeopteryx than chicken, lay before me, and I thought of troubadours and jesters. The stuffing fell into glorious globules and steamed gently on the side of the plate, infused with the green of chard leaves and the scent of gentle spices that wafted into the air.

Pau and the Béarn thrive on *poule au pot*, so much so that I wondered how they managed to get enough hens.

'Well, it's easy here in Pau, but some restaurants have to rely on a specialist who travels around the farms in Béarn looking for good *poules*.'

What a life, eh?

The rain tumbled on, but I felt awesomely content. Madame brought me a slice of *brebis* cheese, a Béarn version of the highly esteemed Ossau-Iraty. It was simply perfect, thick and pure white, fresher and younger than the cheese I had tasted earlier in Espelette. In fact it was so good that I asked her who made it. She wrote the cheese-maker's name down on a piece of paper, and I drifted happily off to bed.

The next day, the storm raged on, and I called in at the chateau. Waiting patiently for the call of the compulsory tour guide, I was summoned, only to realize that I was actually the only soul in the whole world who wanted to be taken around that day. And *tant mieux* for me, for I had the luxury of a guide all to myself. No miserable kids. No one but me, him and the castle. He took me into private nooks and fascinating crannies – 'Ah you can cross here, no one is around' – and helped me get to grips with the populism of *le bon roi Henri Quatre*.

'Look at it like this,' he told me. 'He was a Protestant in a country that was mainly Catholic. He taught tolerance, and encouraged France to think positively about itself. He had vision, and maybe even more importantly, a sense of humour. And after Henri IV, what happened? Everything went wrong again. The country was divided. Louis XIV became an absolute monarch, and then we had the Revolution. Look at us today! Who have we got? Chirac. I mean, do we not deserve something better than him?'

Indeed you do, *mon pote*. Indeed you do.

Come lunchtime, the cheese man beckoned and, stopping off for a few bottles of the finest Jurançon *sec* on the way, I drove high up into the Ossau valley, towards the border with Spain, the mountains and the snow to seek him out. It was still cold, and got colder still as I arrived in cheeseville and saw the tiniest little bistro imaginable, again utterly empty, and the staff huddled around the fire. It seemed my kind of place.

I asked if they knew where Patrick the cheesemaker lived.

'*Ah oui! Bien sûr!* But he isn't around at the moment. He'll be back later. Why not sit and eat something warming in front of the fire?' they said, shuffling away from the flames to let me sit and warm myself a little. I felt a little guilty, but not for long when I saw the magic word *garbure* on the menu, and realized to my absolute horror that I had been about to leave the Béarn without having eaten a *garbure*. How could I face the world? And M. Koffmann?

Garbure. Hmmm. *Garbure!* Yes, they had it. Yes, it was ready. And yes, it was good.

Brought steaming to the table in a huge enamel pot that looked distinctly Chinese, it was thick with cabbage, the softest white beans, potatoes and carrots, and dotted with *confit*.

Well, it seemed that *garbure* was quite happy to be Béarnais.

By now, Patrick the cheese man was back and

chugging around on his tractor. The farm dog, a distant cousin of Lassie, barked and tried to bite me, but nothing can get in the way of a man and his cheese.

Tragically, he had no *brebis* left that day. But I bore this blow with courage and left with half a cheese that was half cow and half sheep. I pushed it into my bag and headed off to Pau airport, where I joined the line to be weighed. What with my ducks, my goose wings, my beans and my cheese, I was way over the limit. I pleaded to no avail. I said I was writing about the Béarn to no avail. I offered them cheese to no avail. Nothing. I was forced to pay a monstrously large fee to get my produce on the plane. It was a farce.

Garbure

The best thing in the world to eat on a cold day. Serves many. Keeps a few days.

Ingredients
200g haricots tarbais/haricots maïs (or borlotti, lingots, coco – any dried bean with finesse), soaked overnight
About 3 litres of good homemade stock, best of all made with ham bones
400g potatoes

200g carrots
2 parsnips
½ Savoy cabbage
2 onions
4 large cloves garlic
100g *confit*
Goose fat
Salt and pepper

Method

Chop the vegetables and garlic, and fry them in goose fat until they begin to colour, adding as much goose fat as you need to coat them lightly. Add the stock, then the soaked beans. Cook for two hours.

Season to taste. Be careful to do this at the last minute: ham stock can be very salty.

Fifteen minutes before serving, dry fry the *confit* and add to the *garbure*. Serve.

7

Estofinado

BACK HOME, I ABSORBED ALL THE BONHOMIE, immersing myself in Henri IV and the Edict of Nantes by night and in copious bowls of duck fat by day, as I cut and cooked my way through jar upon jar of *confit*. By the end of the week, my hands were silky soft and infantile. Into the fridge went the jars, into our mouths went the cheese, and a few weeks later, off I set once more back to the south to follow up the story of one of France's most bizarre dishes, *estofinado*, whose homeland is in the wilds of l'Aveyron, a fascinating, beautiful and deeply rural *département* to the north-east of Toulouse.

It was a Sunday, and on Sundays something rather strange happens in the hills above the weird town of Decazeville. Busloads of rather gnarled and smiling couples, well into their *troisième âge*, all chatting happily away in French with the regional twang of the Rouergue, set off to visit a tiny hilltop village called Almont les Junies. I joined them.

The road winds up, the buses plough on, pushing all comers to the edge of what is most definitely a D road. The earth is a rich and chocolate brown, and healthy, indolent Salers cattle gently chew the cud, fattening their innocent carcasses, for some of the best beef in all of France comes from these Auvergnat cattle. It is all very gentle, very serene, a far cry from the valley below that once bellowed and belched to the sounds of coal mines and smoking machines.

Decazeville is a curious industrialized island in the middle of a profoundly rural part of France. These days, with mining now finished, it inevitably has an air of depression, of rust, of the past. But Almont is different. It has embraced the past, and lives off people's memories. Quite brilliantly, too. This village was once a rural idyll where miners escaped on weekends and holidays, to walk the hills, to relax and, above all, to eat *estofinado*.

Ah! *Estofinado*, thick, warming, speckled with green, this is a dish for the autumn; made, yes, with potatoes as you might suspect, but also with something far more intriguing and mysterious. An ancient food, with something of the Viking about it. This is the one outstanding outpost of wind-dried cod. But let me tell you a little about this town they call Decazeville.

It grew from practically nowhere, emerging from a little village that was once called La Salle, which just happened to sit on a vast seam of coal, a vital resource at the beginning of the French Industrial Revolution and one that had been only lightly exploited in nearby Aubin. So Decazeville has no ancient heart, no glorious cathedral. The town has ridden booms and busts with little choice. During the depression of 1870, troops were sent in to quieten the rioting miners. Many were shot. Zola was inspired by the stories from these 'Pays Noirs' to write *Germinal*.

Stopping off at the Museum of Mines nearby, I drank in the story of depression and profit while snow began to fall outside, and was ushered in to witness a mock underground explosion that was thunderously effective. The fragility of life. My knees trembled. My ears nearly collapsed. The explosion was solid, shocking. I was only looking for *estofinado*.

The mines were first exploited under Louis XVIII, the restored post-revolutionary monarch, the *chouchou* of the British, it was said, yet another plump and secretive Bourbon, not quite but almost the last of the line. And he, too, had his *chouchous*, one of whom was Duc Elie Decazes, a handsome young liberal whom he made Minister of the Police. Decazes was eventually forced to resign after the assassination of Duc de Berry in 1820. His career faltered, but since he was one of the king's most cherished companions he was sent off to become the French Ambassador in London.

Eventually Decazes bought the mining concessions around La Salle, and the town that grew around the mines was named in his honour. Decazes was from Bordeaux and would have been well aware of the importance of the port as a centre of trade, of wheeling and dealing, particularly with the British, whose love for their wine – claret – was crucial to the development of this spectacular city.

Goods were shipped into Bordeaux from all over the old, and then the new, world. Soon Decazeville fed coal to the nation, sending it down the River Lot to distant Bordeaux in thick sturdy wooden barges. Canny barge-owners thought better of returning empty handed, and filled their holds with miners seeking work, and food and wine for the townspeople. Bordeaux had long been involved in a lucrative trade with the far North in dried and salted cod. And it is this that, somewhat bizarrely, became the unique favourite of the miners of Decazeville.

Dried cod is known in France as *stockfisch*, or *stoccafissu* in Provence, both words that derive from the Dutch for a stick, *stok*, and *visch* for fish. In the Rouergue it is known in argot as *estofi*. If you have never seen a dried cod, then let me tell you that it has a hardness and pungency that can kill. Its feather lightness belies its strength. And this, combined with the distinctive odour that you would expect from any fish that has been left out to dehydrate for a few months in the crisp Arctic air, gives any dish that uses it a very characteristic and definitely gutsy taste, which some might find offputting.

Not me, though. No, I travelled for hours to get to this odd little place, stopping in the handsome town of Villefranche en Rouergue to meet a man in the market who still actually sold the stuff. And there they were: flabby white chunks of fish, reconstituted in water and cut into manageable bits and bobs.

'*Estofinado* is still popular here. Especially on the weekends,' he told me as he slowly sold the odd chunk here and the odd bit there. 'If you want to know how to cook it, go to Almont, in the hills above Decazeville.'

I did as I was bid.

The man from the local bookshop was passing by, and heard me asking about how to make *estofinado*.

'We ate some last night, actually. It's always my wife who cooks it, so I'm not too sure about the recipe. But come to the shop, we've got some books about *estofinado* and Decazeville if you want to have a look.'

And off to the shop I went for a mini briefing on *estofinado*.

'Miners by day, peasants by night!' he told me. 'That's what people say about the Decazevillois.'

But they love *estofinado* with a deep passion. There are now very few pockets in Europe where stockfish can still be found. The biggest eaters are in Veneto, in Italy. Here *baccalà*, which elsewhere means salt cod, actually refers to dried cod instead, and they are in reality the market leaders. Even the names for the various cuts and grades are Italian, ancient remnants from a wider trade that once involved the great Italian maritime ports of Venice and Genoa in particular, which forged close links with Bruges and Antwerp, both members of the Hanseatic League.

Now this long upstream journey from Bordeaux just happened to take seven days, which is as long as you need to soak stick-hard *estofi* in water to make it edible. So as they arrived in Decazeville, the barge-owners could pull in the fish that they had bought in Bordeaux and that had been left to dangle overboard, and celebrate their arrival with a warming dish of *estofinado*. It is perhaps the slowest food of all. It cannot be hurried, there are no short cuts.

Weary miners and their families began to hike up to the minuscule hamlet of Almont les Junies on weekends and holidays, to escape all the dust in the valley below and the trials and tribulations of life underground, and to eat this most enigmatic dish.

Estofinado is deeply tangled with the culinary roots of this oddball part of France, and the people of Almont have not been slow to benefit from the powerful folk memory that still exists, drawing people in from far and wide. From as far away as Oxfordshire, for one. It gives the area a strong identity. There are now almost fifteen tonnes – that is fifteen thousand kilos – of *estofi* imported by France every year, and almost all of it finds its way to Almont. And inevitably, there is a *confrérie*. There just has to be.

This is another fabulously esoteric way to preserve the identity of food in France. To translate it as a 'brotherhood' makes it sound too sinister, but a *confrérie* generally involves the people who make or produce a particular food or crop, or raise a particular animal, calling on the local hat-maker to commission something huge, floppy and unique to wear at the annual dinner, which will endure long into the night and involve much merrymaking and singing. There is one in Espelette. And in Bayonne for the hameratti.

Two families seem to control the *estofinado* circuit these days. The Carrier family dominate, and run a thoroughly frill-less restaurant which you cannot fail to notice, since the village only has a very few houses. I arrived for lunch, a little late to be sure, and their restaurant was absolutely humming. Stepping out of the car, I breathed in and thought of Norway. You could hardly help do so, for they have erected the self-same wooden frame that peppers the Lofoten Islands, from which the fat and freshly caught *skreij* (spring spawning cod) are hung to dry in the perfectly desiccating, freezing-cold climate.

I have been to the Lofoten Islands and stayed in a fisherman's *rorbu*, a wooden house sitting at the water's edge. At night the sky flashed with an electric display of whispers and whizzes and ribbons of bright, surreal colours. This was the Aurora Borealis, a vision so sublime, so breathtaking that I wonder now, as I did then, quite what man thought of it all in those heady days when science didn't have an answer to everything. By day, I travelled around the island, went fishing with short-sleeved fishermen celebrating the 'warmth' of minus one. I met the tongue millionaires – kids who were paid handsome sums to cut the tongues and cheeks from the cod, the perks of the filleter's trade. And in warehouses that were warm and dry, but pungent as a fishwife's apron, were pile upon pile of stockfish, all separated into ancient names and types – Hamburgo, Ragno. So it was a little weird, to say the least, to be reliving these memories in the Rouergue.

Inside the restaurant, the buzz was awesome. It has a set menu by day, but closes at night, and the Carriers seemed to be profiting magnificently from this attack of nostalgia. They have built a neat little packing plant, so not only can you sit and eat *estofinado* but you can, as I did, buy your very own homemade takeaway, neatly vacuum-packed, weighed and labelled as our masters in Brussels require.

So I sat down and ordered that which one has to order, and waited for the dish to arrive. *Estofinado* is thick and filling, and yes, it does have a twang to it, but there is something so comforting about its solidity you can begin to understand why the miners were captured so. I sat next to a couple who were doing the memory thing, and were part of a wider jolly group that had the obligatory ruddy cheerleader, a man full of bonhomie and *blagues*, who kept everyone amused as they tucked in with a more silent reverie.

They had once lived in Decazeville, but had retired to the big city, to Rodez, and came here every once in a while to see family and to remember what life was once like. Madame, whose family came to the mines from Poland in the 1920s, had kept house and brought up her children the Aveyron way, a careful woman who never spent too much on her food, bought her fish and meat at the market, and grew her potatoes in the *potager* at the back of her house.

To make a good *estofinado*, yes, you need well-soaked *estofi*, of course, but also good fresh potatoes and parsley. But the really important thing, she told me, was the oil. *Estofinado* needs good fresh walnut oil, which doesn't keep well, and as the harvest is in the autumn, then that year's oil is pretty crucial. And don't ever let your stockfish boil, she said. Cook it just below a simmer, nothing more or the fish will toughen and your *estofinado* will be ruined. And you'll need some garlic, too. We were not too far from Lautrec, where the glorious purple garlic grows. Milder, sweeter than other varieties, it suits this dish so well.

So here, then, is her version of Monsieur Carrier's version of something that has been cooked in the Aveyron for many, many years.

Estofinado

Serves 6–8

Ingredients
1kg stockfish (dried cod)
500g potatoes, peeled and chopped
300ml walnut oil (pure or blended with peanut oil)
6–8 eggs (1 per person), beaten
125g fresh cream
4–5 cloves of garlic, chopped
A handful of parsley, chopped
1 bouquet garni

Method
Soak the fish for at least a week in a large bowl, changing the water twice a day, until it becomes soft. Cut it into large chunks and place in cold water; add the bouquet garni. Heat and then

simmer gently for at least a quarter of an hour. Take out the fish and separate the flesh, removing the skin and bones. Break into medium-sized pieces with a fork.

Boil the potatoes for about 20 minutes in the water the fish was cooked in, to absorb the flavour. Add the hot potatoes to the fish and blend with a fork to a rough mash (not a smooth purée). Make a hollow in the mash and add the eggs, garlic and parsley. Heat the oil till smoking and pour half of it on to the mixture. Work together with a wooden spoon. Mix in the rest of the hot oil and the fresh cream to make the dish creamier. Serve piping hot.

'Can you make *estofinado* with fresh cod?' I asked.

'Well, I suppose you can, but I don't see why you should want to,' she replied.

Which of course raises a very central question. Is there actually any point in recording these unrepeatable dishes? Emphatically yes. *Estofinado* tells a story of a particular past, time and culture of which it is a significant part. It is part of France's distinguished culinary heritage, and its survival is not merely a nostalgic echo, but preserves memories, and gives life to local culture as well. Hence the bus loads. Hence inquisitive journalists like me, who appreciate difference and the discovery of something that is so unique.

But above all, *estofinado* tastes quite wonderful.

It's a hefty, pungent dish, but when made with an expert hand has a surprising delicacy. The smiles, the murmurs of approval that came from the *salle* were unanimously happy. Monsieur next to me started telling me about his days in the mine, and the perpetual disputes. They were a radical lot, it seemed.

'Back in 1961 we all went on strike when the bosses told us they were going to sack two thousand of us. I was only twenty then, but we were all so angry. There was a lot of anger, and there still is. You know, we still haven't forgotten 1961.'

The strike lasted for nearly ten weeks, but little was gained. Many left the area altogether, and moved up north to the mining town of Roubaix where work was then easier to find. Others stayed and joined the heavy industry that grew up in place of mining, but that too foundered.

'When I come and eat *estofinado*, it all comes back. The strike. My old *potes*, most of whom are dead. And just feeling so tired all the time. It was a hard life. You wouldn't wish it on anyone you know.'

8

Tête de Veau, Sauce Gribiche

A FEW WEEKS LATER, I TOOK UP THE JOURNEY ONCE more and was back in Brittany, where I was summarily sent off to scour the butchers of Vannes to buy a calf's head. We had spent the previous evening wondering which of the several thousand homely French classics we should now cook and test and taste, and well, I thought it was time to go the whole hog and savour my father-in-law-to-be Jean-Paul's own favourite, *tête de veau*, boiled calf's head, enlivened by the sharpness of a *sauce gribiche*.

Our wedding plans were well in the air by now, and so it became a time for Claire's parents to reminisce. Out from a neatly tied box came their own souvenirs and photos. 'Dany and Jean-Paul invite you to celebrate the announcement of their engagement to be married.' The whole family was dressed to kill, mutton-chopped friends and severe-looking in-laws thrust together by chance.

I looked at the engagement-party menu in astonishment. There were oysters and pâtés and smoked salmon. Then Faisan Souvaroff, an old caterer's favourite, and *tête de veau*. To follow, cheese of course, and *îles flottantes*. Dany's parents ran a busy *boucherie* in Châteaudun. How relieved they must have been to see her marry such an avid carnivore.

I wondered why it was that a dish that would be considered almost insulting in its barbarity elsewhere was so popular in France. Roast beef yes, but calf's head? No way. But attitudes are different here. Less hypocritical. In France, not only was it an acceptable dish, but part of the traditional repertoire for such a celebration.

During the Middle Ages, while the meat of both calf and cow was mostly destined for the tables of the rich, the offcuts became more popular fare, and it was Paris, and in particular the meat-cutting districts around Les Halles, that started the city's long affair with *tête de veau*.

There is a jolly and widely known French ditty that goes like this: *Parigot: tête de veau; Parisienne: tête de chienne*. In rough translation you would say, Parisian: calf head; Parisienne: bitch head. Which, I have to admit, sounds a little more convincing in French than English. Parisians are generally unloved outside the capital, so it not only neatly manages to convey a nationwide disdain of

Paris and Parisians but plays on their well-known love of *tête de veau*. Oh, and there is a riposte which goes like this: *campagnard: tête de lard*, or as we might say in English, country bumpkin: lard head.

Now *tête de veau* isn't a desperately complicated dish to cook. Substantial, yes. All you need is a willing calf and a skilled butcher. But these days you will rarely see a French man or woman happily winding through the streets from the market laden with a whole calf's head, tongue lolling from the mouth. With families becoming ever smaller, more mobile and distinctly less domesticated, anyone with a love of *tête de veau* tends to buy what they need ready rolled at the local butcher. Or the super-market. Even its classic companion, *sauce gribiche*, is more likely to be found nestling among the boned *têtes* than made at home.

And while the dynamics of family life are changing in France, so these ancient dishes that call for enthusiasm in numbers are beginning to fall by the wayside. We outsiders may imagine that French families are all blissfully harmonious, with granny as welcome as the summer sun, but this is prepos-terous nonsense, the stuff of dreams. French cities are full of single parents and retired men and women who have never stopped to have children. The divorced and separated, the lonely, the miserable. Just like everywhere else in the developed world.

And the superstructure is remarkably similar, too. Increasingly, people have turned to super-markets.

Although when in Vannes we use the weekly street market, much is bought at the local Carrefour, an enormously powerful chain of *très grandes surfaces* (TGS), or 'very big surfaces' in English. This is the term used in French to avoid any possibility of needing a word like *supermarché*. The French, after all, gave us the concept of the *hypermarché*, and are highly adept at this retail business, but their profound love of acronyms conquers all. It appeals to the bureaucrat within.

And these TGS are virtually identical. Again, just like everywhere else. Some are so vast that the staff rollerblade from one end of the store to the other. I cruise the aisles and marvel. Why, even the *pâté de campagne* now comes in mini plastic tubs with several layers of protective film, and there is nothing about it that provokes a single thought of taste. The air is chill. But not all appears to be so anodyne.

French supermarkets are bewitching. They have cuts of meat I have only read about, slices and sections cut with surgical precision, some marbled with fat, others neat and perfectly formed. There might be a whole section devoted to beef from the Charolais, another to Normandie. Over in the fish section I have come across the tiniest fillets of red mullet, still bright and again so damned neat, and sparklingly fresh. Never mind that these fish were all undersized, and had never even discovered the thrill of hormones, let alone sex, they began to excite me.

So here I was on the outer edge of Brittany and I could have easily cooked a *potée* Auvergnate, or a Gascon *garbure*, an Alsace *choucroute* or a Basque *axoa*. I could have eaten horse *cervelas* and a Provençale *daube*. Why, they even sold a *daubière*! There was some Beaufort at half the price I paid in the market last time I was here, and it was *d'alpage* at that and twenty-four months old, so I cheesed myself up. There was even some unusual leavened bread made with a little *blé noir*.

So it will come as no surprise, then, that Vannes, like every town and city in France, is suffering from diminishing-butcher syndrome. While we may spend hours sipping Pinot Noir and recounting tales of marvellous butchers discovered en route in France, the situation out there is grim. And it's not just butchers who are in sharp decline, but bakers, fishmongers, *épiciers*, *chocolatiers*; all those ancient métiers are deeply troubled by competition from those very big surfaces.

But it's not just the downsizing of families that is spelling the end of *tête de veau*'s popularity. There is the same perceptible change in eating habits in France as in the rest of Europe. Many are simply becoming revolted by the idea of eating the head of a calf, much as they are beginning to turn away from roast horse and *saucisson* made with donkey meat. A head is no longer so widely considered 'good to eat'. Of course, this is all profoundly illogical, but logic doesn't really influence what we eat, even in France. It is sentiment, habit and culture, which all ineluctably change. A nascent European food culture is gradually emerging.

While we may very well find the idea of eating calf's head repellent, we may quite happily eat a chicken nugget made from reconstituted slaughter wash, or chickens fed on soya grown on trashed Amazonian forest. These are some of the prime constituents of the fast-food industry and of ready-made meals that are tellingly labelled 'convenience'. Pre-cut meat and meat 'products' far removed from anything animated fill shopping baskets all over the world without the slightest prick to the conscience. But eating a calf's head is considered one step too far.

The further we move from buying our food from artisans and professionals, the more entrenched in our ignorance we become. And the more ignorant we become, the more gullible. The corporate world has a field day, rubbing its hands with glee as it feeds us all those bits and pieces dressed up and prettified, and all the while we are moving away from all things that are recognizably living matter, working bits and pieces.

So have we lost for ever the proximity we once had to our food? Probably, yes. But wherever a market culture survives, as in France, there is at least a chance that we may, just may, preserve and hand down a vibrant food culture.

We may learn that a potato doesn't have to be scrubbed and bagged to be edible. That an apple may have an imperfection yet taste exquisite. That meat comes from animals that once lived, breathed, felt and died so that we might eat. It sounds almost evangelical. We can barely imagine serried rows of carrots standing with their feathery leaves in a field, let alone that they are things of the earth. Or that a salmon was once a beautiful, sleek wild creature that swam thousands of miles before it was caught, a rare and seasonal treat, rather than something mundane, produced by the million for the million to make millions. We are all in the same boat here. All of us are witnessing the dumbing down of tastes and the destruction of our differences.

So let's not get too carried away with the idea that France is the land of gastronomic milk and honey, where loving *mémés* guide future generations through an entire culinary repertoire before they are pubescent. France is a sophisticated urban society, and is not immune to the gradual separation of food from knowledge, from it becoming a mere commodity.

But those mythical street markets, where old ladies sit and gossip next to their vibrant lettuces, thankfully still haven't disappeared and hopefully never will. Where ducks and chickens come with heads and guts and look as if they once lived. Where people queue and haggle and you are asked quite when you are eating your melon. It is another world to most of us, a dreamworld. And also, sadly, maybe a theme-park world. A parody of itself.

I did eventually find my *tête de veau*, neatly boned and rolled and looking remarkably unhead-like. I asked for a massive tongue to be added, by special request of Dany.

'I thought you English didn't eat this sort of thing,' the butcher remarked.

'We don't. My wife is French, and her father loves it,' I replied.

'*Ah, vous avez de la chance, alors!*' Yes, oh lucky man.

I arrived back with my arms a little weary to see that the big pans had already been prepared like surgical implements, laid out by the cooker as if we were getting ready for an amputation. We set the rolled head in the biggest pan and let it simmer for three hours or so. The tongue was to be boiled later.

As the house filled with the unctuous smell of boiling meat, we set the table and Jean-Paul went off to make the *sauce gribiche*, a lovely sauce made from egg yolks, capers, cornichons and mustard. By the way, this is not actually named in honour of a famous chef long gone, a Monsieur Gribiche. A *gribiche* is an ornament on a shoe, and was once associated with the leatherworkers who worked in the shadow of the slaughterhouse district of La Villette in Paris, who of course liked nothing better than to dine on a hearty *tête de veau*. The essence of the sauce is its sharpness, for a *tête* is a fatty thing to eat, another reason why it is losing its popularity these days.

Jean-Paul's sauce gribiche

Serves 6

Ingredients
3 hard-boiled eggs
500ml vegetable oil
1 soupspoon white wine vinegar
1 soupspoon capers
2 cornichons, cut into rounds
2 teaspoons Dijon mustard
1 tsp each of chopped chervil, parsley and tarragon
Salt and pepper

Method
In a bowl, chop the egg yolks very finely, so they become a paste. Add the oil in little doses, then the vinegar, cornichons, capers, herbs and the finely chopped egg whites.

Serve with *tête de veau*, fish, or fresh crab.

The word *gribiche* is interesting. In Paris, before the abattoirs of La Villette were built, most of the slaughtering was done around Les Halles, the old central market, the *ventre de Paris* or 'Paris's stomach', as Zola called it. The butchers or *bouchers* were long established in the area, particularly around Le Châtelet. It was here also that the guild, the *Confrérie de la Nativité de Notre-Seigneur aux maistres bouchers de la ville*, to be exact, held their court. The guilds were hugely powerful in medieval Paris, just as they were elsewhere in Europe. They acted as trade corporations and were given strictly defined rights and duties that were set out in endless rules and ordnances.

These days *confréries* may seem slightly jokey and quaint, but they were once, particularly under the pre-revolutionary ancien régime, absolutely essential to the workings and finances of the State. Rights to trade were sold by the Crown and held in perpetuity by members of the *confréries*, who protected these rights ferociously. This was to cause some fundamental problems for the ancien régime, as we shall see later. But habitual respect for the power of particular interest groups still expresses itself in France every now and again. It was never quite removed by the revolutionaries.

As far as butchery was concerned, no one was allowed to trade freely without becoming a member of the *confrérie*, so it was very much a closed shop. Families not only handed down skills to successive generations, but expanded cautiously, only taking on apprentices to maintain standards. Originally the butchers of Les Halles were allowed to kill the beasts on site, but over the years this became a little crazy, with the narrow streets filled with deliveries of anything from bleating sheep to oinking pigs, while the gulleys ran red with blood.

However, the butchers were not alone in their dealings with meat. Far from it. There were the *chaircuitiers* who dealt in cooked pork, the *rôtisseurs* who dealt in roast meat, and the *poulaillers* were allowed to sell poultry. Every single aspect of the business of supplying food to Paris was closely controlled, protected and taxed, so that the city's central food market, Les Halles, was full of scurrying inspectors ensuring that the complex system functioned.

Les Halles is now a sorry, desolate mess. Cities sadly grow up, outgrow their market. Daft, functional alternatives are proposed, and accepted by daft city planners. The market moved south to suburban Rungis in the 1970s. Bulldozers moved in and created a subterranean shopping centre of such anodyne mediocrity that waves of passionate regret easily overwhelm the senses when you look at it now. Everyone hankers for the past. But, despite everything, you can at least still eat *tête de veau* in this particular cultural fossil.

So, *tête de veau* still has its fans. Tragically for calves, one of them is the presidential greaseball

Chirac, who told the world right at the beginning of his first mandate that he, Jacques Chirac, the fifth president of the Fifth Republic, liked to eat *tête de veau*. That he liked tractors, and la Corrèze, and was truly a man of the people. Sales rocketed. Butchers smiled once more. But time took its toll. The Chirac years ended in even more cynicism, and the sales of *tête de veau* are once again in gentle decline.

9

Pot au Feu

I TOOK THE SLOW TRAIN TOWARDS PARIS A FEW DAYS later, stopping off on the way to try and master one of France's most iconic dishes, the glorious mix of carnal bits and pieces that is *pot au feu*.

Now I am lucky. I can talk butchery till the cows come home, for butchery is in the family. Claire's grandfather, Robert Thibault, or Pépé Robert as we all call him, is a retired butcher, a man once renowned for the quality of his beef, a straight-backed, benign and loveable eighty-year-old, who has lived most of his years in an unremarkable town in central France called Châteaudun, where he is still one of the town's most respected butchers – well, ex-butchers.

Châteaudun has no real claim to fame other than its imposing sixteenth-century castle, where it likes to treat its citizens to the occasional medieval feast.

It is Smallville, gently prosperous and pleasant. Tourists tend to pass by and drive down to Tours and its splendid exoticisms, or the chateaus along the Loire Valley. Or to Orléans, or Chartres. Both are within easy reach.

But I like Châteaudun. Wander around the town – and it is a minor wander, I assure you – and you can still see houses and doors with Renaissance flourishes, and sense its medieval persona and a mild grandeur in the closely aligned streets. And I like it, too, for its weekly *marché*. It's a marvellous market, with a particularly fine fishmonger, a superb *fromager* and one or two itinerant *bouchers*. And one other thing. It is the only place in the world where I have been paraded around town and introduced as '*mon petit gendre*'. In English it means 'my great son-in-law'. And, although it wasn't technically true at the time, it sounded good to me. It helped my sense of belonging. And who needs existential distress when preparing for a *pot au feu*?

I love to talk to Pépé Robert about the life of a butcher, and thankfully he likes to talk, to joke, to soothe troubled souls, to listen and be diplomatic. He is in effect a classic old-school butcher, who understood his clients as well as he knew his meat.

'Ah, you always had to tell the customers what they wanted to hear!' he told me when I joined him on his weekly wander around Châteaudun market, where he shook endless hands, exchanged pleasantries, and confided in one and all. He was on a mission, he told everyone, to fit me out with some really good meat for a *pot au feu*.

The meat stalls and *boucheries* of Châteaudun were heaving that day, full of strange cuts of meat that he eyed and assessed with a practised glance. I am fascinated by the language of butchery. First the cuts, *les découpes*. To the foreign ear, remote, weird-sounding, oddball words abound in both languages, but at least in France you actually see some variety. Many terms used are almost untranslatable, for French butchery is not the same as either the English or American system.

Given that the principle behind a good *pot au feu* is to make sure that you have a mix of the gelatinous and the tasty, you will need at least two, and preferably four or even five different cuts of meat. Most should come from the forequarter, I was told – from the cheaper end, that is. And so we bought a little *macreuse* (who has ever seen any arm clod for sale in an English-speaking butcher's?), some juicy *paleron* (chuck steak), *plat de côtes* (top rib) with a fine bone left in, and some *gîte* (top rump), as well as a few bones that were thick and full of marrow.

Cuts suitable for a beef *pot au feu*
- *joues*/cheeks
- *langue*/tongue

From the forequarter
- *paleron*/chuck steak
- *macreuse*/arm clod
- *plat de côtes*/top rib
- *flanchet*/middle stomach

From the rear quarter
- *queue*/tail
- *gite, gite gite, gite de noix*/top rump
- *jarret*/shin on the bone
- *os à moelle*/marrow bones
- *hampe*/skirt

We were to be seven around the table that night. Any fewer and there would have been enough for a week. But there was so much temptation: I was amazed to see a rolled udder for sale.

'It's much better when the cow has been lactating,' Robert told me.

I bought a slice, and tried it later fried with butter, parsley, onions and garlic. It was excellent.

I saw a rarer cut, too: the butcher's favourite, it is called the *araignée* – the spider, literally – and is much prized, just the thing to buy your favourite carnivore.

For Robert, butchery had always been his great passion. And a curious passion it was, as he would start the week by killing the very thing he loved most of all. Veal. Monday at Boucherie Thibault was the day for *les veaux vivants*, live calves, which were brought to the shop and dispatched with a sharp blow to the head. It would be unimaginable these days. Illegal, too.

The butcher was a respected professional and as such had a particular status within a town, like the baker and the doctor. He knew his customer's every whim. To keep the business functioning efficiently, local butchers, Robert included, used a curious argot called *le loucherbem*, which was, as a rule, totally incomprehensible to outsiders. The fundamentals appear to be quite simple. Look at the word *loucherbem*. It is *boucher* – butcher – with an *l* added at the beginning and the *b* moved to the end: *l-oucher-bem*. *La dame* becomes *l-ame-de*. *Le monsieur* is *lieusiemic*; *bonjour*: *lonjourbem*.

This opened up huge theoretical possibilities to me. I imagined that the *bouchers* of France were continually criticizing and joking about their customers behind their backs, much as we fish suppliers used to do about the chefs we had to deal with. Robert, still famously diplomatic, insisted it was more 'Get the sausages for Madame', 'Madame would like some steak,' that sort of thing. *Informatique* rather than *critique*. It was about perfecting the service, rather than ribald mockery.

Le loucherbem was far from unique to Châteaudun. In the great metropolis, Paris, the wild and busy abattoir district of La Villette also had its argot, called *largonji*, which comes from the

Provençal word *jargon* (which has, of course, successfully moved into English). It replaces the first letter with an *l*, and puts it at the end, followed by an *é*. *Quarante* becomes *l-arante-qu-é*, vingt, *l-in-v-é*. Geddit?

But it was impossible for a butcher to travel around and inspect all the meat he used, so working with him was a trusted middle man, *le maquignon*, who scoured the countryside for suitable animals. His judgement was trusted implicitly. Robert preferred Charolais and Normandy beef, and so *le maquignon* would supply these, but it was up to Robert to bring them to perfection. Whole carcasses were left to mature slowly in the butchery fridge.

The family lived above the shop, in a tiny flat that reeked of meat. Of course, the skill of the butcher was not just to sell '*les morceaux nobles*', but to move every morsel, every tendon, every head and every brain, so *pot au feu*'s popularity helped keep France's butchers in business. However, during the summer months, when Robert's customers migrated westwards to the sea, demand for meat dipped, especially for the forequarter. The answer to this blip in demand was to call up some of his country colleagues, who were still happily selling the poorer cuts for *pot au feu* to rural communities that were less inclined to depart en masse to the beaches. They were the visited rather than the visitors.

Robert's wife Ginette manned the till and took care of the money, while Robert looked after the meat and the customers. The son of a baker, he had learned his skills as an apprentice in Blois, just before the Second World War, and had hair-raising tales to tell of sausage smuggling and clandestine butchery during the Occupation.

If *boucherie* was a thoroughly respectable profession, a métier where skill and trust were the norm and butchers were pillars of the community, their children's perspective was somewhat different. They tell of the unglamorous side. Of Tuesdays when the whole house stank of tripe that boiled and bubbled for hours and hours, permeating the very soul. Of tin baths, and constant work.

The shop always shut at *midi*, though, and the family sat down to eat together. Memories are of simple dishes, well cooked with good ingredients. Of baguettes, and cakes from the *pâtisseries*. The grandchildren talk with misty eyes of playing shop with Pépé Robert, as he wrapped the ends of the *saucisson* and ham for them when the shop was quiet. Claire spent every summer at Châteaudun, cosseted by her loving grandparents. All seem to have benefited. Time spent with grandparents often becomes the stuff of passionate memories. Of food, and tastes, and steaming bowls of *pot au feu*.

So we set off back home laden with bags of meat with strange names and strange shapes, and allowed it all to boil away on the stove while Robert rested, and the kitchen steamed up.

By late evening, all was ready. The table was set, and little pots of cornichons and mustard appeared. The house was sweating with steam and the windows dripped with condensation. We all sat down and talked about the joys of *pot au feu*. Nicole, Robert's partner, remembered how her mother would use pigs' ears, the cheapest cut of all. Her father had died young and money was always tight. *Pot au feu* was, however, very much a family favourite.

The Thibaults around the table were luckier: for them, meat had always been readily available. But to each and every one, *pot au feu* was a changeless, richly evocative dish. Again, remarkably simple to make. Just reliant upon good ingredients.

Families in France all seem to have their own memories and tricks about how best to cook *pot au feu*. You always add an onion, which is always studded with cloves. You bring the meat to the boil, rather than adding it to boiling water – a cardinal rule. This allows the meat to flavour the stock to best effect. Traditionally, you then eat the broth, the *bouillon*, separately. Then the meat, the *bouillie*. Some say you should add a lightly caramelized onion to colour the stock; yet others that you should drop the meat into boiling water to preserve its flavour.

For me, the best thing about *pot au feu* is the

broth, so I always bring the pan gently to the boil and watch all that scum and muck collect. It is a social, familiar dish – the very antithesis of fast food. Hugely comforting and invigorating, everyone should eat it at least once in their lives.

Pot au feu

A simple version could go like this:

Serves 6

Ingredients
1½kg beef shin
1½kg chuck steak
600g top rump, silverside
4 litres water
4 onions with cloves stuck into them
6 good fresh leeks, trimmed, cleaned and tied in a bunch
6 carrots
6 small turnips
6 large potatoes, peeled
Sea salt

Method
Put the meat into the water and bring to the boil. The idea is to get tasty stock. Skim off the scum.

Add all the vegetables apart from the potatoes and boil for an hour and a half. Then add the potatoes and boil for a further hour. Season to taste.

Serve, snipping the string from the leeks dramatically at the table.

So, you skim off the scum and watch the windows steam and the cat stretch its claws. You bring the family to the table, and let them watch as you ladle the burning, boiling broth into a nice familiar bowl. Snip the string around the bundle of leeks, richly flavoured by the *bouillon*. Cut the meat, and marvel at how the gristle and fat have just disintegrated into tender, sweet edibility. Serve, still steaming, wafting its earthy scents, to your family, and watch them as they slice blissfully through those softened morsels, enlivened with the vinegary rush of cornichons and mustard. This is the bliss of *pot au feu*.

Domestic, a little bourgeois even, it is the one dish that truly surprised me in France. Eloquent and simple, profoundly evocative, and so damned good. On one level, *pot au feu* seems really rather mundane. Just meat gently boiled over a slow, lolloping flame. But it is more than that. There is no other dish that allows you to see so much of the story of France and its food. We can watch the guillotine tumble and great chefs stumble. We will see it meander through the Middle Ages, and survive the decline of spices and the subtle, extraordinary cosmic food of the courts. And then on through the Renaissance and into the Enlightenment, *pot au feu* survived virtually untouched, becoming even more popular as France evolved into a semi-urbanized society, with a bourgeoisie hungry for good food and, above all, for meat.

Pot au feu is at the head of what you could call a genealogical cuisine; it is a dish that has given rise to a hundred others, all closely related, all ravishingly delicious. And if there happens to be any meat left over, then that too can be used. Leave it to cool, but not in the stock: it becomes insipid if left in cold stock too long. Take the meat out, wrap it, chill it and use it the next day. You could make a good *hachis Parmentier* (see page 234), or maybe a *miroton*.

And think, too, how to use such copious amounts of the most delectable stock. You can easily freeze it, and use it as you wish. For soup. For risotto. For sauces. But it is this *bouillon* that we will now relentlessly pursue through the streets of Paris. It is time to become immersed in the capital and the Revolution. It is time to dabble in alchemy and intrigue. *On y va!*

10

Restaurant Divin

SO YOU ARE WARM. YOU ARE INVIGORATED. YOU ARE
in Paris, wondering what happened to Les Halles,
mildly depressed, perhaps, at the hideousness of
what you see before you. At the junkies and the
hoodies. At the baddies and the goodies. Paris is
not, they say, quite what it was. There is fast food,
there is slow food. There are bars, cafés, and
hundreds upon hundreds of restaurants. You can
eat African, Brazilian, Thai, Chinese, Japanese.
Even French. You can *croque* on a *monsieur* and
snack on *frites*, but this word restaurant: what
exactly does it restore? Your self-esteem? Your
bank balance?

I left Châteaudun for Paris and watched the city
slowly coalesce through the train's sparklingly
clean window. I had begun to be distinctly
intrigued by the story of the restaurant, even more

so when I learnt that one of the most illustrious of them all, the Restaurant Véry, had the same family name as Jean-Paul. So when I arrived in Paris I walked from the station towards the Palais Royal, where the ancient Vérys once wowed the city's eager gourmets.

First stop: to a street that no longer existed. The Rue des Poulies, now the Rue de Bailleul, not far from the Palais Royal, where one long-forgotten day in 1765 a gentleman called Boulanger is said to have opened the world's very first restaurant. Or so the story goes. Rue de Bailleul is deeply unmemorable these days, a back passage to nowhere. There are no plaques. Nothing. But the story of Monsieur Boulanger is a little more exciting.

Leap back to Paris in 1765 if you will. Louis XVI is king. France is racked by heavy debt and fearful of famine. And along comes Monsieur Boulanger with an excellent idea. Why not allow people to come and choose what they want to eat? It was hardly wheel-inventingly original. One would have thought that Paris, with its reputation for being the gastronomic capital of the solar system, would have worked this one out long before 1765. But until then eating out meant visiting *tables d'hôtes* or cabarets, where you ate what you were offered.

With sparse marble tables and no tablecloths, Chez Boulanger was noticeably different. The proprietor had inscribed above the door: '*Venite ad me, omnes qui stomachio laboratis et ego restaurabo vos,*' 'Come to me, all whose stomachs need attention and I will restore them to good health.' This was to be a place for the delicate, the effete, for foreigners, and young men who wanted to be alone. Even women were warmly welcomed. The cookbooks of the time were full of recipes for invigorating broths. Disease, it was believed, could be prevented by careful eating, and there was nothing more restorative than the essence of a good domestic *pot au feu*: meat stock. And this, in a slightly different form, was precisely what was served in small porcelain cups at Boulanger's. Women, rarely seen in the vulgar crowds that rushed to the city's busy *tables d'hôtes*, were said to be delighted by the lighter food, and were soon to be seen sipping this restorative broth. But there was more on offer. *Poulet au gros sel*: chicken cooked in salt and served with fresh eggs. Sheep trotters served in white sauce.

For a while, Boulanger flourished. He was to be seen proudly dressed with his sword clinking on the pavement, decorated in a cordon of dubious origin. His wife blessed the *salle* with her presence, and there was an air of subdued calm, with little of the ostentation that was eventually to characterize the Parisian restaurant scene. The wig-makers, the city's most notorious gossips, whispered news of the opening of Boulanger's to their clients. Go to the Rue des Poulies, they said. Poets and philosophers were drawn to the bright marble tables. Diderot went and ate there and left well fed, surprised by how much it had cost, lured by the beauty of Madame.

Thus, almost stealthily, was the restaurant born. Its success, however, inevitably caused friction, particularly with the city's powerful guilds. The *traiteurs* were a powerful corporation who controlled part of the business of public eating, and they were wary of such innovation. They saw their power and influence threatened.

Eighteenth-century France had tied itself into a bureaucratic Gordian knot. Various guilds had gained the right to specific parts of the business of public eating. The *rôtisseurs* were allowed to serve cooked meat and deliver it to your home. *Rôtisseurs-traiteurs* were allowed to serve it *en place*. An early guide to Paris (de Blegny's *Le Livre Commode des Adresses de Paris*, 1692) mentioned the excellence of the cooked food at Les Sieurs Guerbois, close to the Boucherie St Honoré, a *rôtisseur* whose hostess was said to be an added attraction. More orthodox were the various *tables d'auberges* or *tables d'hôtes*, where for a set sum you would be served a meal, but had no choice. The food would be placed in the middle of the communal table, to be wolfed down by the regulars, who left any passing and unfamiliar clients stranded at the edge. Foreigners justifiably thought this was all very barbaric.

Many *tables d'hôtes* were run by the *traiteurs*, who had originally offered a different service, cooking to order and delivering the food to your home, but they had begun to have a pretty poor reputation for the quality of their service. Serving anything that was termed a *ragoût* was forbidden to anyone but a *traiteur*.

Ragoût is an interesting word. Originally it referred to something that literally irritated the palate. *Ragoûts* were small appetizers, rather like amuse-bouches in a modern restaurant. A truffle garnished with pomegranate and lemon is mentioned in La Varenne's highly influential *Cuisinier François*. There was to be much discussion as to whether the cups of *bouillon* served in the restaurants were indeed *ragoûts*.

Even the poorest Parisian had to eat too, and they were drawn to the *petites auberges* or *gargotes*, where soup and broth from vast bubbling *marmites* were served as cheaply as possible. Much of the food consumed was bought from *regratiers*, street sellers who shouted their wares above the din and clatter of the city. There were loudmouthed *harenguières*, the herring-sellers. The milk-sellers, the cheese-sellers. Some food came from the surplus of cabarets, and eventually from the restaurants of the arrondissement.

The business of public drinking was just as complicated. Hoteliers, *cabaretiers*, *taverniers* and *marchands de vin-à-pot* were all allowed to sell wine, but not to the same clients. There was to be no toe-treading. Thus the hoteliers served passing horse-riders and carriages. *Cabaretiers* were an interesting case. We now associate cabarets with music and Nazis, but at the time they were loud, licentious drinking dens, where the wine had a reputation of being as bad as the morals.

Rabelais liked a cabaret called the Pomme de Pin, where the vibe was suitably gargantuan. In 1698, cabarets were allowed to serve food, but it had to be cooked by the *rôtisseurs*. The tables could be covered by plates and tablecloths if desired, but no cook was to be employed. Cabarets were supposed to be used by strangers to the area; indeed the statutes theoretically forbade married locals either to drink or eat there. It was presumably a little difficult to enforce.

Taverniers could for a while only serve wine, not bread. But they too became like the cabarets, serving food that was cooked elsewhere. As for the *marchands*, they were permitted to sell wine to individuals for consumption off site.

And we must also mention the *limonadiers*, who far from being purveyors of lemonade had to submit to an insane and almost constant revision of their statutes, particularly under Louis XIV, who dreamt up elaborate ways to increase the State's income. The king decided to sell masterships to the guild, entirely against their wishes. Ah! The joys of absolutism. The *limonadiers* were obliged either to buy them or to see their monopoly gradually dissipated. They paid up. This happened in 1704, 1706, 1713, and finally in 1775.

So amidst all this confusion, along came Monsieur Boulanger with this brilliant idea. The *traiteurs* reacted vigorously to his arrival and took him to court. Was he not serving a selection of *ragoûts*, they reasoned? On the contrary, he replied, his food was meant to restore health rather than feed the general population. But the genie had been released, and Parisians liked this novel way of dining. They could at last choose what to eat. The idea of restoring health was quickly forgotten.

Another restaurant opened nearby, run by Messieurs Roze and Pontaillé. It was called the Champ Oiseau. The story gets a little hazy here, for these two then published an almanac that, unsurprisingly, boasted that they and not Monsieur Boulanger were the first restaurateurs:

The restaurateurs created in the capital in 1767 by Messrs Roze and Pontaillé are part of the *traiteurs*, those who excel or should excel, according to the aims of the founders, in making *potages au riz, au vermicelli*, and other salubrious and delicate dishes. The object of these well-composed establishments is not to provide a *table d'hôte* but to allow eating at all hours, and of particular dishes at a fixed price.

You will notice that they include themselves among the *traiteurs*. It seems they were part of the established order and were determined to appropriate the success of Boulanger.

Roze then listed several other establishments, but singularly avoided mentioning poor old Boulanger. Deslauriers, in the Rue Saint-Honoré, were the successors to the first restaurateur, they said, and *Venite ad me* seems to have been replaced by '*Hic sapide titillant juscula blanda palatum, hic datur effoetis pectoribusque salus*', 'Here pleasant broths prudently stimulate the palate, here health is given to tired hearts' as a slightly less catchy epithet for everyone to muse upon.

By Roze and Co's own admission, the Rue des Poulies proved to be a difficult location, so they moved on to the Hotel d'Aligre on the Rue Saint-Honoré nearby, which had previously been known for its *table d'hôte*. 'The price of every dish is fixed and determined, being served at any hour of the day whatsoever. Ladies are admitted and may dine or sup with an excellent choice of dishes at a fixed and modest price.'[1]

Confusingly, there is yet another version of events. In Jouy's *L'Ermite de la Chaussée d'Antin*, the reader is assured that the first restaurant that opened was in

[1] *Fine Bouche: A History of the Restaurant in France* by Pierre Andrieu, translated by Arthur L. Hayward, London: Cassell, 1956.

the Rue des Prêcheurs, said to be a *table d'hôte* that quickly morphed into this new form:

> Perfection is reached in nothing save by endless striving and experiment. About the year 1772 various *traiteurs* ceased to keep a *table d'hôte* at regular hours and substituted for it small tables for six or a dozen covers, which were renewed as often as the guests appeared.

The menu had already evolved considerably from Boulanger and his *bouillon*. A Monsieur de Védel served *bisque d'écrevisses* and *truffes au champagne*, a whole turbot at a cost of twenty-four *livres*, *petits pigeons innocents* at sixteen. Desserts and wine were beginning to flow freely, but still there was noticeably little meat: this was still the business of the *rôtisseurs* and *charcutiers*.

At the time, food was believed to have highly specific properties whose correct combination maintained the natural balance of the body. These ideas were central to contemporary ideas of health. Foods could alter the production of the body's four humours (blood, black bile, yellow bile and phlegm) and affect the personality. Anyone whose character was thought to be, say, melancholic, could eat certain foods to counteract this tendency, prescribed by physicians. *Der Mensch ist, was er isst*, say the Germans. You are what you eat, say we.

There were many and varied means available to ward off disease. Cordials were concocted to work on the spirit, and as early as the fourteenth century there was an elaborate search for the purest essence of substances that could perhaps ward off the ultimate, death itself. These were called quintessences.

But how to extract these magical substances? Alchemy had long struggled to liberate the great power and mystery of nature, while physicians concocted pills and remedies with fanciful claims. The object was always the same: to restore the natural balance of the body and the humours. Naturally they worked with substances that were rich in quintessences. Thus wine, sugar, gold and the mysterious myrobalan were all subject to a series of fantastical experiments, of which perhaps the most significant was distillation.

From wine came alcohol. Again, an interesting word. It comes from the Arabic *al-kohl*, which once referred to the alchemists' favourite substance, antimony, refined from the mineral stibnite that came from ancient Assyria. The word changed from meaning this refined powder to a powder of any kind, and then the essence of any substance. And it was the essence of wine that truly shook the world. It was called *eau de vie*, water of life.

The twelfth-century Catalan alchemist Arnald de

Villanova was among the first to mention it.'[1] '*Eau de vie* ... prolongs good health, dissipates the humours, rejuvenates the heart and preserves youth,' he said.

Eau de vie became a useful medicine in the physician's repertoire. A teaspoonful a day was the recommended dose. In 1514, King Louis XII gave the *vinaigriers* the right to sell *eau de vie* in France, but they subdivided interminably, so wide was their remit and so popular was *eau de vie*. Street sellers called *placiers* were allowed to sell it in small doses, and in 1678 to place chairs in the street, presumably for those who could stand no longer.

In 1676, the *limonadiers* were brought into the equation. They could already sell distilled rose water, *eau d'anis* (aniseed water) and *eau de canella* (cinnamon water), and in 1704, Louis permitted them to sell *eau de vie* and strongly flavoured alcohols: fennel-flavoured *fenouillette*, *ratafia*, and even gin. From Lorraine came a potion called *parfait-amour* which proved very popular with the Parisians, who took to this new 'medicine' with enthusiasm.

But the logic of distillation could also be applied elsewhere. Why not, for instance, try and capture the essence of good *bouillon*, that most fundamental, restorative liquid, the heart of all domestic cooking and the *pot au feu*? Records show that as

---

[1] See *The Devil's Doctor* by Philip Ball, London: William Heinemann, 2006, pp. 176–80.

early as the sixteenth century, finely cut beef and poultry was being cooked in tightly sealed bottles, with grains of barley and Damas raisins, scented with rose water and cinnamon, and distilled to make what was called a *restaurant divin*, a divine restorative. There were even recipes in existence for a *restaurant* made from live turtles.

The influential seventeenth-century French cookbook *L'Art de Bien Traiter*, written by the mysterious L.S.R., contained several *restaurant* recipes. It was first published in 1674, and was an immediate success. The author wrote:

> The science of cooking is in the decomposition, the digestion and then the extracting of the quintessence of meat, taking from it the nourishing juices in such a way that nothing dominates.
>
> Take a *rouelle* of veal, a *quarteron* of cut ham, the zest of carrots and parsnips, an onion – studded with the habitual cloves, of course – and a chicken cut into four. Add some stock, and cook for six hours. When the meat is done, add some meat cordial and leave until the veal is done.

More refined versions began to appear, called *bouillons en restaurant* or *potages sans eau*. They quickly crossed the Channel, and appeared in several English cookbooks of the time. Elizabeth Moxon's 'soop without water' is a direct crib.

Come the Revolution, the king lost his head and the corporations their raison d'être, but the restaurants lived on, and took to all the turbulence like a duck to water. Many chefs, finding themselves at a loose end, took their skills elsewhere and opened their own restaurants, many of which thrived.

And at the centre of this rejuvenated eating culture was the Palais Royal, just a few streets from the Rue de Bailleul. It was here that the Vérys once held open their glittering mirrored doors to the most discerning clients.

11

Sauce Béarnaise

FOUR YEARS EARLIER, I HAD SAT IN THE SHADOW OF the Palais Royal, having just finished a journey around Italy. I was in love – full of enthusiasm, passion and ribald dreams for all things Italian – so I moaned a little at the surliness of the gloomy Parisian waiters, at the banality of frothy sauces and prettily stacked chips.

But being a glutton for punishment, I now thought it time to revisit, particularly as I wanted to look at this intriguing story about the Vérys. Ghosts and spirits now wander through the breezy emptiness of the Palais Royal, which seems a duller place these days than the ancient texts suggest. The whores, spies and assassins have long gone.

So I sat in the sun – it was quietly autumnal for once – ordered my steak and watched it ooze deliciously as I tipped the little *pichet* of Béarnaise sauce on top and sliced into its meltingly tender flesh.

I took a bite and remembered. The sauce was rich and sang of tarragon, chervil and copious, rich butter, subduing the controlled sharpness of the vinegar. There was sweet skilled harmony between the meat and the sauce, and this was exactly what I needed to be reminded of: that a sauce is a gestalt creation, where flavours, like the colours in a palette, combine and appeal to the accepted tastes of the age. There are some combinations that may now seem awesomely clumsy, outmoded, for tastes do change. But Béarnaise hasn't.

It was a brilliant creation, born of the burgeoning post-revolutionary Parisian restaurant culture, like so many dishes that seem to appeal to the regional in us all but were actually created right here in Paris.

Before the Revolution, the Palais Royal was owned by the Duc d'Orléans, King Louis XVI's much-mistrusted cousin, who despite showing distinctly liberal tendencies and even changing his name to Philippe Egalité, was guillotined during the Terror, going to his end, it is said, with much calm and dignity.

Cash-strapped despite the immense fortune of his wife, the duke had set about transforming his inheritance energetically. And the Palais Royal, Cardinal Richelieu's old domain – it was originally called the Palais-Cardinal – was his inheritance, which he made into a warren of shops, cafés and worse, so that the whole edifice could be sold or rented out, to help the poor man in his extravagant ways.

It quickly found takers. The king teased his cousin: 'Now that you have become a shopkeeper we will no doubt only be seeing you on Sundays!' To the king's dismay, the Palais Royal was a brilliant success.

When the new-look palace was finally finished in 1784, there were 180 arcades on the ground floor alone. Below them was a vast basement area, while two further levels above were made available to all and sundry. The Parisians loved it. They flocked into the gardens in their droves and languished in the bars and cafés, drawn by the sight of Mademoiselle Lapierre, a nineteen-year-old Prussian girl 2.2 metres tall, or the 240-kilo bulk of Paul Butterboldt, or by accounts of copulating savages. And there was the food, of course.

At midday a canon would sound, its fuse lit by an elaborate system that magnified the sun's rays. The Palais Royal was all very cutting edge and innovative. History doesn't relate what happened when it was cloudy.

The gardens were enclosed on three sides by the Galeries de Montpensier, de Beaujolais and de Valois, and you can still wander through the dappled shade of the trees, although it all seems positively somnolent these days.

In the Galerie de Montpensier the extraordinary waxworks of Monsieur Curtius were on display, where for two sols you could see Rousseau, Voltaire and later the villains of the Revolution brilliantly reproduced. Monsieur Curtius's niece was to marry a Mr Tussaud in London, whose famous waxworks still draw the crowds in their thousands.

Ribaldry and risqué behaviour went hand in hand in the Palais Royal. The Café des Aveugles, in the Galerie de Beaujolais, was divided up into twenty private rooms, and entertainment was provided by a small orchestra of blind musicians, who played on while the guests amused themselves, passive witnesses to seduction and debauchery.

Two heavily laden flower-sellers circulated, with enormous bouquets to flatter the ladies. Many were resold at the end of the evening if things hadn't gone to plan.

'*Ici on s'honore du titre de citoyen, on se tutoie, et l'on fume*' a notice proudly displayed at the café door. 'Here we give you the title of citizen, we *tutoie* you, and you can smoke.'

In 1805, the basement was enlivened by Le Caveau du Sauvage, a licentious club run by one of Robespierre's ex-coachmen, where the famous copulating savages could be seen for two sols. Nearby was the Café Mécanique, where food was delivered by a rising plate that ascended in the middle of each table, and orders were placed down a speaking tube. It was immensely popular. Queues waited patiently outside to get a table, and many just stood and watched in awe.

While the restaurants tended to trade on the first floor, above them the whores and the pimps plied their trade. Gamblers gambled. Young men fell into easy dissipation.

At Number 57 was the famous Café de Foy, which had been open since 1725 but had moved lock, stock and barrel into the arcades, attracted by the buzz and the location. The owner paid a massive 500,000 livres for the privilege, gaining the right to be the sole supplier of drinks and ices to the public who flocked into the gardens.

Nearby, in the Galerie de Beaujolais – below which I was eating my steak and musing on my Béarnaise – is one of Paris's most respected and oldest restaurants, Le Grand Véfour. Almost the only remnant of these pre-revolutionary days, it is a Dionysian dinosaur, the old fiefdom of Raymond Oliver, France's first TV chef, who remained attached to his chef's hat and chef's whites throughout a long and brilliant career. Oliver was a highly competent, passionate chef, no relation to Jamie, whose hair is as wild as Raymond's stiffly greased locks were controlled.

Once called the Café de Chartres, it was taken over by the elder – *le grand* – Véfour, and has kept his name ever since. Much plotting and discussion took place in the apartment above, owned by the notorious Marguerite Brunet, la Montpensier, the close confidante of many of the prime movers in the Revolution, including Barras, Hébert, Robespierre and Camille Desmoulins. She became the director of the Théâtre du Palais Royal during the Revolution, and died in 1820 aged ninety.

Not far from where I ate, Desmoulins had stood high on a table top and heckled the crowds, incensed at the demise of the popular finance minister, Jacques Necker, who was dismissed, it was said, at the instigation of the highly unpopular Marie Antoinette. The date was 12 July 1789.

'To arms!' he yelled. Two days later, the Bastille fell. The Revolution had begun.

Then, nearly twenty years later, in 1808, along came the Vérys.

This was the site of their second restaurant. The first had been not far way, near the Tuileries, but the Palais Royal was simply *the* place to be, a highly sought-after location. Stamford Raffles wrote of Véry's in 1817:

> On entering the room, the first object that arrested the attention was the mistress, a young and beautiful woman, most elegantly dressed, reclining at her ease on an elevated seat. Around her the waiters gather to receive her orders and to make reports of the progress of affairs.
>
> The next thing to which our attention was drawn, as you will naturally suppose, was the carte, or bill of fare, at the immensity of which a London epicure would have started. What a boundless variety! Fish, flesh, and fowl – *rôti*,

bouilli, *fricassée*, *fricandeau*, soups, sauces, incon-
ceivable combinations, unutterable names.[1]

The salle was covered in huge, elaborately gilded
mirrors that allowed the diner to observe everyone
else and reflect upon their beauty. Ladies mingled,
and gentlemen entertained their wives and mistresses
in an atmosphere of sensual extravagance. People
gossiped about the voluptuous Madame Véry. She
had charmed the Minister of the Interior, they said,
who had quickly succumbed, and shortly afterwards
the Vérys moved into the Palais, on condition that
'she would favour him with her company to supper
and not forget to put her night cap in her pocket'.

Véry's was among the first establishments to
experiment with a *prix fixe* menu, where you were
allowed the luxury of choosing how much you
wished to spend, as well as what you wanted to eat.
The public flocked in for a while, boosted by the
endless crowds of foreigners and military caught up
in Napoleonic blunders. A Prussian general famously
ordered coffee in a cup 'from which no Frenchman
had drunk'. It was served in a chamber pot.

One of the most fascinating characters to emerge
from the post-revolutionary eating culture was
Alexandre Balthazar Laurent Grimod de la
Reynière. In 1803 he published the first volume of

---

[1] See Jacques Hillairet, *Dictionnaire Historique des Rues de
Paris*, Vol. 2, Paris 1963, pp. 83–6.

the *Almanach des Gourmets*, a protean food guide for visitors to the city of light. Knowledgeable and highly respected, his pen helped make fortunes – and break them too. At first Véry's seemed to thrive, but by 1808, the last year of the almanac, Grimod noted its gradual decline. Too expensive, he wrote. Too many Englishmen.

Paris was full of *nouveau riche* families who had thrived on the Revolution, and bureaucrats and businessmen who sought their fortune. Added to all this were the visiting dignitaries, the military and the Parisians themselves, many of whom were thoroughly entranced at the new order, and revelled in the demise not only of the old order, but of the stifling hand of the guilds and corporations.

Paris quickly became the centre of a vibrant and brilliant food culture, which thrived on the talent that had once largely served the aristocracy behind closed doors. Beauvilliers was just such a place. Monsieur Beauvilliers had been the cook to the Prince Condé, and he too opened his own restaurant in the Palais Royal in 1808, where a large and imperial Madame, the restaurateur's wife no less, presided over the scene, alongside a cashier and a waiter, who was in charge of the desserts and the extravagantly displayed fruit. By six, it was said, there was hardly a vacant seat.

The system of running a restaurant had yet to become formalized. It was still very much evolving. A British visitor, Blagdon, recommended ordering the second dish while you were eating the first, to avoid delays ruining your night at the theatre.

But eventually, along came a man who was to provide systems where they were most needed. Right in the heart of the restaurant kitchen.

Antonin Carême was born in 1784, long after Boulanger had disappeared from the scene, into a poor Parisian family. The story goes that he was sent packing with words along the lines of 'go forth, young man', and he eventually found work at a well-reputed *pâtisserie* called Bailly, not far from the Palais Royal.

He was immensely skilled in creating elaborate set pieces made from sugar, which provided startlingly realistic focal points for banquets and suppers. This was food transformed. The mastery of man over nature fitted the aggrandizing nature of the nineteenth century and Carême's skill came to the attention of the equally skilled French diplomat Talleyrand, who managed to survive the disastrous end to Napoleon's empire, and success-fully negotiated both France's and his own future at the Congress of Vienna in 1815.

The brilliance of food had a significant role to play in the flattering of diplomats' stomachs, and Carême became Talleyrand's chef and Talleyrand his mentor. Both flourished. Carême was well aware that being a successful chef required order and an ability to harness technology, so he set about creating a creature that was long to outlive him, which went by the name of haute cuisine.

In the early years of the nineteenth century, restaurant kitchens were struggling under the weight of expectation fuelled by their very success. Carême realized that imposing order was essential if the bubble was not to burst. So from the chaos he imposed structure. It was he who first created the four mother sauces of classic French cooking: Allemande, Espagnole, velouté and béchamel, each dependent on copious amounts of stock to make them work.

You may wonder why French food is so dependent on sauce. Here I was with my Béarnaise, which could have been a thousand other things. A Hollandaise with poached turbot. A Sauce Soubise. Choron. The list is almost endless. A sauce is so intimately French that we accept it almost without comment.

And yet within such success lies the seed of its demise, for a sauceless world threatens the primacy of French haute cuisine. When produce is allowed to appear relatively unencumbered, another concept of superiority is needed. It is called *terroir*.

The sauce has an ancient ancestry. Medieval sauces such as Sauce Cameline may have been flavoured with cloves and *grains de paradis*, mixed with vinegar and thickened with bread. Then there was the popular Sauce Jance that was prepared by mixing almonds, ginger, wine and verjuice. Many were sweet: '*Sucre n'a jamais gâté une sauce,*' wrote Champier, King François I's personal physician. 'Sugar has never spoiled a sauce.' Colours were often lurid and significant. The popularity of saffron was due to the intense colour it gave food more than its taste, yellow food being seen as heavenly, the colour of the sun, both primal and pure.

Tastes were strong, too. Distilled rose water was used not only in sauce-making, but in *ragoûts* and desserts, and to preserve walnuts. The king was even said to wash his hands in it. Extracting the essence of a substance became, as we have seen, an elaborate chase, a search for the purest of foods that would endow the consumer with power beyond imagination.

In ancient saucery, butter was noticeable for its absence. The classic thickening method of a floury *roux* was still a long way off, and only came to dominance in the late eighteenth century. It too was part of the success of haute cuisine.

Since butter was an animal product, it was subject to the tedious restrictions that were decreed by the Church. And getting round them proved to be an expensive business. Indulgences could be either bought or granted by the Pope. The Normans, in particular, were keen to be allowed the freedom to eat butter. It was in their roots, after all, butter being a staple that these northern sea-borne warriors had long treasured. It is said that one of the huge towers of Rouen Cathedral was built with money paid to the Church by Normans buying exemption.

The marriage of Anne of Brittany to the King of France resulted in first her, and then the whole of Brittany being allowed to use butter freely. Elsewhere, its restriction angered the Reformists. Martin Luther complained in *To the Christian Nobility of the German Nation* that:

> In Rome, they even laugh at the idea of fasting while they force us to eat an oil with which they would not even oil their shoes. They even demand that we pay for the right to eat fat and all sorts of food . . . The people are scandalized and feel that, for the Church, eating butter is as serious as lying or blaspheming or taking part in indecent acts.

The Council of Trent (1545–63) liberated the use of butter to some extent, by issuing a general indulgence that reduced fast days and restrictions on forbidden foods. Butter began to emerge from the cloisters, and by the middle of the seventeenth century cookbooks were beginning to reflect its increased use. It rapidly moved from being the food of the poor to having real social distinction, and by the beginning of the eighteenth century, Louis Lemery, an eminent physician, noted that 'practically no sauce is made without it in France'.

Although its original raison d'être might have been purely functional – it was one way to preserve cream – butter was rapidly elevated into the gastronomic stratosphere, where it long remained, brought there essentially by the arrival of the unctuous buttery sauce that became so much a part of haute cuisine.

With the explosion of restaurants that followed the French Revolution, the sauce-maker became a vital member of a classically trained kitchen brigade. Escoffier, adapting the words and ideas of Carême, divided his brigade into five *parties*, with a chef commanding each section. There was the *gardemanger*, who looked after the supplies; the *entremétier*, whose concern was for the soups, vegetables and even desserts, aided with the latter by the *pâtissier*. The *rôtisseur* was in charge of all the roasting, grilling and frying, while the *saucier*, of course, created those magical sauces.

To this day, mastering a sauce is considered the apogee of good cooking, a culinary rite of passage that all chefs must cross. The magic of sauce-making lives on. Michel Roux writes:

A pinch of this, a pinch of that – the creative process is bewitching. A flame licks up from the pan containing the bubbling steaming potion, illuminating the sagacious face of the 'saucerer'. He inhales the fumes laden with the first aromas. His imagination is fired as he conjures up the magic of his sauce.[1]

[1] *Sauces*, Michel Roux, London: Quadrille, 2006.

Inspiring stuff, and putting aside gender issues here, the chef is clearly portrayed as an artist, a creative genius, who with skill and inspiration can create true magic. The French chef in particular, especially the one trained in the classical style of haute cuisine, is often portrayed as a genius, an alchemist.

The famous French gastronome Jean Anthelme Brillat-Savarin told the story of the Prince of Soubise, who once dared to question his chef's request for fifty hams.

'Fifty hams, sir? Why, you will ruin me!' said the concerned prince.

'Ah, Monsieur, but give me those hams and I will reduce them into a phial the size of my thumb, and make with it something truly wonderful!'

Passion won the day. Chef had his hams, and Monsieur avoided another hissy fit. And what did he intend to do with this extravagant essence? Why, make a sauce, of course!

Carême was heavily influenced by the power of reduced stock, of *pot au feu* and the *sacré bouillon*. But he dressed much of his writing in the language of science. By the early nineteenth century, the search for the essence of meat was still firmly on, and scientists thought that they had isolated a substance to which they gave the name osmazome. Brillat-Savarin wrote in his *Physiology of Taste* about the miraculous properties of this extraordinary substance:

The greatest service chemistry has rendered to alimentary science is the discovery of osmazome, or rather the determination of what it was.

The long reduction of stock in commercial kitchens was made infinitely easier by the development of powerful stoves, where heat could not only be regulated more easily, but accurate temperatures could be easily maintained. The stock was essentially the self-same *bouillon* that was used as a *restaurant* or restorative, and became one of Carême's famous mother sauces, which are still the essence of classical French cuisine. This is *sauce espagnole*.

Sharing the family sauce tree were *sauce allemande* – made of stock, egg yolk and lemon juice – and *sauce béchamel*, which was originally a stock and milk-based sauce rather than milk thickened with roux. The last was a *velouté*, a lighter sauce altogether, made from fish or chicken stock rather than the heavier red-meat *bouillon*.

But there is one further level of reduction that created a sauce that was perhaps even more fundamental: demi-glace. Half stock and half *sauce espagnole*, demi-glace is thick and intensely flavoured, as close to the *restaurant divin* as you will ever get. Recognized as being the key to classical French cooking, it is horribly time consuming to make. Julia Child therefore created her own more do-able version and called it semi-demi-glace.

As restaurant culture flourished worldwide in the nineteenth century, it moved ever further from the realm of domesticity. Diners were tempted by the excellence of the food, its inventiveness and extravagance. The French model dominated and continued to do so until the appearance of *nouvelle cuisine* in the late 1970s, which allowed us all to begin to glimpse a different world. Gastronomy was never the same again.

French haute cuisine was formalized and closely controlled, very like cooking under the ancien régime. But it appealed to a world that was entranced by France and its efficient extravagance. Of course, the story that the restaurant was invented in France has proved so persuasive that we have all forgotten it was the French who were the laggards as far as developing the culture of public eating beyond its self-imposed boundaries was concerned.

And of course we have all taken to the word *chef*. Not cook. And what is our chef? An artist or a scientist? Cooking is an art, we are told. Only artists need apply. Yet, over time, the very chefs who have bathed in artistic glory have had to apply themselves to the strictest principles of science, particularly when it comes to making sauce. The relationship between the art and science of cooking is a theme we will return to shortly, but in the meantime, here is a little interlude. Go and buy the finest steak, serve it with some *sauce béarnaise* and tell your friends the story of Monsieur Boulanger and his restaurant.

Sauce Béarnaise

Béarnaise is a rich sauce and relies on the principle of an oil-in-water emulsion. The liquid – wine and/or vinegar – is reduced, then thickened with egg yolks and finished with butter. The skill comes in making sure that the eggs aren't cooked, in which case you would get an aromatic version of scrambled eggs. The quality comes in the combination of skill with the excellence of the raw materials – the freshness of the eggs, vinegar, tarragon. Indeed, the better all the ingredients, the better the sauce will be.

Ingredients
170ml vinegar or equal parts of wine and vinegar
30g finely chopped shallots
Thyme and bay leaf
5–6 egg yolks
1 tbsp water
450g butter
1 tbsp chopped tarragon
1 tbsp chopped chervil
Salt and pepper
Cayenne pepper
Lemon juice

Method
Put the wine or wine-and-vinegar mixture in a small pan with the shallots, thyme and bay leaf.

Reduce almost completely, then allow the vinegar to cool. Add the egg yolks and a tablespoonful of water. Whisk over a low heat. As soon as the sauce thickens add the butter little by little, whisking until it gets the consistency of mayonnaise. Season carefully.

Just before serving, add 1 tablespoonful of chopped tarragon and half of chopped chervil, season with cayenne and add a dash of lemon juice.

12

Pain Mollet

WHEN THE LATE LIONEL POILÂNE SET OFF TO OPEN HIS bakery in London in 2005, he took a batch of his Parisian starter in his suitcase. Poilâne's customers expect a very particular taste from his bread, one that he felt could only be reproduced by using the same yeast culture wherever his bread was sold.

The rhythm of breadmaking is gloriously eternal. Each batch of Poilâne bread is begat by a little starter kept back from the previous batch, and so on. It sounds almost easy, but yeast is a demanding beast. Humidity and temperature need to be carefully controlled. The flour has to be as consistent as possible, tricky this when freshly milled flour can cause fearful unpredictability, the baker's nightmare.

Pain Poilâne has a fabulous reputation. Chewy and slightly sour, it keeps well and is marvellous sliced and toasted. It is in fact very like the bread that was once baked by Paris's bakers, before a diminutive little upstart called *pain mollet* came along in the seventeenth century.

Now to most of us, the most iconic of all French breads is the baguette. But this was not always so. In fact, it may surprise you to learn that the baguette appeared on the baker's shelves relatively recently. In the middle of the nineteenth century an Austrian aristocrat with the wonderful name of Baron Zang perfected the technique of breadmaking known as *à la poolisch* or Polish-style, which involved adding barm or brewer's yeast to a liquid base of flour, and letting it work overnight, which brings out the flavour. It is a technique still used, and is well respected by even the most fastidious bakers. Thus was born *pain viennois*, and Zang was so successful that he quickly employed a network of delivery men working from his highly elaborate bakeries, many of which were staffed by bakers shipped in from Austria, such was the demand. But the quantity of bread that could be produced was still limited.

Using fresh yeast had been tried less successfully before, and provoked another bout of national soul searching as innovation collided once more with reactionary opinion from surprising quarters. In the 1930s a surge of creativity took place, and there appeared the most famous of all loaves, the baguette. It too was made by adding brewer's yeast directly to the dough, and then letting it rise, knocking it back, and finally baking it, not before adding the characteristic seven *coups de lames* from a viciously sharp blade. Seven cuts are still obligatory. Count them.

This was bread that was just made for mass production. Each batch was started afresh and had no relation to the last. *Pain au levain*, on the other hand, is the direct opposite. The morning I spent at Poilâne's reminded me of the delicate balance that has to be struck, to preserve enough starter dough, to add it at the right temperature, and to make sure that the flour is of the same strength.

Using added yeast is simpler by far. There has long been the temptation to take short cuts to provide the cheapest bread possible. Improvers such as ascorbic acid or broad-bean flour have often been used, until everyone eventually noticed that the bread was not quite what it once was.

The reaction to dull, feather-light bread has been so strong in France that bakers now try to outdo each other with strange names that call the baguette anything but baguette.

Baguette à l'ancienne is perhaps the most popular of all these days. And what is it? Well, bread made with a starter, just as it always had been, until, that is, *pain mollet* came along.

Pain mollet shook seventeenth-century French society to its very core, and sparked off an intense debate that lasted over a hundred years. No mean achievement for a loaf of bread.

To look at, it had something of the baguette about it. Long rather than round, its crust was golden, and the crumb a fine, soft, milky white. *Pain mollet* was pleasing to eat, easy on those rotten seventeenth-century gums, softened with milk and butter.

Pain mollet first appeared in Paris around 1665, a good twenty-two years after the death of Marie de Medicis, the wife of France's ever-popular King Henri IV (he of the *poule au pot*), who is often erroneously said to have 'invented' it. She ordered the royal baker to create something more to her Florentine tastes than the everyday *pain au levain*, the bread made with natural yeast that was commonly found at the time. And the results pleased her so much that the new bread, which originally became known as *pain à la reine*, was soon being sold widely in Paris. It was the conceptual foremother of our *pain mollet*.

Three years after *pain mollet* first appeared, the matter of using barm in breadmaking was controversial enough for King Louis XIV to convene a council of seventy-five *notables* from the Faculty of Medicine to pass judgement on its use.

The problem was this. Traditionally, bread in France had been made using *levain*, just as it is at Poilâne. It was part of the everyday business of breadmaking. Keeping the *levain* refreshed was a complicated business, but the yeast culture gave bread its character.

But contemporary beliefs held that adding brewer's yeast was dangerous for the health. You might have thought that its use would have been widely welcomed: it increased productivity and allowed a wider range of flour to be used. It made one of the most demanding of professions less exacting – night baking was an exhausting business. But it was not to be.

The focus of this dispute was more theoretical, and boiled down to an understanding of the nature of fermentation.

Fermentation was seen as a force of nature that was capable of generating matter, a process whereby constituent parts first separated, then reunited into a new form, which depended upon the matter that was being fermented. Thus, by adding flour to the 'natural' yeast of the *levain*, the bread was thought to take on the properties of the yeast. If, however, an impure yeast was used, then the end result would, if this understanding was correct, be equally impure.

Brewer's yeast was fine for making beer, physicians reasoned, but would cause problems if added to flour. So eat *pain mollet*, the detractors suggested, and you risked blocked urinary tracts, bad skin and worse.

Even the modernizing forces of the Enlightenment turned against the use of brewer's yeast. By the mid eighteenth century, the physiocrats, who were avowedly for progress in agriculture, interpreted the use of barm as unnatural, and reasoned that true bread was worked by skilled artisans from the simplest of ingredients: flour, and water uncorrupted by any added yeast. Such ideas have a distinctly modern ring to them. The heat of natural fermentation was seen as the fire of Prometheus, and was capable of powerful generation. It was this that produced the finest bread.

So the matter went to Parliament and a vote on permitting its use was taken. The result was forty-five against and thirty for. In August 1667, with the matter apparently not resolved to the satisfaction of all, a further council of twelve *notables*, six physicians and six *bourgeois* met to discuss things further. This time, while the majority of physicians favoured a complete ban, the bourgeoisie, who were probably more aware of the implications for the economy, were unanimously for allowing barm to be used, under certain restrictions. After all, it was said that even the king himself ate *pain mollet*. To its detractors, bread with barm was the devil's spawn, impure and doctored, but nevertheless it eventually usurped the round *pain populaire* for good. And became the ancestor of the iconic baguette.

This lighter dough became even more popular when made into *petits pains* or *pains de fantaisie*, rolls that suited the effete nibbling of the time. But they were only a small part of the daily bread supply of Paris. Under legislation put in place by Cardinal Richelieu, the weight and quality of *pain mollet* was far more closely controlled than that of the *pain populaire*, *le gros pain*, whose price was a matter of utmost sensitivity. Richer clients were less likely to riot. Come times of grain shortage, the flour used in *pain populaire* was often doctored, but the price, rarely. It was simply too risky. God help any ruler of France who upset the mob by raising the price of *pain populaire*.

But this dispute was never really about taste. Paul Malouin, a highly respected eighteenth-century commentator, noted that *pain mollet* was in his opinion less tasty than bread made from natural leaven.

The colour of the crumb was important, though. The desire for the purest white bread was deeply entrenched. And not just in France. Dark country bread was the food of the poor, and the cheaper the bread, the darker the colour. Buying highly refined white bread was a social statement. We have arrived. We are rich enough to eat *pain mollet*.

Rural incomers assumed urban habits with ease. The majority wanted their bread to be as white as possible, and made from wheat, and no court case could change that. Rye bread was never popular in Paris.

During Louis XIV's long reign, soldiers were known to refuse to march unless supplies of wheat bread were assured, and complained heartily of the colour of the bread they found in Lyon. Few trekked to the cities expecting to eat thick country bread, or the hardened twice-cooked *pain bis* (the origin of the English word biscuit, by the way). It was white bread they wanted.

Bread was the staple, the essential, Christ's body in the Christian communion. Many kept a small lump of *pain bénit*, blessed bread, in their pockets for good luck, and loaves were always blessed, and cut only after the sign of the cross had been made over them.

Folk memories told tales of poverty and deprivation and eating black, rough country bread. But not all were so smitten. When Napoleon first arrived in Paris, he was astonished by the whiteness of the bread and longed for the black bread of Corsica.

Good citizens were *gagne pains*, breadwinners (they only became *gagne bifteck*, steakwinners, in the postwar years), and if they wished could afford to buy bread every day. Country bread was baked once a week, and could be kept that long at a stretch.

Did bread play a role in the Revolution? The harvest of 1788 was poor, and the *pain populaire*, the four-pound *gros pain*, rose in price from eight to twelve sous. Labourers then struggled on a daily wage of between twenty to thirty sous, so this was a rise they could ill afford. In Versailles a baker who raised the price to eighteen was attacked by a murderous crowd, and only just saved from certain lynching by the military.

Faubourg St Antoine, the most febrile, densely populated working-class district of Paris, within spitting distance of the Bastille, rose up in anger at the hike in bread prices, summoned by the tocsin of Sainte-Marguerite on 10 October 1789. Swarming through the streets, an angry crowd pillaged the Hotel de Ville, and moved on to the National Assembly. 'We don't give a fuck about order. We want bread!' they cried. And then on to Versailles they marched, and the crowd camped outside the palace, shouting: 'Bread, or we'll cut the pretty queen's throat!'

That same night, Lafayette arrived with a massive contingent of National Guards, and the royal family was escorted to Paris. Never again was Marie Antoinette to see her beloved Trianon, nor the king to taste freedom.

If bread prices had remained stable, would the Revolution have been avoided? Who knows. The Revolution had its own complex logic and unpredictable momentum. But the old order was finished, the State bankrupt. The king's apparent willingness to reform only hastened the end of the regime. But his dithering made his end infinitely tragic.

Pain mollet disappeared from view in postrevolutionary France, and it wasn't until Baron

Zang came along that barm was once again widely used, and his *pain viennois* slowly morphed into the baguette. There was no reaction. No court case. France needed its industrialized bread.

Monsieur Bouillard's pain mollet

Take some fresh brewer's yeast, put it in a little warm milk and let it rise, with one ounce of yeast per pint of milk. Mix with some white flour and add more milk, and salt, until the dough has the correct consistency, then knead vigorously. Allow it to rise for 6–8 hours in a warm, draught-free place. Knock back, let it rise once more, and fashion into rolls or loaves as you wish. Bake as usual.

Translated from Paul Malouin, *Description et Détails des Arts du Meunier, du Vermicelier et du Boulanger,* Paris, 1767.

13

Croque-Monsieur

IF THE BAGUETTE IS NOW SO PROFOUNDLY ICONIC, THE
relationship between France and the rest of the
world's iconic foods is complex. Take sliced bread,
for example. There was a time – I lived in Paris
then and can remember it well – when the classy
British chain of not-so-grand surfaces called Marks
and Spencer decided to open a branch near Paris's
Opéra. It seemed a brilliant idea, but when you
looked closely at what the Parisians were actually
buying it was more than a little intriguing. Some
smoked salmon, of course, English tea and crum-
pets, but it was the quantities of sliced bread they
bought that astonished me.

The French equivalent of a sliced white loaf is
called *pain de mie*, a soft and bland bread that is
square and sliced and can be used for one of the
classiest French snack foods, the *croque-monsieur*.

Now I had read that the brilliant and highly respected French chef Pierre Gagnaire had adapted this bistro classic in his own style, which in itself seemed to be significant. Here we have one of the country's finest chefs turning a mundane classic on its head and wowing Parisians with a sense of innovation.

So when I was asked to meet the great man, I hurried along with indecent haste, and looked forward to a taste of the present.

To me, the Rue du Bac used to mean but one thing: stuffed animals. Enthusiasts have been trekking down this elegant Parisian street for over 170 years to visit a labyrinthine shop in the seventh arrondissement called Deyrolles, whose well-trodden floorboards positively creek under the weight of the fruits of taxidermy. Magically coloured dead butterflies, stuffed baby elephants, enraged lions, all are there for you to make that impulse buy of the millennium. Little had changed, I thought, as I gawped in the window, since I last visited.

The neighbours have, though. And animals don't have much more luck next door, where Pierre Gagnaire is grappling with modernity at his popular neighbourhood restaurant, Gaya, slicing and cutting his way through the freshest of corpses, many of them fishy, all in the name of gastronomy.

If it is true that French cooking has become more

global these days, then chefs must wing their way around the planet not just spreading the word, but imbibing subtleties and new techniques. Gagnaire is no exception. He has fingers in many culinary pies. Some are in London, others in Japan, as well as here in Paris. When I met up with him, he had just flown in from Niger.

In France, modernity and tradition are beginning to evolve into a new culinary life form, one that has to some extent eschewed the use of the classic and awesomely expensive key ingredients – foie gras, truffles, that sort of thing. This helps democratize fine dining, for élitism and the everyday financial realities of running a restaurant have pushed Parisian prices way up into the stratosphere. At Gaya, you don't feel the need to gasp and reach for the oxygen as you read through the menu. Drooling is more in order.

Yet these are strange times. There is almost a sense of melancholy in the Parisian air, an intro-spection best described by the French word *nombrilisme*, navel-gazing. Nobu Paris has closed. Senderens has returned his Michelin stars. Bocuse, the grand master, is old now, and new generations seek their leader.

Pierre Gagnaire is well placed to reflect upon all this, and to comment on the apparent waves of gastro-energy that are drifting in from Spain, the US and even Britain, for he is also the power behind the stoves at London's Sketch, a complex, multilayered and, it has to be said, somewhat controversial gastrodome.

'At Sketch, you should be able to laugh and eat, to listen to music, to watch videos. It is a more total experience,' Gagnaire told me with fire in his eyes and gallivanting hand gestures. While Sketch is deliberately trying to innovate, to be radical – revolutionary, one might almost say – Gaya essentially conforms to the classic, well-tried model – the neighbourhood restaurant.

But why have Sketch in London and not Paris, I wondered?

'There are less restraints over there,' he told me. 'And people have more money, but in London people can be so cynical. And it hasn't been easy to get staff with the same level of skill as we have in France.'

It is a commonly heard complaint from chefs on both sides of the water. Maybe it is down to the more vibrant economy in London. Or maybe it is because the French have difficulty with the Anglo-Saxon tradition of the passionate, educated amateur, someone who becomes so smitten by the idea of being a chef that they immerse themselves in its every aspect, sweat and grind for years, constantly learning, questioning and even innovating.

In France there is far less of this impulsive behaviour. There are systems and laws to obey, diplomas to take, the way it always has been in the land that invented haute cuisine. Understandably, perhaps, Gagnaire told me that he found it easier to work with the culinary culture of Japan than that of Britain.

If Gagnaire makes London sound almost vulgar, *moins cultivé*, or less cultured in his words, then Paris in turn seems almost provincial. While we were eating, an ex-prime minister, an architect, a gaggle of eager journalists and even a few hard-hatted workmen came by, all in turn meeted and greeted by Gagnaire. With a neighbourhood that just happens to include the Assemblée Nationale, it's not surprising that his neighbours can be pretty illustrious.

Over an exquisite Chantilly of sea urchins, I asked Gagnaire where he liked to eat in Britain.

'Fergus Henderson's St John. Ah, that was wonderful! And Heston Blumenthal's Fat Duck.'

Not entirely surprising – they are two key figures in British gastronomy these days. Both, I might add, gifted, passionate and self-taught chefs.

'I would say that Heston is the first really great *European* chef to come from England,' he added with emphasis. So are we now entering a new age where European food is beginning to be an entity in itself? Perhaps. It seems more likely that we should recognize an emerging global cuisine, where what we might eat in Melbourne is not in all honesty that different from what is served in New York or London. Or, shock horror, Paris.

The kitchen had by now cobbled together their signature *croque*, with a *mie* that was black from squid ink, and a simple slice of mozzarella, basil and tomato. And although Carême may well have turned in his grave, the result was good. But the artistry was in assembling a curious combination, of defying the traditional rather than in elaborate preparation. It is very much a dish that we could make at home. It is just that we wouldn't have thought of it.

But if star-studded French chefs are no longer trying to be grandmothers with cloches, what are they trying to do? Where once they may have been grappling with the complexities of *sauce espagnole*, they are now almost certainly influenced by the new kid on the block, molecular gastronomy.

While Pierre Gagnaire set off to find a parking space for his partner Sylvie's car and dog, the kitchen sent out a dessert of such perfection, so sublime and beautiful, that this particular cynic trembled like a jelly. It was a parfait topped with whisperingly light, intensely flavoured blackcurrant *cristaux du vent*, crystals of the wind – delicate meringues scented with cassis – a dish made by using ground-breaking techniques suggested by Gagnaire's illustrious partner in food, Hervé This.

Science and gastronomy are stretching the boundaries of the known and the unknown. The highly respected American writer Harold McGee inspired many to question and experiment in his seminal work *The Science of Food and Cooking*. More recently, radical innovation has been fostered by teams headed by Ferran Adrià in Catalonia and Heston Blumenthal in England, both of whom are devoting much of their time to a radical re-jigging. Gastronomy will, I suspect, never be quite the same again, although much of what they are creating is so ethereal that it has yet to filter down to everyday food. But it will, eventually, and is proving to be ideal terrain for skilled technicians who once trained in haute cuisine.

But it calls for different skills. Out goes blind obedience, and in comes inventiveness and a radical, deliberate breaking of boundaries. France's innate conservatism has allowed it to be thoroughly wrongfooted here. The restaurant world likes enthusiastic innovation, but this time it has come from far away, and is more than a little resented by the establishment in France.

Gagnaire is an exception. He is a very cerebral and innovative chef, constantly experimenting, and has established a fascinating working relationship with the renowned scientist Hervé This. It is a class act.

While we were marvelling at the food's complexities, Pierre came back, and reassured Sylvie that her dog hadn't been sent next door to be stuffed, nor had it been molecularly synthesized in the kitchen. 'The policeman looked at me and said,

"You're Gagnaire, aren't you? Leave the car there, Monsieur. Don't worry." '

Vive la Révolution!

A few weeks later, I had arranged to meet Hervé This. I arrived on time, and they buzzed him from afar.

More tomato and basil than Jekyll and Hyde, there is, however, a touch of both in the intense and very public *affaire d'esprit* between Pierre Gagnaire and Hervé This.

'Ah, he is always on the telephone,' the receptionist at the Institut National de Recherche Agronomique (INRA) observed acutely, smiling. An affectionate rebuke from below, where groups of well-heeled Parisians circulated, looking for a conference venue or their lost youth. Eventually Hervé This came down to meet me, glanced down at my grubby shoes, shrugged his shoulders, and swooped me upstairs to his modest laboratory.

Their relationship allows us to peek through an open window and see what exactly science and cooking are doing in bed together after all these years. Is it a *lit matrimonial*, or a *lit de putes*? Is there soul-searching, or selling out? Are they still happy bedfellows?

The couple do, after all, go back a long way. In the early nineteenth century, the great and much-quoted post-revolutionary gastronome Grimod de la Reynière was entranced by the development of bottled food by the French scientist Appert. Then there was the great Antoine-Auguste Parmentier, he of the *hachis Parmentier*, who for years struggled to solve the shortage of bread in the late eighteenth century by turning potatoes into flour. Both were closely supported by the establishment: Appert by Napoleon, who realized the importance of securing a reliable food supply for his military exploits; and Parmentier by the ancien régime, desperate to avoid the catastrophe of famine.

But while science once helped both increase and secure the food supply, particularly by developing ways to preserve food, things are different now. In the developed world the problem is of over rather than undersupply. We all munch radioactive salads and year-round tasteless strawberries without a care in the world, and famine only enters into our thoughts when we see traumatic pictures from else-where.

Science has been liberated and is kicking its heels with joy. It has become seduced by hedonism, and has entered the world of eating for pleasure, of creativity and passion. Technology is used to titil-late rather than innovate. It is becoming part of an ooh-aah culture that gets us marvelling at the feats that can be performed in the kitchen, and we gawp and wonder very much as we do at tantric sex.

So it came as no real surprise to hear that in France, at least, science and gastronomy were cavorting quite happily in middle age. The rediscovery of passion has been helped along by the clinical enthusiasm of This and Gagnaire. Science and cooking are not, never were and never should be separate bedfellows.

Now we humans have to label things, and the press has created a strange creature called molecular gastronomy. Hardly anyone seems ready to admit they are part of this movement, and in France its very existence is often questioned. It is not, you will have guessed, a French invention.

Monsieur This would prefer to be known as a chemist, and in the true style of a French patriot would question quite what molecular gastronomy actually is. Indeed, since he can be a little prickly about perceived Anglo-Saxon terminology, he has come up with his own alternative that he calls 'note by note' cooking, which you will note is written in English. This, he feels, better expresses the gradual experimental progression he uses to lead us to a greater understanding of exactly what cooking, scientifically speaking, entails.

But let's face it, we all want to know what the hell molecular gastronomy is. Whoever I asked for a definition tended to scoff and dismiss it as a journalistic fantasy, to be almost in denial as to its very existence. It is a creation of the press, a convenient label to whip up frenzied interest in a new fad, I was told over and over again.

But definitions do exist. Harold McGee calls it 'the science of deliciousness'. Peter Barham, a scientist based in the UK, less poetically tells us that it is 'the application of scientific principles to the understanding and improvement of domestic and gastronomic food preparation'. I'll go with McGee on this one.

What I thought was so exciting about molecular gastronomy was this sense of innovation, the crossing of boundaries, the questioning of this and that, and the radicalization of our palates.

You may find the idea of a sorbet made from sardines repulsive, but to me it is absolutely thrilling. It is hugely encouraging to see the very nature of what we eat being jolted, shocked perhaps into breaking away from its innate conservatism. The big if is whether this is just a passing whim, a fad. Or whether there will be a lasting shift of the known and the edible.

But I had become a little confused. Who were the practitioners? Gagnaire dabbled, by his own admission. But so consistently was molecular gastronomy reviled in France, that, heaven forbid, the cynic might almost be tempted to think that this was because it had its roots elsewhere. Within the minds of eager foreign journalists, perhaps. Or down in sunny Catalonia, where the mighty talent of Ferran Adrià teases and toys with the palate in a most revolutionary way.

So I sought solace in the words of this Monsieur This, the French master of *goût*, and asked *him* to help me define the term. He began by telling me more about what it wasn't. In a recent conversation he had had with the prodigiously talented English chef Heston Blumenthal, who is party to the inner circle of moleculophiles, This said, 'I was telling Heston that no, he is *not* a molecular gastronomist, he is a molecular cook. It is not the same thing.'

Cooks are technicians. Gastronomists have a broader brush, and look at all matters that relate to the stomach, using the definition that Brillat-Savarin came up with in the nineteenth century. A cook merely cooks. Apparently, Blumenthal looked a little crestfallen when Monsieur This expounded this theory, but This is sure of his ground, indeed scarily so.

I scribbled away furiously, trying to keep abreast of his train of thought as he slaughtered another writer who had dared to commentate on the matter in hand. 'That is completely wrong, it is ridiculous . . . look at this . . . maybe you know him?' he said, looking deep into my eyes with a powerful gaze. I didn't. But I vowed to be as attentive as possible, and felt like beating myself ritually for being a writer.

One of This's colleagues walked in, breaking the mounting tension. I mopped my brow and shook his hand. 'This is Monsieur Black, he is writing a thesis on French food,' he said, with excessive flattery. This elegant neophyte had been researching the colour of French beans for three years. This and his team spend magnificent hours researching into the science and technology of food and cooking for all our benefit.

Read This if you can. Some of his work is now available in English, and it is beguiling, fascinating. But to me, it is the interplay between chef and scientist that is so significant. The fact that Gagnaire and This sit down and discuss and create and test and question in an eternal fugue. All of this is reflected on the equally riveting website at pierregagnaire.com.

While Gagnaire would, I suspect, love to have the freedom to be closeted away in an artist's *atelier* rather than involve himself in the mucky old world of running a business, a.k.a. a restaurant, Hervé This would be just as happy in chef's whites, glorying in all the glory. The two make a happy fusion. Not all the innovation works, of course. When I ate with Gagnaire, we were served a dish on radically square plates with a liquid served separately. But what was it? A sauce? A dip? Innovation can be a little scary, and one wouldn't want to dip when one wasn't supposed to, now would one? What was one to do with it? I waited to see. But Gagnaire wasn't actually eating anything; he was champing at the bit, desperate to get into the kitchen, where he hadn't been for a couple of weeks, and now he was being asked silly questions by me.

Luckily his partner helped.

'Pierre, what are we supposed to do with this? Drink it or add it to the dish?' she asked.

Gagnaire grabbed the bowl and poured it all magisterially over the food, with a *Voilà!* And I poured away too.

14

Génération C

GAGNAIRE AND THIS, WITH THEIR MOLECULES AND gastro love, are establishment figures in France. They have, in a sense, up and come. But where then, one has to wonder, are the up and coming? Where does the future of France and her beloved culinary *patrimoine* lie? It was Hervé This who told me about Génération C. I was actually asking him about le Fooding, the streetwise band of enthusiasts of whom I had already read (I was off to meet them later), and in whom I thought one might get a little *amuse-bouche* of the future.

'Ah, le Fooding, they are finished now,' This told me. 'And why do they use English, anyway? I have said that I would be happy to work with them, but only if they use French. Why not *sentimanger*, for example?' It was another case of

Gallic *Ah bof!* It made me think of his 'note by note'. 'No, you should go and talk with Génération C.'

Well, I did.

Gilles Choukroun is the man behind this particular infant. He is also the chef behind the stove at L'Angl'Opéra, a gastro-pod within L'Hôtel Edouard VII, just within a cantata's lob of the Paris Opéra, where the menu is significant in that it actually accepts that people like to eat, but quickly rather than languidly, at lunch at least. He packs them in and feeds them well, and professionally. It is all marvellously refreshing.

So I sat down to a coffee, and asked him this scorchingly original question. What does Génération C actually mean?

'*C'est Génération Coincée,*' he told me.

I laughed. *Coincé* means tight arsed – restricted, literally. I admired his sense of humour and uncharacteristic self-deprecation.

I soon realized that he was looking at me a little strangely.

What he had actually said was *Génération point C.* The C stands for culture. And for cuisine. It signifies neither chef, nor con, nor concept, nor combustion.

It was, he told me, his own deep concern that France was in a sense losing its culinary way that had caused him to pick up the phone and establish contact with a few like-minded professionals to reflect on the matter. They were mostly chefs in their thirties and forties, who had already expressed either in words or deeds a feeling that all was not well with the status quo in French cooking.

Equally refreshing is the fact that the young stars of Génération C are far from being Paris-bound. There is Thierry Marx, who wows the taste buds in Pauillac in the Gironde. Yves Camdeborde, everyone's darling, who has decamped from the mighty Bristol to open his own (OK, Parisian) bistro in the sixth arrondissement, where I ate later that day. It was packed. The food was simplicity itself. A cool soup of melon, followed by grilled *côtelette d'agneau* or lamb chop, and a slice of exquisite cheese. Food, in other words, that relied upon the primacy of the produce. The skill of the chef was in getting the food to the table in good time, and creating a buzz.

There is not only a sense among the Génération C brigade of the passing of the old guard, the role models of the past, but concern that there was no one in France ready to replace them. There was, Choukroun told me, an alarming and increasing disinterest in the métier of chef within France. And so it was time to try and create a new public image of *cuisinier* both for the profession and for France. Génération C is not about establishing a new cooking style; just a new philosophy of professional cooking, a reinterpretation of *la cuisine française*.

France stood still and ossified, happy for so long in the assumption of its own superiority that it came as a shock to realize that the world had moved on. The dread spectre of them doing better than us has shaken the cobwebs a little. From Britain came the rise of the sexy rock 'n' roll chef, from the States the global fascination with food.

One thing that seems to distinguish the new French model from its illustrious predecessor is a world vision that is, if you delve a little, noticeably and unashamedly global. And it was this that struck me so forcefully while revisiting this country that was for so long the unopposed ruler of the roost.

'Let's look at Japan,' Choukroun explained. 'In the old days, chefs travelled there to re-create an exact replica of a French restaurant, as authentically as possible. Now if I go to Japan, I will listen, and am happy to see what happens outside France. I can learn. There is a constant conversation in my kitchen. I have staff from all over the world – England, Japan, South Africa – and they all have a different perspective. In the old days I don't think we asked the right questions. We used to travel to spread the word. Now it is to learn.'

So Gilles Choukroun travels as chefs have long been prone to, not to create a culinary clone, to offer the Japanese the same eating experience as the Parisians, but to learn and to master new techniques, and to offer tastes that are from elsewhere.

This new vision accepts implicitly that the other is no longer to be feared or dominated, but to be learnt from. It encourages French food to adapt, to savour influence. It is a novel approach in France. But does that mean, I asked, that we are all headed in the same direction? Will we soon all be eating the same fusion food the world over?

'No, I don't think so,' he replied thoughtfully. 'There will always be things that the French do better, that the Italians do better. There will always be difference.'

I am not so sure. Anyone in Europe can now, in theory at least, eat the finest *culatello* with little difficulty. The raw material has been liberated from its *terroir*, and food as a result is in the process of being liberated from its roots. Devalued, perhaps, but there is little point in being too overwhelmed by nostalgia. It is time to move on. Adapt or die!

If, as Génération C thought, there is little interest in food and in eating out among the young, then the future for the restaurant as we know it is bleak indeed. So how can people be recruited into the sector if it seems to be in possibly terminal decline?

Lunch, *déjeuner*, is perhaps the meal that requires the most fundamental reappraisal. Time is of the essence, so Choukroun has introduced his very own *formule* – everyone needs a good *formule* in France – and it appears to work. His restaurant is full, brimming over.

There are sandwiches, some luxurious and others almost simple. Who knows, maybe soon France will even experiment with power breakfasts. Nothing, you feel, is sacred any more.

'It makes me happy if I have someone coming in for one dish and who only drinks a mineral water. Young or old. They are the people who we need to excite, to get them into our restaurants.'

How else then can they energize the disinterested? The young, above all? L'Angl'Opéra has pioneered a scheme whereby anyone under twenty-five is allowed a 25 per cent discount. I was fifty, and thought the idea should catch on. Why not extend the scheme a little? I might even bring my mother to eat here. She is in her seventies. *Egalité* and all that.

This desire to democratize eating out is, to me at least, an excellent idea, long overdue – that kids may experience the complexities of taste, that they might enjoy eating, being social and cooking, and not just eat to quell hunger.

Génération C now has over a hundred chefs, who represent a serious attempt to plot a revival, give a creative boost to a flagging national métier, to energize the image of being a chef. This movement shares a real concern about the future, but Choukroun, at least, was not of the opinion that we were seeing the birth of a European cuisine.

Now anyone who dabbles in these things may well come across a rather confusing babel of groups, trends and ideas, in France as elsewhere. I was more than a little confused by the association of Génération C and another group called L'Omnivore. They are not one and the same, but cohabit.

L'Omnivore, too, is founded on a sense of crisis. A crisis of profit. Of clientele. And of direction. This group publishes a monthly paper, and arranges events that bring life to deadened corpses. Why else choose Le Havre in February to arrange a fabulous collection of the most enthusiastic chefs to perform and to cogitate in public?

But there often seemed to be a little bitchiness in the air, particularly when it came to talking about my own favourites, the boys and girls at le Fooding. For Hervé This, they were past it. Irrelevant, and worse still, using English to communicate ideas that should be intrinsically French. While some chefs decry their amateurish approach, le Fooding does not actually seem dead in the water at all. On the contrary, they manage to attract some of the country's finest talent to their events. But they too bitch. They have criticized the Omnivores for the lack of transparency in their food guide, where visits are far from being anonymous and tabs are picked up once in a while.

And nor was Gilles Choukroun that convinced

by *la cuisine moléculaire*. It doesn't exist, he told me. And as for le Fooding, 'It is nothing more than events. They have no philosophy, no substance.' Harsh words, perhaps. It was time to dabble in a little fooding myself.

15

Le Fooding

IMAGINE THE THRILL AS I STEPPED OUT FROM THE innards of the city of light, up the steps of the Metro at la Bastille, and picked my way through bodies, thousand upon thousand of them, still warm and all deliciously angry. By the way things were, by France and its lacklustre politicians, by an inept president mired in lashings of the muddiest of innuendoes. This time the villain of the piece was Chirac's unfortunate *premier ministre*, Dominique de Villepin, an urbane and elegant *énarque* (a graduate of the Ecole Nationale d'Administration), who although he had never actually held elected office in his life was deemed to be the ideal candidate to represent the people, simply because he had been to the ENA. This being France, his connections were what really counted.

De Villepin was trying to impose a law that

dared to address what was thought by some to be at the very heart of France's growing discontent: a 23 per cent unemployment rate among the young, a stultifying, over-protected labour market, and a lifeless economy that gave little hope and opportunity to the hundreds of thousands of unemployed, especially the young of the urban ghettos, thick with their culture of despair and frustration, and an alarming revolutionary sense of their own.

This was the day I had chosen to meet the man who fronts le Fooding, Alexandre Cammas. So I bounded through the crowds, and sought refuge in le Fooding's office, which is but a Molotov cocktail's throw from the Bastille in Paris's once most revolutionary *quartier*, the Faubourg Sainte Antoine. I climbed the stairs and asked for Monsieur Fooding, to see how revolutionary was the cut of this man's jib.

Cammas is no chauvinist. He has no trouble with diversity. Indeed le Fooding, like Génération C, revel in it. But why is their organization called le Fooding?

'It means food and feeling,' he told me. 'I don't think it matters that it sounds English. Food is much more global now than it has ever been, and even here in France things have to move forward.'

Le Fooding is deliberately and avowedly global in its outlook. Cammas himself has travelled, and happily absorbed the influence of food cultures from far outside France. It struck me that the countries he named as being inspirational – Britain, the US and Australia – were frequently held up as the enemy in the undeclared cultural battle between France and what it refers to as Anglo-Saxon culture. To group three of the world's most vibrant cultures, let alone food cultures, crudely as one is gruesomely simplistic, but you come across it over and over again. Anglo-Saxon culture does not exist, however much some people might wish otherwise. And let me remind you that the Angles were a people from Northern Denmark, and the Saxons from an area that is now in modern-day Germany. But what all three countries share is openness to diversity in food culture, which has trouble expressing itself in France, where the weight of a historical sense of superiority has over-whelmed such vitality.

But what really attracted me to le Fooding was their attempt to bring the best of French food culture on to the streets, to democratize it, if you like. Or to try to, at least. And this in a country where the streets have an almost religious signifi-cance. In Britain, people walk along the pavement with their eyes cast downwards. In Paris the pave-ments are a refuge, a cultural icon in themselves.

Trottoirs speak. They have kept a revolutionary sense of being, they cosset the defiant and allow them to express their anger. They know violence intimately, and have seen hideous *événements*. They are inescapably part of the culture of France.

Citizens once pissed on their edges, and doggies now do so at their peril. They are remarkably less splattered with chewing gum than you would expect, and far better preserved than London pavements.

And it is to the streets that le Fooding turn to spread the word. Every few months or so, they arrange an event, and when I was there in early spring they were busily planning the summer schedule. You pay a nominal fee, which goes to Action Contre la Faim, to come and watch chefs do their thing. The rain, too – it has become traditional that the summer Fooding festival has wintry weather. But people, all effortlessly casual, arrive and fill the space. And fill it to bursting.

When le Grand Fooding of the summer of 2006 did finally take place, it was cold and blustery as usual. But you could have nibbled at Pierre Gagnaire's *lichette de veau au romarin*, or joined the long queues for pizza made by the talented young chef Thierry Marx. This was French food that was thoughtful, capable and conscious of tradition, while wholeheartedly endorsing the experimental.

Much of my inspiration from food has come from producers rather than chefs. Inevitably, perhaps, since I spent so many years as a food supplier. Give me a smiling old *mémé* any day, who ladles thick bowlfuls of soup, strangles chickens bare handed and creates magic from the mundane. And I think, I hope, I am not alone. There are hundreds of thousands out there who love good food – maybe you are one – who simply haven't the means nor the inclination to go and spend their life savings on a meal out. Food culture is far more than restaurants and great chefs, in other words.

And who are these people who spend their time dabbling in the food of the great restaurants of Paris, frittering away ill-gotten fortunes? The highly respected restaurant critic and *Figaro* columnist François Simon doubts that any more than 10 per cent of the punters actually know their onions, as it were. Are those glittering temples of haute cuisine, as the word on the boulevard seems to suggest, really inhabited by culinary ignoramuses?

But having said that, is le Fooding actually a movement at all? Or is it just a feeling? Is le Fooding as empty headed as the average restaurant-goer?

'It's the art of eating and cooking, at your home or in a restaurant, with an open spirit, one that appreciates novelty and quality, that shuns boredom and that takes the time to savour simple foods,' explained Cammas.

I told him about the comments of Hervé This. He seemed unfazed. Le Fooding has just as many fans as detractors. A desire for gastronomic glasnost has led them up the path of élitism and they have an excessive attachment to fashion, bleat their critics. But when all is said and done, le Fooding is at least innovative.

16

Seksu

SOME FOODS HAVE BECOME SO UBIQUITOUS THAT
their origins are well and truly lost. Take the
Frankfurter. Who conjures up images of the Rhine
and *Wein* (let alone pig) when we bite into one of
the world's most popular sausages? Nor, talking of
ubiquity, do we dream of the Mönkebergstrasse in
Hamburg when we schlump our teeth into a
hamburger.

And in France there is couscous. Here is a food
that has been wholeheartedly accepted, but few
know that its heartland is in the Algerian hills of
Kabylie, among the Berbers. Yet almost everybody
in France is familiar with couscous and thinks they
know how to make it. Just add water, they say. Stir
and wait.

Couscous, or *seksu* as it is called in Kabylie, is a
dish that I, like you I suspect, have eaten many

times. And in some of the strangest locations. One of my fish suppliers lived in Casablanca, and I used to love sitting around on the floor, dipping my hands into a dramatic dish of fish couscous, then sleeping it off in the afternoon heat, soothed by endless cups of mint tea.

Back in Paris, I have eaten couscous in some pretty bizarre places, the most memorable being a Moroccan restaurant not far from the Bastille, where I ordered a couscous royale and watched as it came to the table propelled by sparklers. It was all delightfully naff. And then, lo and behold, when writing my book on Italy, I stumbled across a young chef on the island of San Pietro, a weird Ligurian-speaking outpost off Sardinia, who had just won a Mediterranean couscous *concours* in Trapani, wowing the judges with his San Pietran version of the dish. There were Israelis alongside Arabs, Croats alongside Italians: it all seemed impressively multicultural.

Couscous has crossed so many cultural boundaries that it is definitively rootless to most diners, with but the merest hint of the Maghreb, that part of North Africa to the west, where the sun sets (the meaning of *maghreb* in Arabic, by the way).

The day after I met with *les gens du Fooding*, I visited one of Paris's lesser-known arrondissements, the twentieth, where from Belleville to Ménilmontant there was, I had been told, a sense of multicultural harmony rare in French cities.

Cultures, religions were said to coexist happily. I assumed this to be the case, since there were no gum-chewing, gun-toting riot police around to tell me otherwise.

So, to the Boulevard de Ménilmontant, where the lunchtime market was drawing to a close, amid joking and japery. Piles of purple shellsuits awaited their fated companion, the passer-by destined to spend five Euros on nylon heaven. I passed a wedding organizer called Fati, and wondered how our plans were moving on, pulled in my stomach, and thought of lunch. July was getting ever nearer.

The pavement cafés were full and buzzing. The Lebanese was chokka, as was a café that bore a notice reminding visitors that the great Edith Piaf, the Little Sparrow, was buried not far away in the Père Lachaise cemetery, along with Jim Morrison and Oscar Wilde. What a marvellous threesome they would have made for my unplanned lunch.

At the other end of the street, the flavour was distinctly Algerian. Couscous and *briks* were on offer, and I thought yes. It was time.

The busiest restaurant along the boulevard was called Les Quatre Frères. It wasn't actually run by four brothers at all; more bruvs, really, four childhood friends whose idea was deceptively simple. They wanted to offer the same sort of food that one might find in the bistros of Algiers and the villages of Kabylie. France, after all, and Paris in particular, has a vast diaspora of Algerians, whose presence is rarely praised, rarely celebrated. And it was they who initially provided about 90 per cent of the custom.

I sat and talked with owner Kartout Karim, and his friends who passed by, adding this and that to the conversation.

Karim, like his partners, had grown up in the suburbs of Paris. They had drifted through the education system and emerged feeling more Algerian than French, and fiercely protective of their identity. When they all decided to open a restaurant, choosing the location wasn't too difficult.

'Ménilmontant is truly cosmopolitan. There is a Jewish shop around the corner, next to the Arab library. There are Lebanese, Turkish, Chinese, we all get along together. You don't see that too often in Paris. In the beginning it was almost all Algerians who came here. Some of them became quite emotional when we offered them food that they hadn't tasted for so long. We all had our mothers to help us get the dishes just right. We even had Algerians coming over from England. And Canada,' he told me, although that seemed a little excessive just for dinner.

On the menu that day was *chlita* and *chorba*, as well as the inevitable couscous.

'People who come here for the first time eat couscous. Sometimes *briks*. It's the only thing they have heard of.'

197

This said as I finished off my own *brik* and my own couscous.

'But for the regulars, we change the menu. Oh, you should come here in Ramadan. It is so busy. We even have women and children here. That's when we must get the food right. It's a special time for us. We always make *briks* as you would eat them in Algiers. With potato and *viande hachée* and egg.'

So what then is a *brik*? It's a strange word.

Une brique, its homonym, once meant ten thousand francs. Further back it was a million old francs. For years there were Frenchmen and women who clung to the notion of old francs far more rigidly than the British did to pounds, shillings and pence. Yet it astonishes me how easily France seems to have absorbed the Euro.

A *brik* is a food that evokes powerful memories. It is rarely found outside North Africa, and in France has yet to make it to the culinary big time. It is still largely ghettoized. They are made of sheets of filo pastry as fine as veils of voile, which envelop a filling that could be egg, fish or potatoes, and are then fried in oil and eaten at finger-melting heat. In Tunisia they are *briqs*, which has linquistically won the battle. Moroccans call them *briwat*, while in Turkey they become *börek* and in Algeria *bourek*. But however authentic the Brothers would like to be, filo pastry or *feuilles de brik* are bought in.

'Back in Algeria,' Karim told me, 'you still see

women sitting and talking while rolling the pastry by hand.'

And couscous is still occasionally made at home in Algeria, though rarely now, and tastes, they say, much the better for being so. Homemade couscous is a particular treat at the Feast of Eid al-Fitr that marks the end of Ramadan; it is served in magnificent mounds, dotted with meat – lamb or goat for choice.

Couscous can be served sweet, too. *Seffa* is a glorious subtle dish of grain, raisins, sugar and cinnamon served with hardboiled eggs and perfumed with saffron or orange-flower or rose water.

The couscous I ate was rich with mutton, and spiced. Here is a version I have translated from a book I found in the Algerian bookshop around the corner from Les Quatre Frères. Even the kids like it, and it calls for no great skill. Just a little time . . .

Couscous with lamb and vegetables

Serves 6

Ingredients
500g lamb, chopped
2 potatoes
3 medium turnips

3 large carrots
2 courgettes
1 stick of celery
1 handful of lentils
1 cup of chickpeas, pre-cooked
4 cloves garlic, finely chopped
1 teaspoon paprika
1 teaspoon cinnamon
A pinch of chilli (optional)
700g couscous
100g butter
Oil/salt/pepper

Method

Make a *dersa* (a mix that characterizes Algerian cooking) of the garlic, paprika, and some salt and pepper by mashing it to a paste with a pestle and mortar or equivalent. Place in the bottom of a *couscoussier* – a tall casserole will do -- and add the cinnamon, then a little water and the lamb. Bring to the boil and cook for ten minutes, then cover with 2 litres of water. Add the chickpeas, lentils, and the chilli if you like it, and bring to the boil again.

Peel and chop the vegetables. Add the celery, carrots and turnips and cook for a further forty minutes. Then add the potatoes and cook for a further twenty. And the courgettes ten minutes after you have added the potatoes. They should cook for no longer than ten minutes.

Place the couscous in the upper part of the *couscoussier*, or on top of the pan in a colander lined with muslin, above the cooking meat. Leave to cook for twenty minutes.

The couscous can then be put into a wide dish, making sure that it doesn't stick and clump together. Return it to the top if it does, add some salted water and mix well with your fingers to aerate it. Add the butter, mix further and arrange the vegetables and the meat around the edge of the dish, and moisten with the stock.

Translated from *Saveurs d'Algérie* by Fadéla Benabadji,
Editions de Lodi, France, 2005.

Will you ever come across homemade couscous in France? Unlikely. Packets work for us all. But for those purists among you, let me explain how once it was made. It goes like this. Durum wheat flour is first ground, then magically transformed by experienced hands that rub and flutter and coalesce the powder into the finest of particles, combining a little flour and water, salt and oil, then throwing it all high into the air and catching it in a wide sieve. This is but a gastronomic dream. No one will ever do this sort of thing these days in France.

Over the years, Les Quatre Frères has begun to attract an increasing number of Parisians, who love all that authenticity and gobble their way through endless *briks* and couscous, just as I had done.

'And when they come to pay the bill, so many say to me, "You know, you would be so much richer if you sold alcohol!" I say if you want alcohol then you can go over the road and get some and eat there. We don't want to change the way we eat. This is an Algerian restaurant and they should accept that we will do things our way.'

Now lest we forget – and outsiders almost always do – France and Algeria have had a truly gruesome relationship. A war that killed millions is barely referred to in the French education system. So brutal was the reality of the war, so raw is that nerve, that shoving it all under the national carpet has been the policy of generations of politicians, unable to confront the past. Which has done absolutely nothing to address the problem of the tension that still exists between the communities. It has done little to soothe what is essentially unsoothable. Apologies are there none. From either side.

The ferocious seven-year War of Liberation saw France forced to accept Algerian Independence. The highly disciplined Front de Libération Nationale or FLN survived to become the party of power in Algeria, while the French hauled General de Gaulle back to power and eventually conceded virtually all matters in their haste to get out. It was an exceedingly dirty war.

Estimates as to the total number of dead vary considerably. The FLN reckon on about a million.

By the end of the war, French colonization had lasted 132 years. The white settlers, les Pieds-Noirs, became as attached to the land as the indigenous population and they too sought a voice in the conflict, firmly opposed to anything but maintaining Algérie Française. Out of the turmoil emerged the Organisation de l'Armée Secrète (OAS), led by a disparate, vicious bunch of ex-military, serving military, bar-owners and opportunists, who targeted Algerians, be they liberals or extremists, and tried on several occasions to assassinate de Gaulle, so dogged was their pursuit of anyone who opposed Algérie Française.

The war saw the collapse of the Fourth Republic and caused the downfall of the relatively moderate prime minister, Pierre Mendès France. And along came the Fifth Republic, which stays to this day but placed greater powers in the presidency.

The scars of the war still remain. The Pieds-Noirs are still bitter. The *harkis*, Algerians who fought on the side of the French, were largely left to fend for themselves. The new regime saw them as collaborators, and many were brutally massacred post independence. The few who managed to flee the country are still ignored, and feel discriminated against in France.

The French military was implicated so deeply that it took years for it to evolve into the modern postwar fighting force that de Gaulle, always a soldier at heart, clearly envisaged.

Is all now forgotten, over forty years later? Not at all. 'I do not feel French,' Karim told me. 'And yes, I do think that France is still a racist country. At school, we were never told what happened in the war. They were just *événements*.' Events. Just events.

But things are darker still in Kabylie. During le Printemps Noir, the Black Spring of 2001, the Berbers of Kabylie rose up against the increasing Arabization of Algeria, after the assassination of a young Berber, Massinissa Guermah. Over sixty people died, and eventually some concessions were made to the principal demand, the recognition of the language of the Berbers, Tamazight, by the Algerian government.

So if you feel like contemplating the origins of couscous, this is a story far removed from those loving grannies that we all dream of. It reminds us just how barbarous we humans can be when it comes to nationalism and protecting our identity.

The next day I set off back to Oxford, taking Eurostar, which I had begun to love for its untroubled simplicity. I left with books on Algerian cooking, bundles of press clippings and newspapers, and sat in the Gare du Nord whiling away an hour or so, waiting for the train back to London. Being engrossed is not always a useful state of mind; you need to be alert. With my head buried in words, I never even looked up as I felt the most delicate brush against my leg. I just read on.

When the time came, I got up and saw that my precious backpack had been stolen. All my notes. The exact words of Hervé This. Books and a CD – but those notes. It was grim.

The police just shrugged their shoulders and said, Well, whoever took it is long gone now. And at least they'll be able to learn about molecular gastronomy. All I could do was shrug my shoulders with a Gallic *bof*, and thank God I had kept my passport and ticket close to hand.

On the other side of the ticket barrier, I just carried on phlegmatically reading the stuff I still had to hand. I was brought to my senses by a massive explosion below.

What was that? someone asked. Somebody left a backpack unattended down there. The police have just blown it up, we were told.

I watched all those shredded words of wisdom falling on the concourse like snow.

17

Plateau de Fruits de Mer

IT WAS WARM. IT WAS SUNNY. AND IT WAS ALMOST summer. I had been at home in England for a few weeks when Jean-Paul called to tell me of a few food festivals he had read about in *Ouest-France*, so dragging myself from tales of Algeria, the ancien régime and bloodcurdling accounts of Revolution, I set off on another gastronomic foray to Brittany.

Maybe it was the sun, maybe it was the morning market, or maybe it was just that with most of the family back in England it was almost affordable, but one April day, Jean-Paul, Dany and I took the road from Vannes to Quiberon, and dipped down to the sea at Saint-Philibert, tempted by the idea of a *plateau de fruits de mer*, a plateful of seafood, one of the much-praised glories of Breton cooking. Only most of it isn't really cooked at all. Lightly steamed or poached in brine is about as far as it goes.

It is, however, along with the crêpe, the one thing that you are obliged to eat when in Brittany. No one can escape. Both specialities let everyone else in France continue in the belief that Bretons are not great cooks, but are blessed with great raw materials. It can all sound a little condescending at times.

Now there is a busy road that goes down the Quiberon peninsula from Vannes, but if you take the smaller coast road you will eventually come to a bustling little port, stuffed full of yachts and stripy blue sweaters, called Saint-Philibert, and right opposite the harbour, perched just above the sea, is a little place called Le Chantier. It is deceptively tatty to look at, almost unprepossessing.

We sat on the terrace and relaxed as the oyster boats chugged noisily by, and pretended it really was summer. With a staff of two, they were, I suspect, not really expecting anyone that day, but it didn't seem to matter.

We made our choice and waited. I sent Claire a photo of the sun and the sea and a plate of her very favourite thing, *bulots à la mayonnaise*, freshly cooked whelks. So new-millennial. So cruel, too; she was profoundly envious and I felt more than a little guilty. While she was back at home coping with nappies and kids, I was relaxing in the sun with her parents!

Minutes later, a pair of hands swooped down to the table with the grace of a Breton seagull, reverentially placing a heaving plate, dripping with oysters, clams, whelks and winkles, on to a curious frame set centre stage. It almost had a hint of the guillotine to it. The scene had been meticulously well directed. Cups of Breton cider and slices of the freshest *pain de seigle* had already arrived.

I inhaled the scent of damp iodine that drifted from the glistening fronds of seaweed, captivated by the gentle squirming of the oysters and the warm, hazelnut aroma of those sweet, sweet langoustines. This, then, is the beguiling world of *fruits de mer*. The waitress allowed us a gasp, and a moment to reflect upon the glories before us.

Fruits of the sea. Food in its purest state. It seemed a fitting way to remind us that we are all animals underneath the *culottes* and the blubber, just blessed with a little culture.

While cooking transforms us from beast to man, we haven't entirely lost our appetite for raw food. Steak tartare is still served in a Vesuvian fleshy mound, topped with a raw egg and a little green from a gherkin. Sushi – raw fish and rice – is decorated and cut to ancient Japanese patterns, and has now moved way beyond its ancestral home.

From Japan also comes a highly developed appreciation of raw fish: sashimi. Delicate plates of the finest tuna, snapper or yellowtail now tease the palates of enthusiasts the world over, this too a highly ritualized, precisely mannered and humanized form of raw food. Patterns, textures and colours are created by the hand of a skilled chef. This is not simply a matter of grabbing a fish and biting. Far from it. But if sashimi has yet to truly conquer France, every year thousands upon thousands of tons of oysters and clams are still enthusiastically devoured, mostly uncooked.

That morning I had heard an astonishing story drifting across the ether, *grâce à la* BBC. Strange news from Africa. Somewhere in deepest Congo, a wild gorilla had been observed hesitantly dipping a stick into a murky lake to test the depth of the water. Scientists, environmentalists and biologists were all terribly excited by this remarkable event. But what happened next? Did it unravel a beach towel, slip on its Speedos and plunge into the lake? Did it unroll a copy of *Newsweek* and sit passively by the water's edge, cogitating on matters in Iraq? No, it carried on dipping its stick. But this gorilla was being held up as living proof that humankind is not the only creature to be able to dip sticks into lakes. And to use tools. To reason.

But the story had yet to reach fever pitch in *Ouest-France*.

A good *plateau* can be a glorious sight. The oysters still twitching, gently writhing when splashed with a little lemon juice or, as I prefer, a modest dribble of red wine vinegar and shallots. Then we had a few mussels, also raw, and some diminutive clams with fine, shining shells. These were *praires*, ribbed fat bivalves that are encumbered by a ridiculous name in English: Warty Venus. Sales are always slow in English-speaking countries, for some reason.

The rest of the display was cooked. There were of course those succulent langoustines, sleek and sweet, whose bodies and claws need to be sucked of the last of their flesh for true enjoyment. They are exquisite crustaceans. Then there was a neatly cleaved crab, to be picked and delved into with long, probing spikes. It is surgical fun eating a *plateau de fruits de mer*.

Whelks, however, are not to everyone's tastes. They seem too proletarian, for one, and to look at they are no great shakes, even less so when you draw them from their shell, and watch the almost nasal mess dribble from the end. But what a taste! Dipped in mayo with a slice of *pain de seigle*, there is nothing finer. And what's more, you could even go and catch your own, in theory anyway. But that is another story.

Later that weekend, I set off westwards to the edge of Brittany, to meet a man whom I knew by his voice alone. Yvon Madec is one of France's most-respected *ostréiculteurs* or oyster growers, and is based in the blustery *département* of Finistère, the end of the earth, on a beautiful creek called Aber-Wrac'h. When I was a seafood trucker, I would phone him every week, leave my order, and know that without fail his oysters would arrive in Boulogne, to be squeezed into my truck and delivered in the middle of the night somewhere in deepest, darkest London.

Since oysters were my first gastronomic passion, the very reason why I spent so many years hanging around fish markets as I morphed from being an Irish-oyster seller to a global fish merchant, I always respected the consistency and dependability of his produce. Raising oysters is not easy. But his *prat ar coums* were a class act for me, just as they are now for some of France's most respected chefs, who still swear by them.

Take an oyster. Hold it in your hand and smell it. Inhale deeply. It should be clean, and hint of iodine and the sea. Cold-shelled, but full, almost heavy to the hand, it should be tightly shut. Or better still, shut tightly when you drag it mercilessly from the water. It isn't easy to tell at a mere glance that all will be well inside, that the meat of the oyster will be full and mineral rich. But experience helps. Ensuring that the oyster is good and fat is down to good cultivation, and is an area where a good *ostréiculteur* will excel.

And it is very much a matter of oyster cultivation in France. There is a huge, almost scary variety of oysters, all of which, if you can decipher them, have their own message. The majority of French oysters are finished – i.e., fattened – in what are called *parcs* or *claires*, and most of these are cupped or *creuse* oysters, technically of the species

Crassostrea Gigas, the rock or Pacific oyster. They feed off plankton, and fatten according to how much they can gobble, so the more that are stacked within the enclosed *claire*, the thinner they tend to be.

The thinnest are often simply called *fines de claires*, and are stocked at about twenty per square metre for a month. Then moving up the scale are the *huîtres spéciales*, which are held for at least two months at ten per square metre. The difference can be marked. They are fatter and tastier, and yes, more expensive. They also tend to be less salty. A finer creature altogether.

You may come across some oysters that are exquisitely tinged with green. These are the famous *huîtres spéciales de Marennes*, where a rich local population of algae is used to give them a particular mineral taste. Marennes is far to the south in La Vendée.

Monsieur Madec is better known for his *huîtres plates*, or Belons. They are the native oyster and are a far trickier creature altogether.

You may well have heard someone rave about these Belon oysters, be it here or over there. They are so called after one of the main production areas in Riec-sur-Belon, to the south of Brittany, and have long been thought of as the ne plus ultra of the bivalve world, subtle, sweet, but oh so delicate! But the reality is that the native oyster is more expensive not simply because it tastes better, but because it takes longer to grow. In reality it is difficult, over-sensitive and over-priced. To look at, it is disc-shaped, with a concave lower shell, and is happiest filtering sea water and clinging on to a shell in the shallow coastal waters. Oysters open their shell and waft sea water that's full of microparticles over their highly complex intestines, growing fatter and fatter, unless someone comes along, interrupts their reverie and ships them off to be eaten. Or unless something appears in the water to upset their metabolism.

'To be honest, I tend to bring the *plates* in and sell them as soon as possible. You never quite know what is going to happen to them,' Madec told me.

In the 1980s, the sweet innocence of the oyster population was rudely interrupted by the arrival – from America, it is thought – of a deadly virus, which led the *famille* Madec to take the plunge and diversify. And it was then that they introduced the Pacific oyster to Aber-Wrac'h, which has been the saviour of *ostréiculteurs* in Europe, for even if its biological origins are in the Pacific, it has adapted magnificently to life in Europe, growing to edible size within three years, while native oysters can take at least five.

'The oysters need to move around,' Monsieur Madec told me. 'It helps fatten them up, makes them stronger, lessens the risk. We have learnt that the one thing that really gives them a special taste is the year they spend in *eau profonde*, in the deep sea.'

Now, a Breton creek should be a microbe-rich

environment, as perfect a place as any, you would have thought, to raise oysters. As it once was. But there is now so much nitrogenous waste, a.k.a. pig shit, being jettisoned into Brittany's rivers and estuaries that weed and algal growth is getting beyond a joke.

So Monsieur Madec is now obliged to raise his oysters elsewhere. His *claires* sit rather disconsolately and utterly empty within sight of his office, overgrown with seaweed.

But despite all this, since we all love the idea of buying fresh and from source, the Madecs have now opened their depot to the public, so the enthusiast can walk in and buy these mythical bivalves, and more. There are crabs and lobsters, even the occasional langouste. Live langoustines are brought in with the morning tide, and clack mournfully as they wait to be boiled. Tanks of filtered sea water gush and splash frenetically around sections of this and that, around oysters of all sizes, both *creuses* and *plates*. There is a divine scent of sea and brine.

I asked whether we could taste a few.

Or if I could taste a few, for Yvon Madec, like his father before him, never actually eats an oyster. Neither his nor others, which reminded me of that distance the Breton so often has to food from the sea. His appreciation – just as profound as mine, I assure you – is more for the feel and the sight of the oyster. Not the taste.

He picked up a *creuse* from the tank, spun it around and sliced it open. 'There, look at that. Not bad, not the best, but here, taste it.'

The sea water, the subtle, cold mineral blast. Good.

We crossed over to the other side and fished out a *plate*.

It was diminutive. Diminished. A sad little specimen.

'You can see it hasn't been a very good year at all. Too little rain. Not enough nutrients in the sea for them to fatten up properly. But here, look at this one.'

He fished out an oyster, took out his knife and cleanly opened it, laying it throbbingly perfect and gently undulating before me, a full, fat oyster, with a tinge of algal green to it and a jet-black beard, the outer frilly edge. A complex mix of vigour and vitality, of salt and . . . is that a hint of hazelnut?

'I never could understand why some people swallow their oysters whole, straight down,' I said.

'*Ah bon?* It's better to bite a little. They've got to be *croquante*.'

It was excellent.

'Now just try this one and then I'll tell you what it is.'

A *plate*. Very dark-shelled. A good meat inside. Not bad. Not bad at all.

'Well, we call it a "Black". I thought you'd like it. We have some customers who swear by them. They say they are the best of them all. We bring them over from Falmouth.'

Ho hum.

18

Pêche à Pied

I LOVE THE IDEA OF SCOURING THE FORESHORE FOR this and that, chasing chimerical *couteaux* (razor clams) and apoplectic crabs. Of learning to interpret the runes of the sand, the wiggles and the squiggles, that are as alien to us as birdsong in the Amazon. In France there are a surprising number of purists who tramp the foreshore collecting their very own seafood. I used to be among them, until I realized just how unpristine Breton beauty could be. This pastime is called *pêche à pied* and is still deeply popular in France, leading to some nasty winkle-rage incidents as the beaches quickly become filled with bent-backed grumpy old men and their rakes.

As I was tasting the fruits of the sea at Aber-Wrac'h, a friend texted me to tell me of an exciting event to be held that very evening in nearby Binic, in the Côte du Nord, devoted entirely to the pleasures of *la pêche à pied*. Vive parochialism, I thought, and set off.

Binic was hosting a meeting of Les Bistrots de Vie. Every few months, one of the local bistros would organize a get-together, word would seep out – the newspaper plays an important part here too – and a steady stream of visitors would arrive.

So, come 19.00 hours exactly, there I was, champing at the bit.

The marquee quickly filled up.

Starting time had passed, and everyone was getting restless.

'*On voit rien, monsieur!* We can't see a thing!' came a voice from the back, as our hostess for the evening said something incomprehensible into the microphone, which wasn't working.

'*Il faut un micro! J'entends rien.* You need a microphone. I can't hear a thing!'

'OK, here we go. It's working now!' the presenter told us, shouting through cupped hands to make herself heard.

I began to wonder whether the evening was going to be too much for the tanned and vigorous Briochins who had filled this marquee right on the sea front of Binic to bursting. The townspeople, the Binicais, have St Brieuc as their local capital, and they are all known as Briochins. It is nothing to do with a love of brioche, by the way. Just to set the scene topographically.

Was there going to be a touch of tension in the proceedings? Shuffling bones, squinting eyes, an average age over fifty means but one thing: get on with it! And in the end they did.

Now Binic is a perfectly ordinary fishing port, with a few hotels, a line of cafés and the usual gang of crêperies. It once sent its men to sail the seas to America, where they fished for cod on the Grand Banks and helped keep France supplied with salt cod, *morue*. These days the young sail off to Paris. It pays better.

The evening was part of a deliberate strategy to encourage a sense of community, through food and drink. The France that we all think we know and love, dreamland France, is sprinkled with cafés and bistros, full of happy, wine-swilling locals, thick with tobacco smoke and the smell of good food.

A few years back, it would have been unthinkable to read of their decline and distress. How things had changed. The government of the day was so concerned about the rise of evil coffee-bar culture that they were even toying with a radical plan that would allow local establishments to lease games such as the much-loved *babyfoot*, or table football, and one-armed bandits at special rates. What a magnificent gesture!

Yes, all France agrees that something must be done. As indeed it should.

Communities that ebb and flow with the seasonal rush of tourism can suffer from a profound malaise when the summer crowds have gone. Here local memory and history were being harnessed to help define exactly what this place was all about.

But it was more than a collection of ancient souls pounding the *trottoirs* of memory lane. Both the bistro and the café have played their part in moulding French society, in creating that unique French identity. So there is profound disquiet at the number of businesses that are closing for good, at the gradual move away from the ways of the past. The old-style café was a malleable, changing entity, where you could just as well write a book as spend hours drinking a coffee. As I did more than once. Then you could come for lunch on another day. Or dinner. Or an aperitif.

Everyone knows that French café culture is unlikely to survive by being passive. Strategies are being thought carefully through. Binic was evidence of a very genteel rearguard action.

For a while, the presenter wandered uneasily up and down the marquee – called delightfully in French *un barnum* – clinging to her dysfunctional *micro*. Even a microphone seemed to have cultural resonance to it. In France they are held tightly in the hand and pulled almost obscenely close to the mouth, or jiggled like worry beads. You can see them on display most nights on French television.

Saturday night on French television is gloriously tacky, and yes, everyone is clinging like grim death to the *micro*. But what makes it so odd to me is that fifteen years ago they were doing exactly the same thing. Even the presenters were the same. A selection of white middle-class French males who have now swollen and wrinkled with age. But at least there is now *le satellite*, so you can always watch endless documentaries about starfish in Guadeloupe. Or just go out. To Binic, maybe.

The logic of all this was once explained to me. It was government policy, I was told, to encourage people to communicate, to dance, to eat together, and what more effective way, the *énarques* thought, to maintain the old ways than by creating television so awful that no one in their right minds would actually want to watch it. And anyway, they were all out dining, whoring or visiting their masters and mistresses and their *résidences secondaires*.

Fifteen minutes on, and we were still being told in explicit detail what we were about to see, without actually seeing it. There was a selection of *notables* centre stage, and they too had yet to be introduced. But in the end, it all kicked off.

So, say *Bonsoir* to Monsieur and Madame Chenu, a swarthy couple who were there to talk about *le petit train* that once ran along the coast. They began to reminisce somewhat hesitantly about their childhood, about France of *autrefois*. Of those happy days, and holidays marked by the whistle of the little train, *la micheline*, they called it, since it ran on rubber wheels.

'We kids never had a watch. So in the evening we were allowed to stay out until we heard the nine forty-five whistle,' Monsieur Chenu told us all with misty eyes.

His wife grabbed the microphone. 'My father always took the morning train to St Brieuc, with the same lady, in the same carriage, and he always did the crossword.' It sounded positively metropolitan.

There was by now a passionate momentum building up.

'Remember the station master!' one voice called.

His daughter was in the hall, and everyone turned their heads respectfully and clapped. And so it went on, and on, and on, to its own curious, interminable rhythm. It was a collective sigh of nostalgia.

Meanwhile, the projectionist had fired up the power-point presentation and we all gawped at images of a France long gone. Those heady days when everyone thought that global menace had been buried for ever, when clattering Deux Chevaux ruled the roads, and Frenchmen puffed on Gitanes for all to enjoy.

But with a collective toot, eventually and oh so sadly, this part of the evening drew to a close, and we moved to the bar and did the bistro thing. Then images began to appear on the screen of bowed backs, rakes, and buckets full of shells. This was the moment I had been waiting for. An hour or two on *la pêche à pied*.

Scuttling around on the foreshore, *l'estran*, lifting slippery, salty boulders from the sand, really is a magical way to spend the day. To watch the sea slip gently away as the tide ebbs. To see the alarmed, crazed movements of fish trapped in rock pools, and listen to the gentle hissing of barnacles on the rocks as they warm in the sun, and limpets as they cling tighter to the rocks. The tide goes out. Hermit crabs pull their shells over their bodies, and winkles hunker down and wait for the sea to return.

This is the world of *la pêche à pied*: what you can find with your feet in the sea. It is more than infantile, more than poetic. In France it involves looking for something to eat, for food that is still perceived to be pure, untouched, despite all the problems of pollution. It is about the perfumes, *l'iode*, and the sea. Although there are still a few professionals who work the foreshore, not many are left now and they rail against the hordes of amateurs who have ruined it for them.

It is almost alarming to see the lines of hunched, bowed people on a good low tide. Here the talk will be of prawns and shrimps cooked lightly in the sea water, of *palourdes* and *praires* placed under the grill with butter, parsley and chunks of garlic, a sublime, effortlessly simple dish if there ever was one.

And it appeared that *l'estran* was as much a part of the local community as *le petit train*.

A local anthropologist, Guy Prigent, told us, 'In the past, the foreshore was always used by the people of the area. They would put down fishing lines, collect the seaweed to fertilize the soil. Each area had local names that everyone knew. Every stream, every mound, every rock had its name. They used names that came mostly from the farm, or the human body, in either *Gallo* or Breton. All this memory is being lost.'

So much of the French coastline is devoted to tourism that keeping it a truly functioning part of the country with its own sense of community is proving difficult. Incomers buy up houses and push the prices ever skywards. Summer rubbish accumulates and has to be shipped away, and demands for water in the high season are colossal. Being everyone's preferred summer destination comes at a heavy price in twenty-first-century France. Particularly here in Brittany.

I slipped away like an eel after the second hour of blissful memories, knowing that I had been due in Finistère for dinner about three hours previously. And next morning I was off to see an island where the foreshore still played a major part in helping the locals grow some of the finest vegetables in the land.

Rain was pouring once again from the sullen Breton sky as I arrived to stay with friends not far from Lannion, gruesomely late. They brought out a plate of spectacular scarlet prawns, with their anguished antennae forever silenced. They were rich with that marvellous combination of sweet and salt that only the freshest of seafood ever has.

And one of their friends had dropped by to show me an ancient agricultural handbook on one of Brittany's most iconic crops: *blé noir*, or *ed dhu* in Breton. In English it's known as buckwheat. I watched the whisky bottle slowly empty, as we were drawn into spirited conflict. He was a little prickly, and I was being provocative. *Soixante-huitards*, they call them – men still fighting the street battles of 1968 – he was one and happy to blame me for all the wrongs of the world.

'You English! Always following the Americans! How can you support this war in Iraq?'

'We don't,' I told him. 'We didn't enter the war, our government did. I don't actually know anyone who supports the war at all. But one thing I can say is that no one was at all surprised when France took the position that it did. It was to oppose the Americans. Your government is in it up to its neck. It's just playing the same old game.'

We all make assumptions about each other. That French people live close to their roots, and are constantly cooking up marvellous things to eat, for example. That their food is consistently brilliant. But his was one assumption too far. So I retaliated.

I asked him what he thought an average Briton

was really like? What did he think really made us tick, as it were?

'Well, I would say that you lack individuality. That you all always do the same thing. That you are all a little fearful of the State . . .'

I laughed. 'That's exactly what many say about the French.'

19

Hachis Parmentier

AND SO TO ROSCOFF. THE SKY WAS WIDE AND achingly blue, the wind still cold, as I stepped gingerly on to the ferry to the Ile de Batz to meet a potato. And a man called Monsieur Prigent.

I knocked on the door of his solid *maison bourgeoise*.

Jean Prigent was as weather-beaten and tanned as everyone else seemed to be on the island, his hands still hard and cracked despite his retirement, and despite the fact that summer had hardly begun.

'Monsieur Prigent?'

'I have been waiting for you, monsieur. Please come in. Sit down.'

I sat, looked around, and relaxed in the vibe of a kitchen that was full of solid farmhouse cupboards, with immensely thick walls. The fireplace was charred and ancient. I asked how much time he had to talk to me.

'I am not thinking of passing away just yet, you know. I have as long as it takes. I am retired, so talk away. But I'm not too sure I can help you on the cooking. My wife did the cooking, and she passed away.'

He slipped his hand into his pocket, and took out a potato.

'*Et voilà!* There. That's one from this year's crop, but that's what you want to talk about, so take it home with you if you want. I have got a bag of them for you outside.'

It was very sensual, almost perfectly oval, utterly unblemished, delightfully smooth-skinned, and if you held it close to your nose and gently inhaled, it had the slightest hint of seaweed. This was no ordinary potato. It had nothing to do with the morass of monoculture, and the great prairie fields that you see elsewhere in Brittany. Were it not for the fact that it was so clearly of the earth, you could quite easily imagine it nestling happily among the pebbles on a storm-battered beach.

And believe me, this potato, like Monsieur Prigent himself, knew a thing or two about the sea. And the wind. And the warming mists of the Gulf Stream, the gales, and the monumental turbulence that you get in Finistère. The clouds that seem to spring from the earth, and tear themselves away from the land.

It started its life, as tradition dictates, on the twentieth of January under a thick protecting mulch of seaweed, which rots down and gently leeches into the soil, giving Batzian potatoes a taste that is so fine, so delicate that people like me get extremely excited by the prospect of holding, let alone eating, a *pomme de terre de l'île de Batz*.

In the 1960s, life on the island became more difficult, Monsieur Prigent told me. The population continued to decline, and the potatoes were becoming harder to sell. So some of the island's farmers decided to link up with a cooperative on the mainland that began to market their produce far more effectively. The word began to seep out.

And they did have a remarkable product. Not only were their potatoes among the earliest to appear in French – and importantly Parisian – markets, but they tasted as sweet and virginal as a potato can be. A *sirtema*, for example, boiled, and served with Breton butter and a sprinkling of sea salt, is absolute perfection. I know people who eagerly await their arrival. Hundreds are shipped off to treat the pampered gourmets of Paris.

And that's not all. Almost all of the island's production is organic; it's how things have always been. A healthy soil produces a healthy plant, which in turn calls for fewer chemical props. Seaweed is the essential fertilizer on the island, it is mineral rich and abundant.

But when the potatoes didn't bring in enough

money, the islanders decided to diversify. They tried sea kale, *chou marin*, a tricky crop, but so delicate to eat when gently steamed and served with butter. They have dabbled in *crosnes*, tiny, awkward vegetables called Chinese artichokes in English, that were once all the rage in *grands restaurants*.

Whatever the island grows seems to be so profoundly healthy, so vibrant, so alive. Earlier, I had walked past rows of parsley of the deepest, darkest green, carrots of remarkable vigour, cauliflowers and cabbages without a leaf even vaguely nibbled by beast or bird. It made me want to weep. My efforts back home seemed almost tragic.

While we talked, there was a constant buzz of tractors – the island is virtually carless – and noise from the local school. We began to discuss how things have changed on the island, what they used to eat, how close they were to the land and to the sea.

'Well, let's look at how things were in the fifties. The island had more people then, for a start. There were about a thousand islanders. These days I think it's about six hundred.'

Not a population collapse, then?

'No, no, not at all. We all lived off the land then. Every month somebody would kill a pig, salt it down and leave it in a pot, a huge clay pot like that one outside' – which was now stuffed with a fuchsia in the rudest of health. 'We'd exchange it for whatever we needed at the time. Everyone worked like that. So when a pig had been killed, then there'd be *jambonneau* to eat. That was good with a purée of potatoes. We all made butter, of course, *en barattes*. Everyone had a churn, or a wooden bucket where you moved the stick up and down like this.' He moved his hand up and down like that. 'And when the cow was in calf, there was veal to be had, although we didn't eat it. Veal was too valuable. We sold it on the mainland.'

By now a friend of his had joined us around the table, the old lighthouse-keeper, he too now happily retired. They talked of the war.

'You know, some of the Germans were good to us. We used to follow them around all day and pick up the food they dropped, and nick things from them as well. I remember right at the end, they lined up thirteen people against the wall, we all knew they were about to be shot. One of the village women came running up and pleaded with them to be saved. And they were . . . But when they left, they destroyed everything. Many islanders, they went to Paris, you know. The Parisians used to say we Bretons liked to *baragouiner* too much.'

To this day there is still a large Breton population in the capital, known for their love of the *craich* and drink. The word *baragouiner* means to talk endlessly, to gabble, and is said to come from the Breton habit of offering bread, *bara*, and wine, *gwin*. Wine? Hmmm. Breton cider, maybe. We stuck to water.

Now Batz is by any account a special island, for it has consciously decided to keep its agricultural soul alive, and hasn't entirely sold out to tourism. But while we chatted about farming, I noticed that the talk was of meat and drink, milk and potatoes. Never about food from the sea.

'No. It's true we mostly ate meat and potatoes. Sometimes we would go and get *patelles* (limpets) from the beach, always the smaller ones higher up on the rock, they tasted better. My mother would put them in a casserole. We used to give the bigger ones to the pigs.'

And there were abalone, *ormeaux*, caught when the tide was low and the tidal *coefficient* was high – at least 110 for you *pêche à pied* freaks. Abalone were slowly fried in the *billig* (the thick iron crêpe pan that was found in every kitchen on the island), with sea salt and lard, then preserved in glass jars for the winter. Soft velvet swimming crabs (*étrilles*) were made into soup, and *crabes dormeurs*, the best of all thick-clawed and sweet-tasting edible crabs, simply boiled.

'Batz was always a working island until recently. We never really had any tourists until *Amoco Cadiz*.'

In 1978 a massive oil spill plastered the whole Breton coastline with 67 million gallons of Iranian crude oil, wrecked oyster beds, killed thousands of sea birds and millions of fish, and ruined the ecosystem for a generation. Yet people were so drawn by the spectacle that they began to think, Hmm, Finistère, let's go and stay there, it looks so beautiful.

'Have you walked around the island yet?' he asked me. 'Just round the back here, they are putting seaweed on the fields for the potatoes. Go and have a look.'

Come high summer, the island's population quadruples. Rubbish accumulates and water becomes scarce. This is the price the local population pays. And the tourists? What do they know of all this? They come for peace and quiet, always difficult to find in France, where tradition has it that most of the country, indeed most of Europe, heads in the same direction with the regularity of migrating swallows. In the winter, the islands and resorts are full of houses shuttered tightly, enclosed, quite dead. It all seems so soul-destroying.

But Batz at least has its potatoes, and its *primeurs*, early produce which springs from this sandy ground, teased to premature growth by the mild air and the light, as well as the island's great secret ingredient, seaweed. The place is living proof of the power of *terroir*. The farmers of the island would never be able to compete against either the world's or France's enormous potato industry, but here they have found a niche that, if it doesn't exactly make them wealthy, allows the island to survive as a living, breathing community, on the reputation – justifiable, it must be said – of the excellence of their vegetables, in a country where taste still survives as a guiding light for people who enjoy good food.

Hachis Parmentier

This is a classic dish that uses cooked meat left over from a stew or pot au feu, and tops it with the finest mashed potatoes.

Parmentier was an eighteenth-century scientist who spent a lifetime seeking alternative sources of flour to relieve the constant threat of famine. His treatise on the potato bigs up the vegetable so massively it makes you think it the world's panacea. As many did, of course, until the Irish potato famine came along . . .

Serves 6

Ingredients
800g cooked meat, chopped
A handful of lardons
2 Roscoff onions, or a mild equivalent
2 cloves garlic
2kg potatoes

Enough grated Emmental or Cheddar to cover
50g butter
A pinch of grated nutmeg
Salt and pepper
Olive or vegetable oil

Method
Cook and purée the potatoes with the butter and a little nutmeg. Add some milk if the mash is too thick. Meanwhile lightly fry the lardons, onions and garlic in oil, and add the meat.

Season, and place in an ovenproof dish. Top with the potato and cover with cheese. Cook in a moderate oven for 30 minutes.

20

Gratinée

BACK ON THE MAINLAND, MY THOUGHTS TURNED TO another vegetable. Maybe you are old enough to remember the days when French men with bicycles really did work the cities and suburbs of Britain selling onions, and without recourse to a single shot of testosterone. Just a little cider. They arrived dangling unfeasibly large tresses of onions from their bicycles and were called Onion Johnnies. Almost all were Bretons, seeking their fortune over the water. Right opposite Batz is the mother town, Roscoff, which also benefits from the mild warm salty air and grows the most exquisite sweet-tasting onions. The famous *oignons de Roscoff*.

I had assumed that all this toing and froing was dead and long gone, the stuff of memories, until I noticed that Roscoff had opened its very own Musée des Johnnies. Which was where I breathed the life and culture of Johnnyism, and where I discovered that there were still living, breathing Onion Johnnies. I know. I met one.

So, welcome Monsieur André Quemener, Dédé to his mates, a man who is still so profoundly attached to his métier that he now takes the ferry to Cornwall every year, reliving a more comfortable, post-retirement version of his past as a traditional onion-seller. Dédé has become un homme avec un white van. He tried to stop selling onions back in 1972, but found that he just couldn't. 'It was like a drug!' he told me. 'I just missed going across the water every year. It has been in my blood for too long now. I cannot stop.' So off he sets just like in the old days, but with his onions stuffed into a white van.

His story is fascinating, and he can tell it in French or English, or rather English with an Edinburgh brogue, for he spent his formative onion years in Leith. He has that defining lilt which when crossed with a French accent is alluring, to say the least. But then, as he pointed out, it was Breton that he and his family spoke at home, and he still speaks, so onion-selling was actually a tri-lingual business.

But it was often very difficult for a young Johnny, when confronted by Scottish voices trying the odd word of French, to understand what was being said. Dédé learnt to love Scotland, and the mining families of Leith in particular, and it was there that he finally mastered English. There is a real empathy between Celts and Bretons; both sides express it. Somehow you might have expected a gentle slumping into Frenchness, but Dédé felt, and still feels, closer to Celtic ways than French.

Being a Johnny was not a job to be looked down upon at all. However hard life was, however poor families might have been, it seems to have been a blessing to be able to earn hard cash and to follow in the path of fathers, cousins and uncles. While the women largely stayed at home and tended the young and the livestock, the men crossed the water and sold onions.

As soon as the harvest was in, boats were filled to the gunwales with sack upon sack of sweet Roscoff onions, and set off across the water. To Leith, in Dédé's case, where they would arrive some seventy-two hours later. As soon as they could, they disembarked and set off to find lodgings, and to brush the dust off their bikes and get ready for the season.

It was all highly organized. No dreamy wanderings were allowed at all. Each team had a master at its head, who tied an apprentice to work '*en gage*' for the season. Sometimes money was advanced as a loan, a crucial source of income for many of the families who stayed behind. Those few who didn't smoke were entitled to tobacco money, which could also be paid upfront.

Dédé was soon captivated by the bonhomie of

the Leith mine-workers; less so by the grand houses of Edinburgh with their maids and butlers, and the huge Georgian mansions. They may have been good clients but they lacked the warmth of the mining communities.

'Once I met one of my old clients, a rich gentleman, walking in the street in Edinburgh,' Dédé told me, smiling. 'He asked me to go and deliver his onions to the kitchen, and paid me then and there. So I went and knocked on the kitchen door, and the maid looked at me and said, "No onions." Well, I tried to say that I had met the governor and he had paid, but my English was not good then, so I had to go back and try again. "No, enough onions," she said. She was very cross this time. In the end I put my foot in the door and said "Monsieur has paid. Yes onions," and dropped them on the floor. And left quickly.'

'Enough' was apparently one of the first English words an Onion Johnny would learn.

'Aye, it was hard. That's why they called us bell-breakers.'

I thought his accent had got the better of him, and said, 'Don't you mean ball-breakers?'

'No, no, bell-breakers. We rung the bells too hard, they said.'

A Scottish play on words, I thought.

It was a long week. On Sunday they would sit down and write home, and tried to avoid going to the pub, where it was all too easy to spend the week's wages. However, Dédé still has a nostalgic fondness for pubs, smoky pints of bitter, crisps and that human side of what must have been a pretty exacting job.

And what of these Roscoff onions? I never knew that they were so particular, so soft, so sweet and delicately blushed with pink. I always presumed, as I suspect many others did, that they were just regular, everyday onions that were being sold by the Johnnies, as harsh and unsubtle as the next.

But there is more to the onion than meets the eye. Much more. In Italy I had come across the famous onions of Tropea, which are so sweet that they can be, and are, eaten raw. In Tuscany, too, they grow the most exquisitely sweet onions. But the Roscoff onion is, I think, the best of all to cook with. Not just for its beauty or the appeal of its woven tresses, but for the delicacy and subtlety of its taste.

A few years ago, sales of Roscoff onions were declining alarmingly, so a few producers came up with a plan to form a cooperative. It seemed to be a very Breton solution, and it has worked well. Roscoff onions have quietly slipped into the wider culinary consciousness in France – I have seen them as far south as Biarritz, and indeed they can be found all over Europe. Who knows, next stop world domination. Regional products go nowhere unless they become supra-regional.

As to their origins, there is the usual escapee-priest story. All Roscoff onions, so they say, are derived from seed that was brought back from Portugal by a Capucin monk in 1647. The onions grew well in the walled monastery garden. The moist Breton air suited them. And they slowly emerged to become one of the prime crops of the region. But it wasn't until 1828 that a pioneer Johnny, Henri Olivier, first decided to cross the Channel and open up a new market in Britain. His success didn't go unnoticed. By 1860 over two hundred Johnnies had made the journey, selling over a thousand tonnes of onions.

And now here we are in the noughties, and the Onion Johnny is little more than a folk memory. There are one or two still going strong, and there is always Dédé who is happy to talk. And happier still to sell you a string of his most delectable sweet Roscoff onions.

Gratinée

This rich onion soup is traditionally eaten in Paris, but, hey, tradition stultifies, and it is absolutely wonderful made with Roscoff onions and stock from a pot au feu. Gratinée *is one of the most invigorating, soul-warming soups to eat on a cold winter's day.*

Serves 4

Ingredients

800g peeled, chopped Roscoff onions
100g best butter
1 litre homemade stock
200g grated Gruyère
A good baguette
2 eggs
1 tablespoon port
Salt

Method

Fry the onions in the butter for 5 minutes, then boil them in the stock for thirty minutes. Check seasoning. Chop the bread into rounds and put one or two slices into each bowl.

Grate the cheese, and sprinkle some on the bread. Pour the boiling stock over the bread. Whisk the egg yolks with the port and spoon a little into each bowl.

Finish with more cheese, and brown under the grill. Serve sizzling.

21

Crêpes and Galettes

I KNOW OF NO FERRY PORT THAT HAS MORE CHARM and quietness about it than Roscoff. Where boats laden with onions and Johnnies once set off across the sea, now there's the odd car ferry to Ireland and that is about it. A little way from the old harbour is the gorgeous, evocative Chapelle Sainte-Barbe, where the annual exodus was blessed and sanctified; for we shouldn't forget that the crossing was long and arduous. It was not an easy life.

Poverty was the way of things, and the Breton diet reflected this. *Blé noir* is a plant that suited the soil and climate admirably, and has become the source of one of the region's most instantly recognizable creations, the galette. *Blé noir* grew, they said, in forty days, and thrived on the poor Breton soils, particularly the acid terrain inland.

The annual Fête du Blé Noir is held at Pleumeur-Bodou, a little village not far from Roscoff, and takes place, bizarrely, in the shadow of an ultra-modern listening station, with antennae and weird globe-shaped buildings as a background. Thus the old theme-park Brittany and the new techno persona co-exist a little falsely for at least a day a year.

So it was off to the fête, along with a few hundred others, where I met a seasoned galette-maker from a local farming family, whom I knew only as Renée. With a grizzled chin and a practised slurp, Renée the Breton farmer's wife, Renée the mother and Renée the cook merged into one. With her sleeves rolled up, she was at ease with the earth, and with the rich, damp, agricultural heartland of western Brittany.

She looked up, caught my eye, smiled and beckoned me over. '*Venez, m'sieur!*'

Renée made crêpes with a practised rhythm. I watched her calloused, bent-knuckled hands, entranced at the speed of it all. Swoosh, sploosh, fizzle, as she poured a ladleful of grey unctuous batter on to a thick *billig*, a devilishly dark iron plate heated by a raw gas flame below, the pan that Breton cooks traditionally use to make crêpes. Once more, she dipped into the earthy bowl that was by now dripping with thick grey batter. It looked more like necromancy than cooking, but the end result was a little tastier.

Hence the bags of freshly milled buckwheat flour, the black wheat or *blé noir* that has been undergoing a modest revival of late in France. It's also known as *sarrasin* in French. But don't panic over the etymology. All will be crystal clear.

I watched entranced as Renée poured a little more of the *pâte* on to the centre of the seething *billig*, which sizzled and spat once again, then ran a small T-shaped wooden raclette across it, working from the centre outwards, flattening the few remaining pockets of air, smoothing out the rougher edges and setting the crêpe on its way. It darkened. The edges curled lightly upwards in a brief death throw, and less than a minute later she reached for her spatula, flipped it over, waited, and placed it on the steaming pile next to her.

She passed me a fresh crêpe, dressed simply with salty Breton butter, and I felt it hot and soft on my tongue. I looked at her and wanted more. The next was more elaborate, cooked with a slice of ham, some cheese, and an egg that had a glowing golden yolk. This is a crêperie classic, *une complète*.

Crêpes are deeply moreish. Fine food for the hungry and the toothless, they are cheap, nutritious, and easy to cook.

Asking Renée what exactly made a good crêpe, she answered with the wisdom of her age. '*Ah, il faut de bons ingrédients, m'sieur!*' You must have good ingredients.

And were they easy to cook?

'So long as you get the *billig* hot enough, and you work quickly, yes. But if it is too cold your crêpe will not be good.' Maybe that had been the problem back home. Our *billig* was too cold. Or maybe it was that we didn't actually have a *billig* at all.

So, good ingredients. And a thick *billig*. A fine philosophy.

Anyway, the fête. This was, above all, a day to muse on the rising fortunes of a plant that tells of this distant past, of poverty and backwardness, the Brittany of *autrefois*. Nostalgia and food seem to play a complicated game in France. The past becomes appealing when it is sufficiently distant, unknown, of another time and another age. We forget that such a life would have been quite unbearable for most of us twenty-first-century Europeans. Nostalgia taints reality with its siren call, and has become a mere marketing technique. France sometimes seems in danger of becoming a heritage centre, a theme-park world of nostalgia.

French supermarkets vie with each other in trickery, creating labels that speak of tastes of *autrefois*, of tradition, with elaborate earthy labels and elaborately high prices. One has to be prepared to pay for nostalgia. It has become part of the repertoire of beloved added value, so dear to the bottom line, but the sad truth is that almost without exception these pastiches have flavours that are dumbed down and banal. Such is the awesome power of nostalgia.

Just as the Romans celebrated their courageous

ancestors, so they heaped praise on their simple food. In the eighteenth century, Enlightenment thinkers and philosophers were constant in their discussion of man's basic nature and the search for a society that allowed him to express it, seeing society as a corrupting influence. Thus the image of the noble savage took root. Such thinkers favoured simple unfussed foods. Rousseau was a committed vegetarian.

The relationship between France and her food is often retrospective, backward looking. Modernists seem to be keener on re-establishing the dominance of French food than actually creating something new from within. Implicit is not only the idea that the past was a better time, when taste was true, but also that the best is past. That French food is in decline.

Blé noir makes the odd appearance elsewhere in France, but was never quite as wholeheartedly accepted as it was in Brittany. It was grown down in the Cévennes, and in mountainous Savoie, where you can still find a dried form of buckwheat pasta called *crozets*, minute little rhomboids of *blé noir* that make exquisite winter food when served with the local sausage, *diots*, and grated Beaufort.

Rude and elementary *blé noir* may seem to be, helping to perpetuate the myth that Breton food is not among the finest in France, but it also appeals to that increasingly dominant interpretation of French food: that it is rustic and simple, rather than urban and sophisticated.

Brittany is rich in raw materials but poor in cooks, people say. But in 2006, headline news: to the north of Brittany, Olivier Roellinger at his Maison de Bricourt gained his third Michelin star, the first ever in Brittany. Now, you could say that this is evidence of Monsieur Michelin trying to move with the times, trying to tell his diminishing fans that there is life away from Paris. And with the emphasis once again on simplicity and the freshness of ingredients, Roellinger fits the bill perfectly, and shows the world that Michelin really is desperately trying to keep up with les Jones.

While I listened to Renée's crêpe elegy, a slowly pumping steam traction engine gathered speed in the background, its belts tightening, its wheels spinning, helped by generous squirts of engine oil that kept this ancient machine happy. A group of Breton singers encouraged a line of dancers to perform, which they did, singing odes to poverty and starvation in the purest Breton. And everyone felt happy to be there, well fed and Breton.

To add to this study in atmospherics, a tiny, ancient, wizened man trudged endlessly to and fro, bucket in hand, to keep the engine cool with water from a nearby lake. He was almost bent double as he poured it into this massive locomotive, so it could fill its innards with steam.

At the other end of the threshing machine, a whole host of merry Breton farmers were tipping and shovelling in long branches of buckwheat, and watching the seeds emerge, which were rather beautiful, purple and geodesic. I pocketed a few and vowed to start my own ode to poverty back home.

In a masterpiece of canny planning, I had signed up to a day's intensive crêpe-making at L'Ecole Maître Crêpier in Maure de Bretagne, near Rennes, where they promised to sort out the serious problem of leaden crêpes. For those of you who fancy the idea of honing those crêping skills, there are either daily courses or more professional weekly courses in French or English. Since the school is attached to one of France's biggest milling companies and the supplier of the best *farine de blé noir*, Treblec, flour is fresh and to hand.

Despite its size, Treblec still feels like a family business, and seems to fill the village with silos and car parks, but their school has been a remarkable success.

The thing is that running a crêperie seems to appeal to a pretty disparate bunch of people, who are almost without exception disillusioned with something profoundly fundamental. With accounting, or teaching, or life. Of course, being one's own boss and working from home conjures up images of happy, smiling families, and harmony with the world wherever you live. If only it were so easy.

So here they may at least be able to teach you to make a fantastic crêpe. Or galette, come to that. It's the rest that is so difficult. Making a profit. Keeping the books in order. Keeping the family in order. It can all turn so easily into a grim nightmare. Hiring staff is almost inevitably traumatic, so tight are the labour laws and the rules that surround working hours.

I watched the professionals at work. First, to the *billig*. You can actually go into your local Breton supermarket and purchase what is called a Krampouezh, a *billig* that runs on electricity. I was told they work extremely well, but they cost a small fortune, so for those whose fortune is pretty small, you may prefer to use a pan. This odd word Krampouezh is actually a brand name; it's like saying Hoover for a vacuum cleaner. It's a sign of commercial success, you see.

We use a non-stick crêpe pan at home, and that works pretty well, but there is nothing like the heat that you can get from a professional pan, the nearest to the ancestral *billig*, that stays at the crucial temperature of 300°C. Give or take ten degrees either way, that is what you need, they told me: good strong heat. So those with hopeless cookers, please abstain.

Galettes

This is the base recipe for galettes used at the Ecole Maître Crêpier. It will feed an army: vary the quantities accordingly.

Ingredients

1kg *farine de blé noir* (or white flour for crêpes)
20–30g salt (equivalent to 2–3 per cent)
2l water, or 1½l water and 500ml milk
2 eggs

Method

Mix all the ingredients briskly and leave to rest for 4 hours at room temperature. This allows a little mild fermentation, which improves the taste.

Whatever you are using, be it pan or *billig*, should be at 300°C for a galette and 230°C for a crêpe. If the surface is too cool the galette or crêpe will be thick and indigestible. The diameter of the pan should be about 35–40cm.

Oil the pan with lard or vegetable oil (used more frequently these days because of religion). When making galettes you will need to oil the surface every time; with crêpes, after every three crêpes.

Using a 70–80ml ladle, pour the batter on to the centre of the cooking surface, and smooth the edges. This is usually done with a *rouable* or raclette, a little wooden T-shape that you quickly run around the outside. You can use the ladle or a spatula.

Cook for 45 seconds, until you begin to see the edges curl up. Turn it over, cook for another 15 seconds, and it's done.

If you do decide to look for a recipe, despite my having just given you one, you will soon realize that there is not only a mad mess of variation, but the terms galette and crêpe are not consistently used. '*Il y a autant de clochers que de recettes*,' they told me at l'Ecole. There are as many bell towers as recipes.

Much of the variation is down to precisely where in Brittany the recipe actually comes from, for far from being the homogeneous entity many imagine, Brittany is divided into departments and also by language. Breton is spoken roughly to the west of a line that runs from north to south halfway along – that sounds horribly simplistic, so let's say from St Brieuc down to Vannes. To the east of this line lies an area called le Pays Gallo where a variation of French and of *la langue d'oïl* is spoken. The *langue d'oïl* is so called because the word for 'yes' was *oïl*, which has become *oui* in modern French. The distinction is with the *langue d'oc* in the south, where 'yes' was *oc*. Rennes, the regional capital of Brittany, is known as Resnn in Gallo and Roazhon in Breton. This division also roughly corresponds to what is called Haute (Upper, Pays Gallo) and Basse Bretagne, the western, Breton-speaking zone.

Now I tell you all this because it helps sort out an issue that we haven't quite put to bed. When does a *crêpe au blé noir* become a galette? There is a difference in the interpretation of the words crêpe and galette on either side of this line. To the west, they say *crêpes au blé noir* for buckwheat, or *crêpes au froment* for wheat. In the Pays Gallo, *une crêpe au blé noir* becomes a galette. However, in the middle of Brittany, in the Black Mountains, a galette is much thicker and can be made with potatoes. Just to keep you on your linguistic toes.

Gallos love their galettes to be stuffed with sausage, or the lovely alimentary *andouillettes de Guémené*. Hang around outside Rennes football stadium on a match day and watch as galettes wrapped around the most succulent sausages fly through the air. Figuratively speaking, of course. And they also prefer a little more thickness to their galettes, while the Bretons love the translucent thinness of perfect *crêpes sucrées*.

So, please now go forth and be etymologically correct. As soon as you cross that line and get to Brittany *pure et dure*, then remember you are in crêpe land.

22

Sole Normande . . . and an Omelette

THERE ARE FEW PLACES QUITE AS DRAMATIC AS LE Mont St Michel. The glorious abbey sits on a mound of sombre granite, right on the edge of Normandy and its lush pastures, peering out on to the Bay of Cancale, and the flat countryside far below.

Pounded by the wind and the elements and a constant stream of visitors, Mont St Michel is a beacon for gastronomes – many of whom have trekked for thousands of miles to join the happy throng. My trek was a little less daunting. Just a leisurely drive across Brittany got me there in time for lunch with Michel Bruneau, the man who now runs La Mère Poulard, which is about as iconic a restaurant as you can get in France.

Many are magnetized by the appeal of an

omelette. The world's most famous omelette, no less. Where else in the world can have welcomed Zhou Enlai and King Edward VII, Trotsky and Claude Monet, Ernest Hemingway and even Margaret Thatcher to sit and eat an omelette? Sadly not at the same time. If only they could all have been there now, chit-chatting away about revolution and eggs.

I was actually on my way to eat a fish, but, well, the omelette is so ubiquitous, as is the image of doughty Madame Poulard, that I too happily succumbed to its eggy charms.

Why an omelette? In the 1870s le Mont opened up to the world, having served as a prison in post-revolutionary France. As pilgrims, tourists and the curious re-emerged from the post-revolutionary gloom, their arrival depended on tides and horses, since there was no causeway connecting the island to the mainland. Just a long stretch of mud and a track.

So what better to cook *à la minute* than an omelette? All you needed were some fresh eggs, a fire and a little Norman butter. But being a canny woman, Madame Poulard created something a little more alluring and slightly mysterious. A slightly modified omelette, that has drawn in the punters in their thousands over the years and is now deep in culinary mythology.

'It is still by far the most popular dish we cook here,' said Chef Bruneau almost wistfully. 'In the week, at lunchtime especially, it's about 80 per cent omelette these days.'

And although he won't actually tell you how they are made, enough has been leaked over the years to let you know that the fluffiness is a matter of whipping and thrashing the egg white more than you would expect.

If you do feel like playing Mère Poulard at home, then remember that recipes are not writ in stone. This, then, is her version of the recipe that was told to an inquisitive journalist years ago. It is lovely in its brevity.

Monsieur Viel,
Voici la recette de l'omelette: je casse de bons oeufs dans une terrine, je les bats bien, je mets un bon morceau de beurre dans la poêle, j'y jette les oeufs et je remue constamment.

Je suis heureuse, monsieur, si cette recette vous fait plaisir.
Annette Poulard

Monsieur Viel,
Here is the recipe for the omelette: I break some good eggs into a terrine, and beat them well. I put some butter in a pan, and add the eggs, and mix constantly.

I hope, monsieur, this recipe gives you pleasure.
Annette Poulard

And why should we always be led gramme by

gramme, cup by cup by the hand? Perhaps it is inevitable, the more culinary understanding we lose. Shame, though.

Yet cooking an omelette is one of those things that seems so simple but in reality calls for genuine skill. It sorts, as we say, the sheep from the goats.

London's most famous French culinary god-father, Albert Roux, used to see if his cooks could really cook by asking them to make an omelette. Fernand Point, a passionate, enormously fat and hugely respected chef who worked himself to an early grave in his restaurant La Pyramide, not far from Lyon, would boom to his apprentices, '*Faites-moi un oeuf sur le plat!*' 'Fry me an egg, young man!' and judge them accordingly.

At Mère Poulard, the entrance is brilliantly theatrical. You walk through the restaurant door to be met by a *commis* with a giant whisk in one hand and a copper bowl in the other, battering an egg to death. It is all delightfully vaudevillian. The clack clack clack continues throughout the service, interspersed with Chef's booming commands.

I was ushered to a table, and watched as the omelettes poured in from the kitchen. The dining room is full of worshipful gastro tourists, many on day trips from Tokyo, who pick and giggle and look perplexed as they try to interpret the heavily accented English that has become the lingua franca here. An old couple hobbled to their table. Madame took so long that it was painful to watch.

'Can you tell me where the toilets are?' she asked, as she slumped into her chair.

'Oui, madame. On the first floor.'

I sat and observed all this, nibbling bread so warm and fresh it was impossible to resist, especially with a dollop of finest Norman Issigny butter.

Not far away, the tide rushed in at a dangerously stealthy speed, as the kitchen was preparing my Sole à la Normande, more often called Sole Normande these days, a dreamy dish of lightly cooked sole, crème fraîche and yes, a little butter, as well as the odd shrimp, mussel, whatever comes to hand. It's a symphony of Normandyness. A creation, you might think, that owed its very soul to its location. The bay is rich in nutrients, warm and salty, and has long been an ideal location for the odd sole and prawn to swim happily through the richly murky sea water. It is also a marvellous place for raising oysters and France's sweetest mussels.

The Bay of Mont St Michel is where the famous *moules de bouchot* grow like entangled serpents around wooden stakes that are driven deep into the muddy ground, just as they have been since the fourteenth century when, the story goes, an Irish monk set his nets to catch any game winging past and noticed, so long did he wait, that mussels had grown on the wood. And *moules de bouchot* were born. Where would gastronomy be without priests and monks?

And here, too, the salty marshes of the foreshore, *les prés-salés*, are grazed by local lamb that is treasured for its succulence and delicacy. *Pré-salé* lamb is not unique to the bay, though. In the Bordelais, you will find *agneau de Pauillac* which is also highly esteemed. There's something ravishing about the slightly briny succulence of lamb raised on salty grass and sea air. Add to that some of the most delectable carrots – *carottes de sable* – that are grown in the soil just inshore, also sandy and tinged with salt – and you begin to see that this is a part of France that is rich in products that just shout out *terroir* at the top of their soulful little voices.

So why not, I thought, eat a dish that seemed to be as *terroir* as you can get, Sole Normande?

Solea solea is a flat and rather protean fish, a culinary star, its flesh both sweet and firm, and in a brilliant bit of Norman serendipity appears in its tastiest persona as Sole Normande.

'I change the recipe all the time,' Michel Bruneau told me, reminding me that recipes should be open to the odd modern fugue. Except, that is, for something as sacred as the omelette, which is so famous he would tweak it at his peril.

But, well, I love fish. And Chef Bruneau had agreed to cook me his latest version of this classic, something that I couldn't actually remember ever having eaten before, just reading about in all those glossy magazines that show fishing boats and chintzy tablecloths and tell tales of marvellous chefs with toothy smiles and a passion for *terroir*.

This magical mix of *mer et terre* is pretty easy to make, but entirely reliant on the excellence of those raw materials. The butter was from Issigny, the mussels from the Bay of Mont St Michel. The sole was fished up the coast at St Quay Portrieux. But not, as you may be thinking, hours previously.

'People talk a lot of rubbish about fish, you know. If you try and use a fish that was caught the night before, especially a flat fish like sole or a turbot, it tastes like rubber. It needs time to develop its flavour.'

Which may sound odd, but is true. Extremely fresh fish tend to fall apart when cooked (it's called gape, by the way) and taste of very little. Leave them in the fridge for a few days, and lo and behold, they move through rigor mortis to become floppy and edible. This is when they will taste their best. It is, in a sense, a process of ripening, *affinage*, but is seldom deliberately practised, for most fishing boats are out for so long looking for the few fish that remain in the sea that the issue never really arises. Or they are frozen on board prior to rigor, a reason why frozen fish can tend to taste of very little.

Now the sole is an expensive fish, one of what the French call *les poissons nobles*, the élite gang whose qualities are in their eating. Noble fish, in other words. Turbot, halibut, red mullet and John

Dory form the rest of this privileged group, whose prices have become almost stratospheric, so scarce is their supply.

It's not just the species that matters, but the way they have been caught. You will see some fish labelled *pêche de nuit* or *petit bateau*, a sign that the fishing has been short and sweet, overnight usually. Buy some and savour wild fish at their very finest.

But more often these days, sea bass, *bars* or *loups de mer* in French (the latter a term mainly used in the south), are farmed. As stealthily as the incoming tide, our fish stalls and shops are being filled with fish that are farmed and raised for the table. The days of wild fish are numbered, so poor is our ability to catch them sustainably.

The sole became popular in the nineteenth century when restaurants expanded exponentially all over France. Its fate was sealed by the invention of the beam trawl, which dragged a weighted net along the sea floor and scooped them up in huge numbers as they sheltered in their ancient spawning sites in the English Channel, or La Manche as I should call it, and in particular the North Sea.

Have you ever stopped to wonder why the sole has such pristine white flesh? It's all down to its muscle fibres, or more exactly to the way it feeds. The sole has what are called fast twitch fibres that enable the muscles to contract rapidly and allow it to swim quickly from a standstill. The sole lives in relatively shallow water, and has the ability to slob, lying prone on the sea floor and burying itself lightly in the sand. And there it waits patiently, swivelling its eyes this way and that, until along comes a tasty little crustacean. Then suddenly the sole becomes a crazed speed machine, and snaps up the little creature showing it no mercy. It sits back, digests, and fattens its lovely pure white flesh on its prey.

A creature like the tuna is different, constantly hunting, swimming with eternal grace. It never sleeps, and ironically once it stops moving it will drown. Tuna have fibres that are rich in myoglobin, which enable it to use its fat reserves and swim huge distances at a constant speed, and chase its prey. It is this myoglobin that gives the flesh its deep-red colour.

Since sole love the brisk cold waters of the north of France, there has long been an equally brisk trade there in the fish. The Norman fishing ports Dieppe and St Quay Portrieux in particular, which are among the closest to Paris, have long supplied the city with fish. These days the whole continent is cluttered with fish trucks clattering along motorways from Lithuania to Greece, but during pre-combustion-engine days, getting fish to Paris was infinitely trickier.

Many of you who know Paris will be familiar with the various city *portes*, gates of entry into the once-fortified inner city centre, and their particular names. Fish was rushed into the city by means of a network of what were called *chasse-marées*, literally tide-chasers – fast, shallow fishing boats that linked up with a network of horse-drawn carriages with fit and flighty beasts, which allowed the fish to be delivered to the city's famous central market, Les Halles, well before trade started in the early morning. Fish and oysters dripped down these well-trod routes and into Paris via the Porte Poissonnière, and were sold at a premium. The alternative supply line for oysters, for example, was by barge down the River Seine, a far longer route altogether.

Not far from the Boulevard Poissonnière/Rue du Faubourg Poissonnière is the location of what was once one of Paris's most famous fish restaurants, Les Rochers de Cancale, which opened in 1837 to great acclaim, and immediately attracted the glittering gourmerati to its tables, drawn by the freshness of its fish.

Since written menus called for names, and the restaurant kitchen had by now become technically sophisticated enough to create variations to the famous four mother sauces, the culinary repertoire evolved rapidly. Restaurants constantly invented new dishes to appeal to a Parisian clientele hungry for that sense of authenticity and novelty, as fickle then as it is now. Les Rochers de Cancale used a lot of sole, a fish that was now appearing with admirable regularity in the city's markets, and served it with a few shrimps and mussels. Thus was born Sole à la Normande, a dish dreamed up by Parisians for Parisians, but one that these days is considered the epitome of regional French cooking. From Paris its popularity reached to the furthest corners of the country. Why, it even got to Normandy in the end.

My sole arrived and it was superb. A fresh and meaty fillet of the whitest fish, the odd mussel, and a giant and distinctly non-*terroir* warm-water prawn gave it a harmony that was truly excellent.

And then, after a polite pause, came the omelette. It was so huge it made me blush. But so fluffy was it from that endless beating that my spoon floated through, just as hundreds of thousands had done before.

Afterwards, I went and had a coffee with Chef Bruneau and marvelled at his enthusiasm. I thought it must be an awesome responsibility to keep the Empire Poulard under control.

'I love my métier, you know!' Bruneau told me with passion. 'I never dreamed I would actually work here, and run the place. But I am a chef above all, a Normand, so where better could I work? Just look out there.'

I did. At the bay, at the abbey, and at the endless lines of chubby legs trekking up and down the ancient steps.

Sole Normande

Serves 4

Ingredients
8 fillets of sole
A dozen or so cleaned mussels
8 oysters
8 langoustines
A few freshly cooked winkles
2 bowls of dry Norman cider
5–6 teaspoons of crème fraîche
A large teaspoon of butter
A bunch of chervil or parsley
Salt and pepper

Method
Place the fish, cider, langoustines and shellfish in a large casserole. Bring to the boil and cook for a few minutes. Remove the fish and keep it warm. Reduce the sauce by three-quarters, then add the butter and crème fraîche. Leave to cook for another minute or so.

Serve on heated plates, and sprinkle the fish with the chopped herbs, surrounded by the langoustines and the shellfish.

Translated from Michel Bruneau's recipe, first published in *L'Express*, 16 August 2004.

23

Filets Doux

I SPENT SO MANY YEARS CROSSING THE CHANNEL IN A rusty stinking ferry, with a truck stuffed full of fish and produce that I had bought in France, that it almost seems like cheating to just take your car across, burrowing underground like a mad mole. Take the Channel Tunnel, and wow, there you are without the slightest need for Kwells or Vomostops.

And where are all those friendly customs men and women who protected each country from the iniquities of the other, and made my life such hell?

On a day trip to Boulogne, memories come flooding back. There's the smell, for one. The town has a strange and not entirely pleasant whiff to it; more than a hint of *poisson* circulates the fetid air of this curious, almost isolated town. Boulogne-sur-Mer is still France's premier fishing port, after

266

all, having fished and frolicked with the sea for centuries. But it can be a dismal place. Bombed and blasted in the war, Boulogne is still scarred, but what it lacks in looks it makes up for in character, for it has a heart as well as a smattering of sole.

In the early 1990s I lived and worked near Boulogne, and fell if not passionately, then gently in love with Boulogne and its people, the Boulonnais, with that smell, an odd mix of sawdust, fish and fumes, and the distinct, almost incomprehensible patois. Everyone was '*mon fieu*'. Shit was *brin*. And that's about all I can remember.

I loved the people for their deep and proud parochialism. In one of the bistros where I used to eat, I would chat to the lady who ran the place.

'Where are you from?' she asked me one day.

I told her.

'When I first started working here,' she said, 'people used to say, "You're not from around here, are you? Where do you come from?" It was true. I was born in Montreuil.' All of thirty kilometres inland. 'And I'm still not really local, even after all these years.' I think she had worked there for over twenty.

I used to spend the early mornings in the fish market, grappling with a system of Byzantine complexity. You never actually saw a fish, but bid looking at strange numerical codes written on a line of sliding blackboards. To make things even more complex, the bidding was done not in francs (remember them?) but in *anciens francs*, just to keep you on your toes, so that sixty francs was six thousand ... *six mille* ... *six mille* ... *six mille*. Four or five auctions took place simultaneously, in the same room, so your powers of concentration were tested to the full.

Old francs were used, so they said, to help the rhythm of the auction, the *mille* being so much more melodic, rolling riotously off the auctioneer's tongue. The auction, *la criée*, was unique in France, tightly closed to outsiders, as is so often the case in fish auctions. I couldn't possibly have bought more than a limp sardine without the help of Charles Hiard, a Boulonnais who had a Gitanes glued firmly to his lower lip, and a sense of humour that was even more sardonic than mine. He knew everything there was to know about the auction. About the boats to avoid, and how to be as modest and as unassuming as possible if you wanted to get those fabulously fresh red mullet. It was almost always red mullet I was after. Chefs loved them and so did I.

I worked with twenty-six other fish-packers and filleters downstairs. Not one of them had ever been to England. In fact they could never really make me out, although I think they did eventually respect my obsessive desire to get the freshest fish I could find. It was what I had done for years, and I loved it. They helped me pack the truck, stacking the endless boxes into the back, which was stuffed tight as a Christmas stocking, and laughing uproariously as I struggled with their argot. So, week in week out, I crossed the Channel. But none of them was ever really curious about England. They thought we all drank too much and that the Queen was a lesbian, and that was about it.

But France then seemed to be a country that was sure of itself. For months they tried to convince me that the French had the best food, were the best lovers, and had the most beautiful language in the world. I almost began to believe it. But I no longer sensed that pride and sense of natural superiority. There was almost humility in the air. France then had the habits of a crochety old man. Come *midi*, everyone set off back home for that traditional two-hour break that was for me an absolute *casse-couilles*, a ball-breaker. I was brought up on London's get-everything-done-and-piss-off-home school of business. But no, things were different then.

The French would argue that a long lunch break defended family values, protected family life, and was so essential that it should remain as it always has been, and nothing should ever change. It was part of their Frenchness.

So while everyone would go off home at lunchtime, switch on the telly and eat, or go and *boire un coup* with their mates, I would set off for lunch in town. On Mondays I would go to a profoundly grotty-looking restaurant called Chez

Soi. Its name was hand painted with neither grace nor style. It was almost always empty. The owner did all the cooking himself, and liked to talk. But this being Boulogne, the fish were utterly fresh, shimmering with the subtleties of the sea.

There was one dish that he cooked sublimely well, the deceptively simple *turbot poché sauce hollandaise*. Poached turbot with a Hollandaise sauce. The turbot was, strictly speaking, a *turbotin*, a chicken turbot as we would call it, a portion-sized fish, all the better for being cooked on the bone, as turbot, and indeed all fish, always are.

So we chatted or not, as the mood took us. If I buried my head in the paper he never seemed to mind. The décor was naff, delightfully so. A hard tiled floor, lace curtains and a dodgy wooden bar. That was it. On the wall were a few plates of fish, three-dimensional crabs and scorpion fish, dusty in their ceramic stupor. I collected a few, years later, because they reminded me of Chez Soi. But don't rush off and look for the place. It was bulldozed to make way for a car park. That's progress for you.

On Tuesdays, while I was wound up by chefs and orders, I would pack endless boxes of fish, then slip off for a fortifying, proper lunch at a workers' café called Le Chatillon. This was where everyone would congregate for their morning coffee before the auction, and the air was always thick with tobacco smoke. It was where I fell in love with the herring.

Around the corner from where I worked was a little depot where one of Boulogne's most highly reputed herring-curers still worked. Inside, the walls were thick with tar, and the whole place, like the town, stank of wood shavings, smoke and fish.

The curing houses or *saurisseries* of Boulogne have now largely closed, but a few still produce what are called *filets doux* – a sweet fillet, literally, a lightly smoked morsel of herring that is finding life in twenty-first-century France particularly difficult.

It is an old bistro favourite. Years ago, when the cure was much stronger, people ate *harengs saurs* or soured herrings, but no one likes them much any more. The taste is too strong. *Filets doux* have taken their place.

You know the feeling that you get as you are driving through France around midday, and your thoughts turn to food? At *midi*, as the offices empty and the morning markets pack up. It's called hunger.

When I was a trucker, everyone knew the best places to stop on the road down to Paris. So as the clock moved ineluctably towards midday, the trucks began to pull in at their favoured restaurants and miraculously filled themselves up with diesel, while the drivers filled up with food and smoked *une clope*. We drank a little wine, and went on our way. These were the *routiers* restaurants, and *routiers* were, as they said then, *sympas*.

There was a familiarity about such places. There were always chips, and in the less trucky ones what was called a *chariot hors d'oeuvre*. It was almost as predictable as the British and their sweet trolleys. There would be *oeufs mayonnaise*, *salade russe*, *saucisson sec*, *salade verte*. Beetroot, perhaps some *pâté* too. And herring. *Filets de hareng à l'huile* to be exact, those sweet fillets laid in vegetable oil, coloured by neatly cut, evenly crenellated carrots, a few slivers of sweet onions, and little else.

Filets de hareng à l'huile

The bistro classic.

Ingredients
A 250g packet of *filets doux*
2 mild onions, finely sliced
2 medium carrots, finely sliced
Milk
Good-quality vegetable oil

Method
Soak the fillets in milk for a few hours, then lay them on a bed of onions in a terrine. Layer them with more onions and the carrots, cover with oil and leave overnight.

Serve at room temperature with cooked

potatoes, mixed with a little vinegar and chopped shallots.

So these herrings take me back. They make me think of days spent reading through pages of faxes and even, laughably, telexes, with intricate details of fish that had been landed, of ducks that had been strangled, and mushrooms that had been plucked from wild autumnal woods. Back to that France that doesn't really exist any more.

So what is it that strikes me now? *Morosité*. The French are consumed by worry. By soul searching. Their sacred cows seem hollow. The Tour de France is a pharmacological sham. The multicultural 2006 World Cup team was criticized for being 'too brown' and fell into self-destruct mode at the last minute. The world dominance of their wine industry is now but a distant dream and millions of gallons of French wine are turned into ethanol. The French language has no global future in a world where English, like it or not, has assumed unassailable primacy.

Change seems to be forced upon the country from without, so the reaction is to hunker down and become even more introspective. So here I was in Boulogne once again, eating a dish that looked backwards, in a country that preferred to look backwards, wondering quite what the future held.

24

Pieds et Paquets

IT WAS MAY, AND WE WERE ABOUT TO SET OFF TO STAY in the sun for a few days, en famille, en Provence.

Claire's sister lives in a Provençal village called Bédoin, which nestles in the shadow of Mont Ventoux, a mysterious barren mountain in the *département* of Vaucluse. It has a weekly market, the usual cluster of bars, a minuscule supermarket, a Maison de la Presse or two, a couple of restaurants that open up when the summer warms the air and the tourists arrive, and a particularly chatty dentist who loves to talk while watching you writhe in agony. He works entirely alone, in a bleak room that reminds me more of a retired priest's sitting room than a dentist's surgery. If you look closely there is probably blood on the walls.

Now to most of us Provence means the sun, the sea, and tomatoes, perhaps. Maybe olive oil.

Lavender. To others, it's the Front National and a pronounced tendency to hang right. But whatever way you look at it, you know you have arrived as soon as you see those bouquets of dried lavender, and sunny tablecloths inimitably designed with floral patterns. Everyone loves Provence. Or at least the idea of Provence.

Bédoin is not far from Avignon, but closer still to Carpentras, a town rare in France for having a particularly fascinating collection of tracts and records that allow you to glance right back into the Middle Ages. Carpentras was once the capital of the papal enclave called the Comtat Venaissin, and only became truly French in 1791, compelled by the reality of the Revolution.

And the town sadly still has a reputation for intolerance. Of outsiders. Of Parisians. Of immigrants. In 1989, the Jewish cemetery of Carpentras was desecrated, to the shock and disgust of many. And six years later the mosque was attacked. Here, as is often the case in Provence, the Front National is strong. Families of Pieds-Noirs settled in the south of France after their exodus at the end of the disastrous, brutal war in Algeria, a war that has largely been forgotten outside of France, but has left bitter memories here that are scarcely concealed.

My brother-in-law is fiercely proud of his Pied-Noir roots. As Pieds-Noirs generally tend to be. Pieds-Noirs are French citizens who were born and raised in the old colonies of North Africa, primarily Algeria, and who left hurriedly and unceremoniously after the Algerian War of Independence was comprehensively lost in 1962. Their feet are said to be black not because they were the first French settlers to colonize the 'dark' continent of Africa, but rather for the black boots they wore, part of the classic colonial uniform of white casque, white trousers and polished black boots.

One lovely morning, we took off to Mont Ventoux, still topped with snow, and glided down the hill with a barely two-year-old Lola, who was utterly entranced, fascinated by the brilliance and the annoying habit of snow to melt so quickly in the hand.

Scene set. To the food. Whenever I thought about what dish would truly represent Vaucluse, it was *daube de boeuf*. Bah, everyone said, it is too easy. Beef stewed endlessly. But we always eat a *daube* down there, thickly simmering in its sealed pot. Open the lid and whooom!

'Try something a little more exciting than that!' they said.

And whenever we discussed food, I was told to talk to Carmen Rouillet, a smiling, solid woman, a true matriarch said to be the best cook in the village. But there was something odd about her. Nobody knew quite what. But people talk.

And word was that that very weekend she was

preparing *pieds et paquets*. So Madame Jean the butcher said, she being a constant fount of knowledge. Now this is a dish that actually originated a little further to the south. *Pieds et paquets*. Feet and packets, literally: a languid stew of sheep's trotters and tripe, cooked for many hours, a dish that was once and is still popular in the working-class districts of Marseilles.

So I trudged up to meet Carmen, stopping to talk to the village butcher on the way, an indomitable, hard-working woman who has gained a reputation – entirely justified – for the finesse of her *andouillettes*, thick chitterling sausages whose gutsy smell can turn delicate stomachs in seconds. Provence is hardly their homeland, but good food is defying boundaries these days. There is culinary creep going on under our very noses. France is in post-regional flux. *Andouillettes* are available almost anywhere, largely, it has to be said, thanks to those huge supermarkets whose strength has helped ring the death knell for regional cooking, if not necessarily regional products.

Madame Jean is a voluble, passionate woman, perpetually busy behind the counter, always with a smile on her face, darting past the lively blood-red carcasses of *agneau de Mont Ventoux*, delectable lamb fattened on the mountain herbs, hay and grass that give it a prized and subtle nuance.

We talked a little of this and that, of how sad it was that so few people seemed to be interested in food these days. Sad, I agreed, just as a twenty-year-old walked through the door and bought a whole lamb.

'It's for my *mémé*,' he said.

I asked Madame Jean what she would choose, if she had to, as her Provençal desert-island food, the one thing that she couldn't do without, a food that sang of the hills and the warmth and reminded her of Provence. I was half expecting her to turn towards the lamb, or to roll her tongue around a tomato, but she veered off and took hold of something that was far more familiar.

'This – this is what I would take!' and she thrust a slab of pork towards me. *Petit salé*. Lard. Cured pork, thick and fatty, and, it may surprise you to know, about as Provençal as you can get. She thankfully passed on the dried *herbes de Provence*. She passed on the *agneau de Sisteron*, and chose something that you rarely see cooked and served as it is, but which is used and used and used every day.

The records in Carpentras prove the point. By the fifteenth century, salt pork had become the second most prevalent food item after grain and remained so until the eighteenth century, when record-keeping dipped a little in the chaos of the Revolution. And to make the English speaker feel even more at home, salt pork was then called *bacon* in Provençal. These days it is better known as *petit salé*. And yet, perhaps oddly, there was little fresh pork on display at all. Just unmarked chunks of lard, so familiar that there was little need to mark it at all.

Pork has always played a complex role, a mix of the domestic and the religious. Although pigs were raised by many households, fresh pork was seldom bought. Pigs lived off waste and whey, and were expertly fattened for slaughter, which usually took place as the winter drew in and the supply of fresh food diminished.

Post mortem, the pig is magically transformed into hams and fresh sausages, and cured to make magnificent *saucisson sec* infused with herbs and pepper. Those that Madame Jean had hanging in the window were all locally produced, fat and succulent: they would be wonderful thickly sliced and eaten with a glass of equally thick red wine. Come Bédoin's market on Monday, the supply quadruples, with hams and sausages piled high on the heaving shelves of the market-traders.

Fresh pig meat was not just forbidden to Jews and Muslims, but was also considered unclean by Christians, and was long suspected of transmitting leprosy. So again, salt pork benefited. It was not only good to eat, but good to cook. Cheap and popular, it was one of the many valuable by-products of rearing a domestic pig.

Simmering noisily in the background, behind all Madame Jean's fresh meat, was a tall casserole that filled the *boucherie* with a sumptuous smell, divine, spiced, warming, nostril-invading, an enticing mix of the meaty warmth of lamb and something else. Was it cloves, I wondered?

'I know you are off to see Carmen,' she said. 'And I know that she's going to make *pieds et paquets* this weekend, but I'm not too sure if she'll tell you everything. She's *maligne*, that one. Beware!'

So Carmen was clever, crafty she told me. For Carmen was a *tzigane*, I had heard. A woman with gypsy blood. A woman gifted. A woman with power over the stomachs of others.

'Her cooking is the best. She always manages to make her *pieds et paquets* taste better than mine. And if she doesn't give you any to try, come back tomorrow. I'm making some to sell in the shop.' At that she pointed to the pot simmering on the stove in the corner.

'Ask her how she made her stuffing, by the way. See if she says that she bought it from me!'

What's it made of, I asked?

'What can you smell? Yes, there's cloves and then there's . . .' and she rattled off a long list of the rest of the ingredients.

Carmen lived a little way up the road, in a house that seemed to be but one vast kitchen. Not a house to hide its face. You open the door, and there in front of you runs a long table with the oven to one side. I introduced myself, a little daft really since she knew full well who I was. Though she wasn't quite sure why I was there.

Carmen was sitting by the table, which was piled high with decapitated sheep's trotters. She picked each one up in turn, scrubbed them briskly and placed them on one side.

'*Ah, les pieds et paquets.*'

'Well, I'm not going to tell you all my secrets, you know. People always ask me how to cook this and that, and I'll tell them, but I always leave something out. That way nobody can be quite as good as me.'

Like fleas to a dog and babies to a nipple, so Carmen's family were drawn to the matriarch, eating and adoring her food. This was a Saturday, and they were all to eat together on Sunday. And they, the family, her pride and joy, had chosen *pieds et paquets*. It might just as well have been a *daube* – 'Too easy,' she parroted – or a *civet*. 'Ah, that's not so easy. I'll tell you about that later, but to do *pieds et paquets*, listen.'

And she began her hymn to this most exquisite dish, all the time surrounded by these delicate little sheep's trotters, that seemed to call for ballet shoes and music, stranded as they were from the body. Now for the cooking. There are the preliminaries, of course. Finding your *pieds*, let alone your *paquets*, may prove tricky, but at least Carmen had Madame Jean the butcher to help. Carmen's family alone needed sixty-five, yes sixty-five trotters. That made 16.25 legless sheep.

The sheep tripe were bought washed but

uncooked, but as a sheep is generally a little smaller than a cow, even in these days of Dolly and genetic engineering, ovine tripe are easier to deal with, less thick and flubbery than bovine. One *panse*, a stomach, needs to be cut in three, and folded around the stuffing, about which I was supposed to be so innocent.

But first, unusually, came a huge slab of fresh *couenne de porc*, pork rind. Carmen placed it skin side up, solid, uncut, on the base of the pan and allowed it to gently melt and ooze its fat for a few minutes, while she chopped the onions and the garlic and tipped them into the pan. And then came some *petit salé*, followed by the *pieds*, now cleaned, washed and porcelain white. Then the *panses*, neatly buttoned up, like a pet's innards. It is a little tricky to keep the *panses* from falling apart during cooking, so you have to cut them into roughly equal triangular shapes and tuck in the single end, while placing the stuffing in the middle and rolling the lower edges around them.

And then, well I had to ask Carmen what she had used in the stuffing.

She looked at me, smiled. 'Guess! What do you think I used?'

A result. I rattled off the list that I had heard earlier. '*Blettes*?' Chard.

'*Non*. Leeks. You could use *blettes*, though.'

'*Petit salé*, onions, garlic, parsley?' Correct. The spices, the gastronomic tinkering, came from cloves, which at times seem almost omnipresent in French domestic cookery. And nutmeg, and then those famous *herbes de Provence*.

She almost looked impressed.

Many are tempted to buy jars and bags and bouquets of *herbes de Provence*, assuming that just with a mere sprinkle the sun and warmth will come flooding back, when you return to the suburbs and try to remember what once was.

But sadly, oh so sadly, this is so often a gastronomic souvenir too far. It can be anything. It can be nothing. Carmen's mix was quite specific, made from as many herbs as could be picked in the hills, and importantly picked in flower, then slowly dried. First, there was a little wild oregano. Then marjoram. A little thyme, but not too much. A few juniper berries, and some *pebre d'ail*, a fascinating herb, pungent, almost peppery, very much part of the flavour of the *garrigue*. She didn't seem to use dried basil. But then it loses its flavour quite quickly. Or maybe she was just keeping it secret, who knows? Dried basil has a musty, almost unpleasant taste to it, nothing like the fresh. So, no herb dust. No pretentious bags and lavender innuendoes were allowed into this working kitchen. Her herbs were used, not abused. Nor were they kept on show for the neighbours.

To most of us trapped in cold climes and urban society, herbs have completely lost their subtlety, their point almost. A bunch of fresh oregano grown on hydroponics in Holland is not going to have the complexity of taste of a bunch of dried herbs from anywhere in the Mediterranean, be it Crete, Croatia, or here in the Vaucluse. It's that old thing called *terroir* again.

Herbes de Provence may be part of the clichéd Provence and the stuff of cruel deception, but they have their roots deep in the thin calcareous soil of the *garrigue*. The Mediterranean has mile upon mile of scrubby, stony land, rich in thick-leaved, stunted trees, such as the Kermes oak, also called the Garric in Provençal. The word *garrigue* has its origins in an ancient prefix *kar-*, or *gar-*, which signified a stone and came to be used to describe the shelters hewn from rock. So all over the Mediterranean we find words such as *karst*, Carcassone, chalet even, as well as *garrigue*, that owe their meaning to this old, now-lost word for stone.

The *garrigue* may seem wild and romantic, it may drive you to poetry and inspire your very soul, but it is not a natural environment. It too is deceptive, created from centuries of deforestation and land clearance that effectively removed the natural cover and replaced it with opportunistic plants that have taken over from the original forests and thick woods of evergreen oaks.

Wood was a critically important commodity in the Mediterranean: it fired ovens, it was cut for beams and fences, and was used for shipbuilding and making ash, quicklime and charcoal. An area rich in wood had a tremendous advantage, but we blew it on a massive scale by having no concept of just how to manage a resource rather than plunder it to extinction. Wood enabled. It was a giver of power. Its absence created great difficulties for the aspiring and warring sea powers of the region, Venice, Genoa, Marseilles, Seville, Barcelona to name but a few.

By the sixteenth century Venice had begun importing oak from abroad, and King Philip II of Spain, he of the Armada, was obliged to ship it from as far away as Poland. The *garrigue*, then, has grown on man's inefficiency and destructiveness. So much for our *herbes de Provence*.

One final ingredient should be mentioned: dried orange peel. You will need it for your *bouillabaisse* and *daube*, but try as you may, you rarely see *écorces d'orange* for sale. Originally the oranges used would have been from the bitter *bigarrade*, a heavily scented fruit that pre-dated the sweeter orange, whose blossom appears so miraculously in the spring and whose wildly intoxicating perfume warms the spring evenings so beautifully.

But back to the pot. In went each and every *pied*. Each and every *paquet*. Carmen poured on a bottle of thick tomato passata that she had bottled in the summer, the juice dripping over every cloven hoof. A bottle, or was it two? (that would be telling), of red wine, her wine, their wine. And she left it to cook for a while. Twelve hours, she said, it will taste better the next day. Flavours improve. They mingle and mix, they harmonize.

We sat and talked a little more. Her son came in to check how things were going, his voice rich and nicotine stained. Magnetized by habit, or the odour, perhaps, her husband arrived and wondered why an Englishman was at all interested in *pieds et paquets*.

Carmen then began to tell me about her childhood, and despite the softness she showed her grandchildren there was steel in her eyes.

'When I see kids with their parents these days I can't believe how easy things are. They answer back all the time, there's no respect. I never once answered my father back, I was too frightened. He would have whacked me. That was our way. Life was very hard back then, you know. We never stayed in one place for very long, but that sort of life has no meaning any more. But you know I have been here for over forty years now, and still I don't feel like I belong. People are jealous. They are always talking behind your back. No, I don't think I'll ever really belong here.'

What was this? The plaintive sigh of an ageing woman? Or the feeling that despite all the mobility, the freedom that we have now to live and move just about anywhere, small communities can be as restrictive and cold as the city, especially if you are seen as an outsider.

If tastes encountered can prove so frustratingly

elusive to reproduce, then there are limits, too, to being French. It is not something you can become, that you can create. You may wonder why so many people choose to up sticks and move to France, knowing that they will never truly belong. Despite the warmth, Provence can be a cold place. It will take time for the Dutch, the Belgians, the Brits and the Germans to integrate. It will only be their children and their children's children who become truly attached to the land.

But there is a freedom now that allows the adventurous to voyage and to experience life and that would have been unthinkable not long ago. And this must surely ring the death knell for provincialism and prejudice, as we all slowly begin to learn to tolerate and celebrate difference.

The thing I love about these close encounters of the gastronomic kind is that talking about food allows you to glance elsewhere, and everywhere. It allows you to play the role of a detective, ticking off one by one the subtleties and nuances that give food and the people who cook, eat and enjoy it their character and culture.

Is cooking difficult? Can anyone do it? Can someone, say in London or Paris, create or re-create what was going on here in Bédoin?

'Of course you can, but you have to taste the food first if you want to cook, and I don't think they eat *pieds et paquets* in Paris, do they?' Taste. What food is all about.

As if on cue from the matriarch, another daughter, a granddaughter and a son-in-law breezed in, smiling and no doubt salivating inwardly at the thought of tomorrow, and the *pieds et paquets*.

Well, I never did get to taste Carmen's *pieds*, so it was back to Madame Jean the butcher the next day, who ladled the thick stew into a bowl for us to take home.

Warmed and bubbling, our *pieds* were brought to the table with their wafting spicy essence and the almost rubbery excellence of tripe. We all savoured the subtlety and the sheer effort that had gone into this marvellous dish. As we sat down to eat, we toasted Carmen, Madame Jean, and tolerance.

25

Omelette aux Truffes

MARKET DAY IN CARPENTRAS, AND I STUMBLED ACROSS a tiny, weathered man with a few truffles on an equally tiny table in front of him. He almost seemed to be a truffle incarnate. Gnarled hands deeply marked with soil. Wrinkled face. And the sweetest smile.

I couldn't pass him by, now could I?

I stopped, picked up a truffle and listened to him trying to entice me deeper into his web. 'They have been grown on the Tricastin, m'sieur. Not down in the valley like they do here, but high in the hills. Go on, smell them.'

I brought it to my nose and inhaled the extraordinary, sweaty, earthy aroma.

Carmen, the *pieds et paquets* lady, had shown me a huge jar full of truffles she had found on Mont Ventoux in the autumn, and had given me a brilliant idea. The thing with black truffles is they need to be cooked. The flavour develops, unlike the white truffle which is always best just grated and eaten raw, on pasta, with eggs or whatever. As simply as possible.

'Have you ever had an omelette made with *truffes noires*?' Carmen asked.

Well, yes but no but. Not for many years.

'Well, if you find some truffles, keep them with some really fresh eggs in the fridge overnight. Then make your omelette. Clean the truffle, and then grate it into the omelette. That's the best way to eat them.'

Which is just what we did the next day. Followed by a salad. It was simplicity itself. Uncluttered food. But truffles are odd. Not just to look at: some people simply cannot abide them.

I am intrigued by truffles. But then so are dogs and pigs. What is this curious thing, this subterranean fungus that some people find so attractive, so damned good that they are prepared to pay such dizzy sums to procure them? The jury is out on this one inescapable luxury of French cooking.

We are talking aroma here, the truffle's defining particularity. And it can be almost overwhelming. The pleasure is in the taste and the aroma. It is of the nose rather than the eye, for frankly a truffle is mundane to look at. But then there are truffles and there are truffles.

The very best, the most exquisite, are white truffles, but these are rarely eaten in France. It is the Italians who love these *tartuffi bianchi*, grating them over fresh eggs and pasta. And I do too. But in France it is *Tuber Melanosporum*, sometimes known as *Tuber Nigrum* and usually called *truffe noire*, *truffe noire du Périgord* or *truffe du Périgord*, that is so highly esteemed. It is this species about which there is so much knee weakness. No other variety of black truffle is really worth getting excited about.

Beware of these in particular: *Tuber Aestivum*, the summer truffle, called in French *truffe de la Saint-Jean*, *truffe d'été* or *truffe blanche d'été*. It is a tasteless impostor, a waste of money, and it is often these that are chopped and added to various pâtés and pastes to give them the alleged class of a truffle. *Tuber Uncinatum* or the *truffe de Bourgogne* was once preferred to the black, and has a decent aroma and a chocolate-brown inner part. I have a suspicion that we see more of these truffles wrongly named than we should. But then I am a suspicious guy. You can probably forget about *Tuber Mesentericum* or the *truffe mésentérique*, which is mostly found in Lorraine. But you cannot forget about the thoroughly woeful impostor from the Far East, the Chinese truffle *Tuber Himalayense*.

The problem is that the Chinese truffle looks horribly similar to the *truffe noire*, unless you have a microscope with you. Remember that a truffle has to have a strong aroma for it to be effective. But is it just a matter of the species? Not at all. If only it were so easy.

Firstly, during the normal cycle of a truffle, and let's say from now on we are talking *Tuber Melanosporum*, black truffle, the aroma develops. The truffle matures. And just to make the restaurateur really edgy, it can begin to do so just before Christmas. But this is not always the case. In fact the best time for *truffes noires* is in January, February even, just when things are calming down after Christmas and people are no longer so keen on spending money. So for all of you who fancy the idea of giving your loved one the taste of truffle for Christmas, caveat emptor. Restaurants are not always quite as honest as they should be when it comes to serving truffles that are mature and in season. To many, just offering truffles seems to be enough, and they assume that few will question the matter if the truffles are not quite ripe.

So how do you tell? To be sure that it is a black truffle, check the outer skin first of all and look for tell-tale diamond, snake-skin scales on the outside, as neatly fitting as a jigsaw. Next, if you can, scratch the surface lightly to see if there's colour beneath the skin. A mature *truffe noire* should be a dark purplish black, with light veins running through the ascocarp. The paler the inner part, the less mature it is. Now pick it up and cup it in your hand, warming it slightly. It should feel neither feather light, a sign of dehydration, nor too heavy. Make sure there are no excessive clods of earth attached to the outer skin, and then breathe in. Inhale. And savour that complex, glorious, earthy, jet-black aroma of such ravishing subtlety, of warm velvet, sex, food and pleasure. Without this a truffle is worthless. It is its raison d'être, gastronomically speaking.

Science can now tell us more. There are over fifty different substances that have been detected in truffles: sulphides, ketones, aldehydes, alcohols and esters, but the most interesting and the most characteristic is dimethyl sulphide, the self-same substance that is added to natural gas to make it smell gassy, that gives the fart its characteristic odour and boiling cabbage its tell-tale pong. The idea that the magnificent truffle shares its odiferous roots with farts and cabbages may just confirm the worst suspicions of many.

But does this explain the association of truffles with love and sex? Few find cabbages particularly attractive, or farts erotic. However, don't despair. Research in France with an artificial truffle aroma and a key pheromone, a complex chemical called androstenol, has shown that neither pigs nor dogs were drawn to the scent with it removed. They all preferred either the real thing, or a scent with androstenol added.

On average men produce two to three times more of this pheromone than women, especially when they are ripe and fully sexual in early maturity, and it is said to be able to alter appreciation, often a key concern when it comes to love. Scientists devised an experiment to see what effects androstenol might have on people. So a group of volunteers were asked to participate in an experiment to assess the stress of wearing a surgical face mask. They were shown pictures, of lovely trees, fluffy kittens, that sort of thing, as well as a number of images of humans. All were asked to assess whether they felt the images were threatening or not. Their comments were duly noted, and the participants were asked to reassemble two weeks later. This time, some androstenol had been added to the mask, and again their comments were noted.

And surprise, surprise, they had become somewhat more telling. While no one found trees or kittens particularly erotic, it was the assessment of the human characters that had changed. They were interpreted as being more attractive, sensitive, intelligent, good, where previously observations had largely been neutral and objective. And where else do you find this magic substance? In the armpit. On the skin. And also in the truffle. Perhaps we can now understand why this enigmatic little tuber has contributed quite so much to gastronomy.

But science also tells us that we are not all able to sense this curious substance. Hervé This told me he was truffle blind. Does that mean that such people are also blind to love and attraction? Luckily, as we all know, love is blind.

26

Bouillabaisse

'HERE ON BUSINESS?' I WAS ASKED BY THE TAXI DRIVER who took me through the busy Marseilles streets, past the football stadium and the glorious Corbusier block of flats, where I stopped and wandered and wondered, and stretched a little after taking the slow train down from Carpentras.

My jeans and scruffy hair should have told him better.

'No, just looking for *bouillabaisse*,' I said.

'*Ah, vous êtes tombé sur quelqu'un qui est vraiment passionné par la bonne cuisine!*' You have fallen on someone who really likes good cooking. As if I had tumbled from the sky. And he told me of this magical place, a little creek not far from the city where they served the best *bouillabaisse* in Marseilles, so they say. He was from the *calanques*, born and bred with his feet in the sea, so I asked him to take me there the next morning.

Marseilles was overwhelmed by clutter. The station was shattered into dusty dismembered pieces, surrounded by *grillage*, reconstruction, dust and men in hard hats. But despite it all, the city's hotels were full of bankers, accountants, beauticians and musicians, all flocking to the sunny south and wandering around hotel lobbies with curious name tags in case they forgot who they were, herded into sessions of uplifting discourse and rejuvenating sales.

By night it was loud dinners and forced camaraderie. The hotel restaurants offered scintillatingly grim things to eat. Getting into the swing of things, I chose a *gratin de tomates Provençale* that was so carbonized I felt it worthwhile calling their cooking skills to task.

'Ah, monsieur, the chef says if we don't serve it like that it wouldn't be cooked enough,' I was told brusquely, and I tried to disentangle the crazy logic that came from within.

And then there was the illicit congress. The call girls and rent boys were busy, diligently pleasing the visitors with their ancient skills. *Les baisers volés*. Stolen kisses. And there was me, desperately looking for a really good *bouillabaisse*.

Rested, spruce and well shaven, we set off the next morning as planned, me, myself and the taxi driver, and a bag of the most exquisite Provençale cherries that I simply could not stop eating.

No one can really understand Marseilles without seeing the *calanques*, Jean-Louis, my taxi driver, said, and the most beautiful and beguiling of them all was here before me at Sormiou.

He pulled up the taxi and let me breathe the view. It was but a few kilometres from the city's edge, lost, remote, wildly beautiful, the most incongruous sight when just over the hill there was so much urban bustle.

Jean-Louis was born in a minuscule fishing port called Carry-le-Rouet. 'You should go there one day. You can still buy fish off the local fishermen. But if you want to make a good *soupe de poisson*, get there early in the morning.'

Of *bouillabaisse* he was a little less enthusiastic. 'I cook it once a year on Mother's Day,' he told me. 'But what is it but boiled fish? I prefer a good fish soup. Or red mullet grilled with wild fennel,' he said. 'Anything caught fresh from the sea is good.'

Bouillabaisse is almost always cooked the restaurant way these days. This involves making a fish soup first of all, and then lightly cooking another tranche of whole fish in the soup, which are then served, often with a lightly spiced *rouille*, a mayonnaise that is almost walking with garlic, and saffron. This economy means that the restaurant can double their menu, two for one. It makes for good business.

The fisherman's method, the origin if you like of *bouillabaisse*, was to put all the fishy detritus from a day's fishing into one pot, and bring it to the boil. That's the theory, anyway.

Now Sormiou really is a particularly special place. Sheltered from the fierce winter mistral that blows from the north-west and churns the sea into a forbidding, spumy mass, local fishermen long ago found shelter here from the winter storms and built low, sturdy huts, *cabanons*, that allowed them to live and fish a little, protected from the elements.

And they still stand. The fishermen have nearly all gone now, but incredibly none of the huts have been prettified and sold, for they all belong to a Comtesse, whose family has kept them virtually unscathed by civilization. It's a very benign form of feudalism. There's no electricity. No water. Just peace and quiet. And the odd visitor. Well OK, thousands of them in season. But this was May, and things had yet to gather momentum.

Water has to be brought in, and electricity, if it is used, is generated on site. Which of course gives Sormiou great charm, especially to the hordes who trek down the hill in summer to swim, or to eat at either of the two restaurants, one of which is called with modernistic simplicity le Lunch, and has been serving fish upon fish for many years. And the most exquisite *bouillabaisse*.

Three years ago the Negril Brothers took it over, after a career that took them to Paris, where they served, they are proud to tell you, even the prime minister. I didn't ask which one. But their roots are here in Marseilles, if not exactly in the *calanques*, and the restaurant is now run with a smooth and professional simplicity. Where better, I thought, to learn the secrets of a good *bouillabaisse*?

Now you might have thought that with their feet virtually lapping in the salty sea, they would naturally catch the fish in or at least near the *calanque*, but restaurants cannot run on romanticism alone. The sad truth is that the two working fishermen left at Sormiou get more money for their fish at the local market, so the fish auction has proved a more reliable source of fish for le Lunch.

Not that that detracts from the quality of the fish served. It is all perfectly fresh. Now these are not everyday fish at all. They swim and nibble around the rocky creeks, famously heralded by the enigmatic, startling, thick-headed scorpion fish, the highly esteemed *rascasse*. This glowering creature bristles with thick, poisonous spines, but despite being the must-have for any self-respecting *bouillabaisse*, it is still regularly caught in the nets that float around the *calanques*. At times it has an almost liquid dark-purple colour, at others it can be a livid scarlet. But *rascasses* are hunted primarily for the flavour they give to a fish soup, and they find little peace all over the Mediterranean. In Greece they are drowned in a *kakavia*, in Spain a *zarzuela*. In Morocco they are sent off to Europe. There are no doubt stocks of fish that will be found in Libya and Algeria. Tunisian waters are already overfished, so little hope there. No, the *rascasse* is too loved for its own good.

But larger *rascasses*, called *chapons* – the same word is used for castrated male chickens, i.e., capons – are getting pretty rare these days, and are often flown in from the North African coast in particular. Since local lore has it that they are simply indispensable in a *bouillabaisse*, demand far outstrips supply. Beware of too much authenticity.

Another miraculously flavoured and equally poisonous fish is the weever (*vive* in French), which sits on the sea floor with its body cannily buried in the substrate, eyes swivelling, searching for prey, such as the odd shrimp or passing crab. A close cousin, called *le boeuf*, often appears in the nets, squarer jawed but still highly esteemed. Scientifically, this fish is called a *uranoscope*, but also becomes a *rascasse blanche*, or *rat*. The naming of fish can be awesomely confusing in France.

The *girelle* is perhaps the most beautiful of all these *poissons de roche*. Brilliant blues and greens mingle along its body, with a red flash flowing from one end to the other. The only thing that perhaps lets it down is its goofy face and thick lips. It seems to be one of the more cerebrally challenged members of the undersea world. The *girelle* is a wrasse, of which there are numerous varieties, a fish that grazes on weedy rocks but is not that good to eat. The *girelle paon*, or peacock wrasse, is ravishingly beautiful, with a fabulously vulgar display of colour on its body. A similar fish is the *roucaou*, more delicate, less brash than the *girelle*. All of these can be used in fish soup.

Then there is the gurnard, *rouget-grondin* or *galinette* in the south, a fish famous for the bizarre grunts and groans emitted in everyday discourse. This at times startlingly red fish has a face that resembles Donald Duck, beaky and protuberant, and three barbels that act like weird proto arms behind its gills as it crawls along the sea floor, delving and disturbing the gritty surface, seeking out shrimps and worms to eat. These fish are found widely in European waters, and if they are ever allowed to reach a decent weight before being plucked from the sea can grow into handsome beautiful beasts, with glorious fan-like side fins tipped with the most brilliant blue.

These, then, are but some of the fish you might find in the local markets. Exquisitely coloured, intensely flavoured, they are the essence of a good *soupe de poisson* and *bouillabaisse*. And into the pots they tumble.

Le Lunch has the air of a cubist experiment stranded on the water's edge. But with the beach to the left and hills behind, it is, to be absolutely honest, the most staggeringly beautiful place to eat that I have ever come across in more than twenty years of travelling around France.

This is the restaurateur's tale of how you should set about making your fish soup. Heat a little oil,

'Which always means olive oil down here,' Monsieur Negril reminded me, 'and then fry some onions and garlic. Don't be tempted by any new season's fresh bulbs. They must be concentrated, dry and pungent. You will need some dried wild fennel from the hills, some dried bitter orange peel and sea salt. Keep a glass of *pastis* handy, to add at the end. And then the fish. You can go to a *calanque* and haggle, or the old port in Marseilles where you can buy fish that are still alive.'

I have even bought a bag of frozen Mediterranean fish in an Ibizan supermarket, packed them in my bag and flown back home, and made a brilliant, richly perfumed fish soup. Frozen fresh is a better bet than not-so-fresh fresh, if you see what I mean.

I stood and watched the fish being prepared at le Lunch and slowly filling a vast pot, their last-gasp heads and bodies enveloped by the perfumed brew. Into the oil with the fennel, onions and garlic, then cover with water – to 4kg of fish add 8 litres of water – and cook over a fast flame for no more than fifteen minutes. The first divergence from the protean version is that fishermen would have used sea water. Then mince it all up with a powerful mouli, and pass it through a fine sieve or *chinois*. Monsieur Negril told me that they might do this ten times or more. They are the professionals, I suppose, but that seems like overkill to me. There's nothing wrong with a little texture, after all.

Savour the intense fishiness, and watch the colour drain from the fish as you turn up the heat. They seem almost to transfer their beauty to the complexity of taste and scent of this mouth-wateringly lovely dish. Then, right at the end, add some saffron. Caution here, for however alluring the colour, saffron can overpower. And bad saffron can make a fish soup taste almost rancid. But saffron in a fisherman's soup? Unlikely. It is and always has been an expensive – the most expensive – ingredient in the restaurateur's repertoire, and hardly suggests spontaneity and poverty to me. But this is what we are told. And as a final flourish, don't forget the glass of *pastis*. For the pot.

Easy, you may think. Yet this is only the first part. You then need a second tranche of firmer fish to make the soup into real *bouillabaisse*, fish that will keep their shape and texture when poached in the broth. Inevitably this will mean conger eel, *fielas* in the local dialect, the cheapest and bulkiest of rock-dwelling fish. But use only the middle part; the tail is so prickled with irritating spines and bones that it will drive you insane trying to eat it without choking. Be wise, and eviscerate.

The same goes for the spectacular moray eel, *la murène*, a doomy black fish with awesome teeth and a bright-yellow dapple, which make it fascinating if monstrous. Aggressive nasty fish these, they attack octopuses with venomous speed, pulling and tearing at their flesh until they die. I like octopuses.

Then there is the lugubrious St Pierre, or John Dory to English speakers. Its strange telescopic mouth darts and swallows its unsuspecting prey with incredible alacrity. When alive, it has an absolutely marvellous golden khaki colour, with iridescent bands of pure gold that seem to flow along its body. On its back are long flowing fins that sweep into the sea and give it great manoeuvrability. On its side is an anomalous black splodge, the famous thumb mark of St Peter, it is said, left in divine recognition of the fish being drawn from the Sea of Galilee.

Baudroie, called *lotte* elsewhere in France and monkfish in English, are also popular. This fish is deemed so ugly that it is wastefully beheaded in Northern waters, although people who live in the Mediterranean, and the Atlantic Spanish are strong enough to face up to the ferocious wide jaws and dripping teeth without passing out. The heads are excellent for soup, and the cheeks contain two gorgeous morsels of flesh that are greatly appreciated by the cognoscenti.

The idea is simplicity itself: the smaller fish make the soup, the larger ones can be served poached in it to make the soup into *bouillabaisse*. No great myth should put you off the attempt either to make it or take it. If you follow the recipe, you will have a fish soup that is sublime and evocative, that sings of the sun and the south.

So, restaurateurs who specialize in *bouillabaisse*

almost always offer fish soup as well – they do at le Lunch – and for those who prefer not to spend triple digits on meals, a bowl of *soupe de poisson* will serve you well. I sat in the sun while the rain tumbled and dripped from the dank dark sky in England, and all was well with the world. A glass of Provençal rosé, a salad of the brightest green and a bowl of fish soup, looking out on to the *calanque* at heavenly Sormiou. It was perfect.

And made me wish for a siesta, and dream of bed. It was not to be. Over on the other side of the *calanque* I had arranged to meet Sormiou's most famous fisherman, who was, oh lucky man, sleepily dozing in the shade, his gnarled and wrinkled hands completely still, his head bowed. But he, unlike me, had been up at the hour when rats scurry through the gutters of Marseilles on the other side of the hill. Jean-Claude Bianco had quite a story to tell.

Bouillabaisse

Serves about 8

For the soup
One kilo of small *poissons de roche*, which should include:
Some small *rascasse*/scorpion fish
St Pierre/John Dory

Raoucou or *labres*/wrasse
Vive/weever
Baudroie or *lotte*/monkfish
Galinette, grondin/gurnard
Tail of a *congre, fielas*/conger eel
Some live *favouilles*/shore crabs

You will also need:
150ml extra-virgin olive oil
About 100g chopped onions
6–8 cloves garlic
200g potatoes, peeled and cut into small chunks
1–1.5kg small Mediterranean fish
Dried orange peel
A can of Italian tomatoes, or 500g of fresh, peeled and
cut into chunks
2 litres mineral water
Some dried fennel branches, or some fresh wild fennel
A pinch of good-quality saffron
A small glass of *pastis*

Method
Some say you should scale the fish first, but if they
are small and include most of the above, they don't
have many scales and will be armed with poisonous spines which makes scaling hazardous, to say
the least. You could gut the fish and make sure the
cavity is blood free, but if the fish are freshissimo
then there's no need.

So, heat the oil, cook the onions for a few

minutes, add the garlic (lower the heat a little), then the potatoes and the fish, and wait for it all to take a little colour. Add the orange peel and the tomatoes, then the water, and bring quickly to the boil. Add the fennel, and the glass of *pastis* if you like. Boil over a fast flame for fifteen to twenty minutes, add the saffron, and cook for another five minutes. Lower the heat and mouli the whole lot, then pass through a *chinois*. (A sieve may be too fine, but if that's all you've got then it will have to do.)

This then is the *soupe de poisson*, which you can serve as it is on some dried rounds of good baguette in shallow bowls. *A volonté.*

To make the *bouillabaisse*, you will need even more fish: a whole *rascasse* (scorpion fish), St Pierre (John Dory), *baudroie* (monkfish) and the middle part of a conger eel. In Toulon and Sormiou, they use mussels and the odd *chambi* – slipper lobsters. Look for fish that sing of the sea and the sun, that are fresh, lively – if not alive – and colourful. If you prefer, fillet them first and then use the bones in the broth. Then poach them in the soup, and serve in chunks surrounded by the soup, or separately, as you wish.

Rouille
Bake a large potato in its skin and mash it finely. Add a little cayenne pepper, and two or three strong cloves of garlic, peeled and finely chopped.

Add an egg yolk if you like, then some olive oil in dribbles as if you were making mayonnaise. Just add the oil without the egg yolk if you prefer. Check the seasoning, and serve with the *bouillabaisse*.

Tradition and etiquette have it that the *rouille* is added to the bread that is served in the soup. I like to spoon a little on, and then let it gently absorb the fish soup. Others stir a little into the soup. Tradition is there for no reason other than to comfort traditionalists. So extemporize. Be liberated!

The Fisherman's Tale

Protected by the massive cupped hand of the white limestone escarpment, Sormiou seems at ease with the world. Wild scented herbs grow in the hills, while out in the sea that glints turquoise and blue, a light wind ruffles darker patches where the seaweed grows beneath.

But is all so serene in this bizarre paradise? While Monsieur Bianco snored, I fell into conversation with one of the settlement's most devoted tenants, who had the glorious name of Dédé Orus.

'Oh, I don't think you'll see Jean-Claude for a while. He likes to sleep, you know!'

I have real sympathy for a man who by force of habit wakes and works at dawn, and savours the world for its solitude and beauty. A man passionate about the sea and fish, happiest with his feet placed firmly on his open fishing boat and his companion next to him, both darkened to an almost chocolate brown by the sun and the wind. I wish I were he at times. I, too, spent years rising inhospitably early, and have fish in my blood. Only I woke to the dark, cold and rain more than the sun and the song of *cigales*.

Dédé was also a son of the sea. His father worked in the port but died when he was fourteen. Retired now, Dédé nods and smiles at one and all, and regaled me with tales of derring-do from above and below the water.

'You know, I had to work to help my mother, to help us all, from when I was young. I was the breadwinner, so I decided to become the first diving instructor here after the war. I worked with Cousteau, on the *Calypso*. In those days there were more than two fishermen here. Maybe eight or so, but never more. But the harbour was busier then. There's just Jean-Claude left now who fishes these days. That's his boat there.' And he pointed to a little open-decked boat with the lines of a Roman galley. Little had changed, it seemed, around these parts.

'In the war, the Germans built a concrete blockade over there, and a net to stop any submarines, so when it was all over, there were suddenly these huge fish, groupers and moray eels swimming around. That was good for fishing. And for diving, too. So I did all right. But for me, the real beauty is under the water. There was some coral here once, and we used to see the odd amphora. And over there, just under the cliff, the sea is over forty metres deep. There are some incredible things there.'

He pointed to the east. 'Have you heard of *les caves rupestres*? They are the most beautiful things I have seen. They are caves that you can only get to underwater, where there are these drawings that are thousands of years old.'

Sormiou was beginning to sound quite mesmerizing. The sea. Fish. Undeveloped tourism. A great restaurant where you can sip your fish soup in the sun, and laze on the beach. Little noise. And in May, not too much bustle.

And then this magnificent underwater world.

During the Ice Age, the sea water retreated as it froze and the caves were open to life. Ancestral Marseillais have left simple handprints, enigmatically coded, that have been dated at 27,000 years old. Slightly later drawings express movement, perspective and shadows, and begin to tell a story.

That humans hunt prey. That the world is full of riches to be exploited. There are charcoal figures of great auks, now extinct, and short-legged horses, wild and square jawed, much like the Przewalski horse that roams the Mongolian plains. There are leaping chamois, bison and auroch, the ancestor of the domestic cow. Strangest of all is the emblematic head of a horse, sketched with the horns of a bison.

Speed and food perhaps, the stuff of Palaeolithic dreams.

Elsewhere in France, flutes have been found dating to the same period, so can we imagine that we were even then drawing, singing and socializing? It seems to be self-evident. Mighty phalluses and vulvas are etched on to the walls. All human life was there, and with Marseilles over the hill, *plus ça change*, I thought.

Well, Jean-Claude did turn up, as promised. Rested and refreshed by his siesta, he stumbled slightly on the steep path down to the minuscule port, slipping out through the gate that guarded his *cabanon* from – well, what exactly? Prying eyes? They are mostly welcomed. Friends? Definitely welcomed. It was more symbolic. These low-slung cottages have the magic appeal of simplicity, shaded from the summer heat and with the most fabulous view. Vines tangle through fences and cover terraces.

He invited me on to his boat, to talk while he cleaned his nets. Of *bouillabaisse* he had much to say. Yes, it might be a dish invented by fishermen, but it has become a little too bourgeois for his tastes, too gentrified. To which he has no objection, for demand pushes up the price of the exquisite little fish that he catches, the ne plus ultra of the gourmet and fish enthusiast.

His idea of *bouillabaisse* was a little different from that of le Lunch. 'Fry an onion or two and some garlic in olive oil, and fill the pot with the fish, washed and scrubbed if you want, or just as they are, fresh from the sea. Add some fresh new potatoes, sliced and peeled. Sometimes we add a *chambi*.'

Chambi are odd crustaceans and are now pretty rare. Overfished, of course, these slipper lobsters have a curious flattened body, and are almost boringly brown, but their skin has a surprising velvet softness and their flesh is a sublime delicacy. Most are caught in nets rather than pots, so are stressed and near death by the time they are landed, which is probably why we see so few of them elsewhere.

'But you shouldn't be governed by rules. The idea is to use all the fish that remain in the bottom of the boat. So we would hardly ever use *rougets* (red mullet), for instance. They were far too valuable. Nor *loup* (sea bass), nor *dorade royale*. My father used to say that fish are at their best when they are with eggs. Afterwards they taste of very little. So we made our *bouillabaisse* in the early summer. That was when it was really good. And when we made *bouillabaisse*, we would use one pan, and put all the fish in. We'd never cover them with water, just fill it to a little below the surface. The flavours are better that way.'

I wondered about the local fish stocks. The word on the water was that the Mediterranean was one of the most overfished of the world's seas, which made eating *bouillabaisse* a little troubling for anyone worried about the state of the fisheries. Excessive consumption of immature fish tends to spell doom and gloom, but a controlled, well-managed fishery should permit at least some fishing.

And like a true fisherman, Jean-Claude reassured me: '*Non, non!* There are still a lot of fish out there, and I know where to find them. My father worked the sea, and I learnt with him. But you know, if there's one thing I can say about the sea out there it is that, despite it all, honestly, we know nothing, nothing at all. Every day I learn something new.'

This was what drew me to fish, too. Despite being driven half crazy by chefs who constantly asked in the autumn for fish that appeared in the spring, and vice versa, the immense variety of fish that I was offered, that I saw in the markets of France, always astonished and excited me.

The ebb and flow of the seasons was the essence of getting the best from the sea, the planet's last great wilderness, threatened now, overfished and forever marked by human greed.

'I love this life. I mean just look out there!' Jean-Claude scooped his hand generously towards the sea. 'But you know, after all these years, I cannot say that I really *understand* the sea. It is another world.'

27

Pieds de Cochon Farcis

AT MARSEILLES, I STEPPED ON TO THE TGV, FOUND MY seat, and at the almost neurotically exact appointed time, the doors sighed shut and the train slipped quietly out of the station. I had my bag. My baguette. My *Opinel*. And a cheese, a St Marcellin bought on a whim in a stoppi or a shoppi.

I was off to Lyon, the proud gastronomic capital of France, a city that is so rich in the culture of food it seems almost ridiculous to pit it against anywhere but itself. Lyon straddles the confluence of the mighty Rhône and the lesser River Saône, and is said by some wags to have a third river, flowing with Beaujolais. But these days, its star has waned. Beaujolais has become one vinous embarrassment too many.

Lyon's potted one-minute history could run like this. City grows up in rich hinterland, discovers the

European textile trade and encourages the production of magnificent silks. It has never had any pretensions to be anything but a regional city, and is essentially pretty *bien dans sa peau*, as they say in French. Good in its skin, in other words. And the Lyonnais famously like to eat and drink. The cradle of gastronomy? Perhaps. But what of the city today? Is all well and comfortable, or is Lyon suffering from a touch of indigestion?

I watched the countryside slowly evolve through the window as the TGV scudded through strange towns and cities, desperately trying to focus on names to give it all meaning. But unless you had the head of a snake and the eye of an eagle, this would have been biologically impossible, so grand was the *vitesse* of the train.

Eventually, and exactly on time, the train arrived in Lyon Part Dieu. I felt far from being a part of *dieu*, but noticed emblazoned on the edge of the concourse the name PAUL, denoting a stand that was selling bread, and good bread at that. This is a baker who has rolled out, expanded and still kept his reputation for quality relatively intact. I bought a *baguette à l'ancienne*, thought of *pain mollet*, and scurried off to the hotel to read some dense books on the ancien régime, thinking about France and its strange Revolution that still obsesses and divides ideologues and historians. How can we mere interested mortals attempt to understand it all, I wondered?

The haunting images of the Palais Royal and

1789 still gripped me. I had this stark picture of Robespierre's last night, of his smashed jaw hanging loose from his face, the wound left for all to see as he too was dragged off to the guillotine in a blood-spattered wooden tumbril. Poetic justice, perhaps. Every time I closed my eyes, gruesome images of sweaty, drunken mobs, of heads impaled on pikes and sticks, appeared and lingered. It was the cheese I had been nibbling earlier that had done it, I thought. Cheese and obsession. A horrible combination.

Morning came and I wandered off to meet up with an old *éminence* who, like me, was getting ever more *gris*. Highly respected chef Pierre Koffmann is an excellent companion, immensely knowledgeable, opinionated, and one of the best French chefs in the world. Who better, I thought, to tramp the streets of Lyon with.

We pushed through the hallowed doors of Lyon's central food market, Les Halles. Every time I do this I am drawn to the vision of Doctor Who and his Tardis. Hideous on the outside, but mysterious and comforting on the inside, Les Halles is a slice of brutalism à la lyonnaise that makes you want to slash your wrists as you walk towards it, especially if you know that, just as in Paris, Lyon's Halles were once housed in buildings of solid industrial beauty.

So rush through those doors, do not dawdle. Then breathe in the quiet, bourgeois air. Savour the sight of blue-legged *poulets de Bresse*, the serried rows of cheese. Look at the splendours before you. Toss away thoughts of suicide and architecture, for despite its exterior this is still one of the world's most brilliant food markets, and it is for the produce you will come.

You will find a range of food unrivalled anywhere in France. Products of such quality it makes your heart leap. We stopped at a poultry-seller's stall, and asked, foolishly perhaps, how sales were going, despite all the worry about avian flu. The response had a little of the Dunkirk spirit about it.

'Ah, no monsieur! Our clients know that there is no real danger! There is no problem at all!'

We wove our way through stalls laden with wine and fish. Past piles of aubergines, and salads, and citrus fruit that glowed with that almost worry-ingly radioactive shininess. I thought how even here the seasons had long ago been forgotten.

I stopped by a pile of dried morels. These mush-rooms are the key to Koffmann's most famous signature dish, *pieds de cochon farcis aux morilles*. It has been copied and tweaked, as great dishes are, and not always credited. It was the dish that drew thousands to eat at his famous London restaurant, la Tante Claire, once my morning-coffee stop. I would always go there first, to offer him the best fish I had bought that morning. Over the years he taught me so much. How to taste food. How to buy, how to cook, and how to appreciate. So these curious cone-shaped mushrooms always remind me of those days, my apprenticeship, if you like. They have an exquisite pungency, especially when dried, better by far than the rather unreliable fresh morel.

Much of the problem comes from their provenance. Morels are spring mushrooms, found on poor, acidic soils, in pine woods and on mountain slopes. Demand, particularly here in the French gastronomic heartland of Lyon, is high, and never really manages to satisfy the Lyonnais, let alone anyone else. So mushroom dealers spread their tentacles wide.

To Turkey, for example, where morels are still found in good supply, if the conditions are not too dry. But they tend to be disappointing. *Fade*, they say in French. I asked the lady manning the stand where her mushrooms were from.

'They're French, Monsieur, I assure you.'

We are back to *terroir* again. Is this the last bastion of French superiority? Is there really something fundamentally better about morels from France, as we are led to believe? There are certainly many who will tell you so.

Despite the ribbon, the price and the location, her *morilles* were actually pretty good value. Koffmann picked them up, inhaled, and nodded in approval. I did the deal.

How then to use them? Keep them. Savour them, by all means, but don't let them join the host of the unknown in the store cupboard, with condiments and sauces so obscure that you almost dare not open them.

No, use them. Make a *pied de cochon farci*. It is a brilliant dish, a mongrel, like most of Koffmann's food, half haute cuisine, half cuisine paysanne.

This is what I like best about French food. A subtle fusion of styles, inventive, rough yet refined, and based upon the most humble of ingredients, the pig's trotter.

Pieds de cochon farcis aux morilles

Serves 4

Ingredients

4 pigs' back trotters, boned
100g carrots, diced
100g onions, diced
150ml dry white wine
1 tablespoon port
150ml meat stock
225g veal sweetbreads, blanched and chopped
75g butter, plus a knob for the sauce
20 dried morels, soaked until soft then drained
Another small onion, finely chopped
1 chicken breast, skinned and diced
1 egg white

200ml double cream
Salt and pepper

Method

Preheat the oven to 160°C.

Place the trotters in a casserole with the diced carrots and onions, the wine, port and meat stock. Cover and braise for three hours.

Meanwhile fry the sweetbreads in the butter for 5 minutes, add the morels and chopped onion and cook for another 5 minutes. Leave to cool. Purée the chicken breast with the egg white and cream and season with salt and pepper. Mix with the sweetbread mixture to make the stuffing.

Take the trotters out of the casserole and strain the cooking stock, keeping the stock but discarding the vegetables. Open the trotters out flat and lay each one on a piece of foil. Leave to cool.

Fill the cooled trotters with the chicken stuffing and roll tightly in the foil. Chill in the fridge for at least two hours, before steaming in the foil for one hour.

Remove the foil and put the trotters in a serving dish. Pour the reserved stock into the casserole and reduce by half. Whisk in a knob of butter, pour over the trotters and serve very hot.

From *La Tante Claire: Recipes from a Master Chef* by Pierre Koffmann with Timothy Shaw, Headline, 1992.

But is there really something so different about morels picked in the hills of the Jura from those of Turkey? Has France, like Maradona, simply been brushed by the hand of God and given divine superiority? Is it all in the mind? How do you measure taste, anyway? Divine superiority was the answer once: France was believed to be superior in all things, and food above all. It gave the nation self-confidence. It even nourished a sense of what was often seen as arrogance.

Let's take our morel. While it grows in the soil, the mushroom is nothing more than the fruiting spore of a wider network of minuscule living threads, the mycelium, invisible to the eye, which spreads through the soil. Air, rain, climate, humidity, soil fertility, all combine to give the morel a very particular characteristic. Then it is picked. The concept of *terroir* is used to explain that, at that very moment, the French version is superior. That the particular combination of time and place makes it noticeably better to eat than, say, a Turkish morel.

But there is more to the equation than that. At what stage in the mushroom's life cycle was it picked? How was it dried, packed, stored, transported? All of these call for expertise, and show that *terroir* is only part of the equation. There is knowledge, in other words, that comes from a lively and confident food culture. From generations of families handing down recipes and words of wisdom, which give France a fabulously rich reserve of indigenous knowledge.

It may be technique and process rather than innate superiority that allows us to say that French morels are better than Turkish, for these are something that France still has in spades. For now at least. For young chefs are getting harder to recruit, families are dispersing more widely, and the fast-food culture is thriving in France, just as it is everywhere.

Now let me say, in case you think I am mad, that I have bought and sold a few fresh morels in my time, and they were always disappointing. Exciting yes, challenging yes, but their taste was dim and dull. Plucked really fresh from the soil, they were always bought from a dealer who had been supplied by another dealer, and been sent for miles in a truck to me, who then took them for miles in another truck and hoped that my tricky chefs would be pleased. They seldom were. Nor was I. And nor was Pierre Koffmann, who stuck to what he knew were best: dried *morilles*. Eventually I gave up the challenge, and stuck to dried ones as well.

We moved across to the cheese section. 'In the absence of an external threat,' de Gaulle famously remarked, 'how can one govern a country that has 246 different cheeses?'

Follow your nose to the cheese zone, and look for la Fromagerie la Mère Richard, and you'll see what a great *fromagerie* really looks like. This is the land of the immaculate cheese conception, with a display that makes you positively want to moo with happiness. Pyramids, cylinders, rounds and squares, the whole panoply of geometry was here, with rumpled surfaces, some peppered with ash, others of a brilliant virginal whiteness. Labels, light, and that wonderful deep sensuous scent of cheese. Variations on the theme of white, from beige to the brilliant purity of goat's cheese, and the solid rounds of Beaufort and Gruyère.

The Richard family has gained a reputation for supplying the very best cheese, and in particular the very best St Marcellin. At its head is Madame Renée Richard, who rocketed to fame on the recommendation of the eloquent patriarch Paul Bocuse, and is an elegant matriarch of la cuisine lyonnaise. It was, however, the cheese that did it for Bocuse, for Madame Richard had perfected the art of *affinage* (the process of bringing the cheese to perfection) to such an extent that one can be almost certain that her cheese will awaken and please the palate. Pierre had met Madame Richard years ago, and shook her hand warmly.

Affinage reveals the character of a cheese. It is the fine tuning, if you like, the elevation of a food to a higher level. It is in a way an extension of *terroir*, where particularity is brought out by the hand of man, or in this case woman. *Affinage* is often taken to be an almost mysterious art, relying on unquantifiable microbiology, evidence that it is only by human interaction and the accumulation of experience that a product can be brought triumphantly to these dizzy heights of perfection.

But the cheese would be nothing if it wasn't fit for transformation. It must have the ingredients to enable the *affinage* to succeed. The story, then, must start with the cow, the grass and the climate. The *terroir*, no less. St Marcellin was once a goat's cheese but is now made exclusively from unpasteurized cow's milk, and in order to reassure the customer that any St Marcellin will be good enough, they are trying to make an Appellation d'Origine Contrôlée of the cheese. We see those magic letters AOC and we breathe more easily. No fraud. No trickery. It is in a way *terroir* in legalized form. Inevitably, anyone making a valuable cheese which tells tales of time and place wants to reassure their customers, to keep a hold on the palates and the purse strings, so the system is crucial.

I left Les Halles a little poorer that day, but laden with the most exquisite produce. Shame about the architecture, though.

Lyon has a unique place on the world map of gastronomy. Gifted, spoilt, many say. With so much produce on their doorstep, the Lyonnais not only have the finest poultry in the world in nearby Bresse, but some of the most brilliant chefs, so inevitably there is a vibrant food culture. Lyon even has its own version of bistros, called *les bouchons lyonnais*, which allow you to experience something that is still almost unique in France.

Bouchons serve neither *grande cuisine* nor fast food, but have refined a repertoire of solid bourgeois fare, elemental earthy dishes, a *pot au feu*, for instance, or a *tête de veau*, cooked with the minimum of fuss. Most are family run, and they are intimate, clubby even. They remind me of those tales of eighteenth-century *tables d'hôtes* where strangers felt intimidated by the familiarity. The food they serve relies on the primacy and excellence of the raw material, and seems in a way to represent the triumph of bourgeois cuisine. Refreshingly unglamorous and constantly busy, Lyon's *bouchons* bristle with a buzz and a sense of camaraderie that is, let's face it, difficult to find in a McDonald's. But then they are fulfilling entirely different needs.

Part of their uniqueness comes from their very particular culinary genealogy. A *bouchon* is said to be the direct descendant of the cabaret, which was part auberge, part tavern, rather than the restaurant. Although the word *bouchon* may make you think of wine, or dream of traffic jams, it actually comes from the old French *bousche*, meaning a bundle of branches: tightly knotted pine branches woven into a circle were once the sign for a cabaret.

Inevitably wary of imitators and falsifiers, the

326

true *bouchons* have grouped together and created a charter, a suitably chatty and familiar one at that, and to gain your enamelled door plaque you must adhere to it. Among the articles that *les authentiques* sign up to is this:

> *Les bouchons, établissements faits de convivialité et de cuisine simple et de qualité dans le droit ménager, appartiennent à la tradition lyonnaise et contribuent au rayonnement de la ville, en France et au-delà des frontières.*

> Bouchons, places of conviviality, simple cooking and quality in the matter of domestic science, belong to the Lyonnais tradition and contribute to the influence of the city, in France and beyond its frontiers.

So off we went to Chez Paul in the Rue du Major Martin. It has no knotted pine, but is intensely convivial. There is a cosy shopfront, which is almost as welcoming as an Olde Englishe Tea Shoppe. It has a warm fuggy *salle*, checked tablecloths in neat French chintz, ornaments, and photos that give it an almost alarming sense of bonhomie. Madame Josiane Chanaux rather than Paul runs the establishment. Enter and you will be enveloped by a feeling of competent domesticity.

You sit down at a communal table that is most un-restaurantish. While others pick at a luscious *pâté de campagne*, Madame brings a bowl of *filets de hareng*, that old bistro favourite. Lyon is known for the finesse of its charcuterie, as well as the excellence of its poultry. Specialities are so thick on the ground you have to batten down your imagination.

At Paul's you may find a *saucisson lyonnais*, a *sabodet*, a *rosette de Lyon*, or a grilled *andouillette*. Happily the menu is restricted and changeable; it has to be, for the only way that a *bouchon* can remain conceptually separate from a restaurant – keep those staff levels low, in other words – is to create a menu that is peppered with classics, *pot au feu* one day, *quenelles* another. And all of these are so enticing that they keep the punters from revolting.

Hungry? At Chez Paul, for a mere €21.50, you can eat well:

MENU €21.50
Le défilé des saladiers,
gratons et charcuterie

Tête de veau ravigote
Saucisson chaud
Andouillette à la ficelle
Foie de veau persillé
Viande rouge à l'échalote
Tablier de sapeur
Poulet au vinaigre
Civet de porc

Quenelle de brochet
Blanquette de veau
Boudin paysan

Fromages au choix

Desserts maison

And what bliss it is to see a whole meal through for the price of a gastronomic whisper of la Cuisine Michelin. The *saucisson chaud* was served *en brioche*, tender, exquisite, ample, and just so satisfying. Ditto the *poulet*. Simple, unremarkable dishes, but served with directness and even a sense of humour. Not that there was any sense of amateurism: the machine was well oiled and when we ate there all the service was done by Madame Chanaux alone.

This is exactly the sort of place that Pierre Koffmann, a chef's chef, a man who has seen the likes of Gordon Ramsay and Marco Pierre White pass through his kitchen doors, feels at home in. He is a modest patriarch, a chef who prefers the buzz of the kitchen to the click of the abacus. A Gascon by birth, Koffmann gained his three stars and played the Michelin game, but his food always seemed to me to be more *paysanne* than *haute*. Which is exactly what most of us want from French cooking.

The upper stratosphere of techno-molecular cuisine is beyond the regional, just as haute cuisine once was. But while the unapproachable heights of *la grande cuisine* are quite beyond the skills of Everyman, *la cuisine paysanne* has moved into the realm of the everyday, via gruesome *plats cuisinés*, ready-made meals, the culinary kiss of death for our taste buds. It has been debased. This is a double whammy for French food.

The *bouchons* are in a way a last outpost, arguably an evolutionary backwater, particularly as they have become so deeply associated with Lyon and *la cuisine lyonnaise*, and neither wish to nor should move out.

Pierre, an enthusiastic *rugbyman*, immediately fell into conversation with *le patron* about something arcane and rugbyish. The three remaining guests all joined in this conversation, which was so deeply French that it was easy to forget that *le rugby* had travelled across the water from an élitist English public school. Way beyond its *terroir*.

Why has the south-west of France taken the game so keenly to its heart? Walking along the sea front at Biarritz, I was astonished to see kids creating rugby mauls and kicking rugby balls. The passion for rugby here is fierce. It explodes at rugby time, and escapes into ancient rivalries that feed on identity, even hatred. Biarritz and Bayonne, for instance, two of the greatest rugby teams in France, cordially loathe each other.

The next day dawned, and there were more streets to be tramped. We had been told about le Carnegie Hall by the concierge. Go there if you like meat. Which we did.

Le Carnegie Hall is a little off the beaten track, and you may be better off taking a taxi, but we got there, and wandered a little around the old abattoir district of the city, and walked into the immense, vibrant space that brings the art of cooking meat to higher levels.

Every conceivable morsel is on offer, and while you eat, the splayed carcasses of beef are hanging there to remind you of what you are about to receive. And we were truly grateful. An *araignée*, that butcher's favourite, was brought lightly cooked, chewy and delectable. A vast T-bone steak arrived, cooked *à point* and oozing with blood, but tender to the bone. It was all deeply copious. A St Marcellin from Mère Richard to finish. Perfect. Some brilliant wine, chosen by Pierre and forgotten by me. Sorry.

The buzz is awesome. Packed at lunch and, we were told, side-splittingly crammed on match days, the Stade de Gerland is next door. Carnegie Hall was the brainchild of Jean-Baptiste Killijian. And where did he get the idea from? Why, Gallagher's Steak House of New York.

28

Fondue Savoyarde

THERE IS MORE TO FONDUE THAN CHEESE. TO A Burgundian, a fondue involves dunking raw flesh into boiling oil and then dipping the lightly cooked meat in a sauce. Or the really racy could replace the beef with horse meat. Then there is the terrible aberration of a chocolate fondue, where you dip strawberries that have been jetted around the globe in chocolate that tastes of nothing. No, fondue is no longer just about cheese. But since real people want real fondue once more, I thought I should go mountainwards and visit fondue land.

Which allowed me finally to visit Beaufort, to witness thousands of litres of delicious Beaufortain milk being gently heated and pressed into those ancient moulds, to see at last how what I firmly believe is the finest cheese in the world is made, and how milkmaids lead a double life as ski instructors and chalet helpers.

Fondue is a fun, sexy dish that first flourished away from its ancestral Alpine home back in the 1960s, just as free love came, like a social disease, to the heartlands of Europe. At the very moment that Danny the Red was manning the barricades, and students were scrawling slogans in red paint on Alma Mater's ancient walls — IT IS FORBIDDEN TO FORBID; YANKS OUT, that sort of thing — fondue was wowing the bourgeoisie into a false sense of *montagnard* security.

So beguiled was the Western world by the idea of free love and lots of sex that they went to great lengths to make feeding the guests as easy and novel as possible, and found themselves spending huge amounts of money on fondue sets, and hostess trolleys that allowed the hostess (never a host) to spend more time with the guests, or upstairs in the bedroom where she hadn't been for so long, and where Monsieur liked to lounge while she worked her socks off in the house. So it wasn't just the contraceptive pill that helped her on the way to liberation. The fondue played its part, too. Women were now free to become enslaved by paid work. There were packets of instant mashed potato and instant whip, although tragically the pot noodle was still confined to NASA's canteen. All this made feeding the family less daunting, but many did away with families altogether. There were TV dinners for those special days, and then there was the fondue set to be used on those really, really special days, when making an impression was the thing to do. The fondue was groovy party food. Melted cheese, a tinny bowl, a few long plasticky forks and a burner were all that was needed to make that evening go with an Alpine zing.

And, boy, was fondue sexy! As knitted sweater touched nylon blouse, sparks flew. Nervous arms reached across, entangled in cheesy love. Even the dipping was suggestive. Drop a piece of bread in the cheese, and your *forfait* was to kiss all the men. Mmmm! All those beards. Those sideburns. These were real men, and their forfeit was to drink a glass of wine instead. Many of them might have already experienced new deviant forms of love and food, such as sodomy and quiche.

Skiing was ultra glam, and chalets enabled huge groups of sweaty degenerates to share baths, beds, and, well, one thing led to another, and before you could say Babycham they too were all eating fondue. Some of them had families in industry, who in order to keep their bottom lines more manageable allowed fortunes to be frittered away designing fashionable fondue sets made of highly toxic metals, with garish plastic handles. You can now find them easily on eBay.

They gradually filtered into homes all over Europe. Nay, the world. Lazier lovers of snow (*neigeophiles* in French) migrated to Courchevel, Megève and Gstaad every year, and would come home with these fondue sets hidden among their skis. The civilized world was bitten by the bug: free love and fondues.

But fashion is a bitter fruit. For just as we all began to get that mountain vibe, feeling cool with our sideburns as snowmelt and mulled wine coursed through our veins, lulling us into a false sense of security, along came the *paella* pan, and things were never quite the same. The sun conquered our hearts, and the fondue sets were placed in the top cupboard to gather dust. The sunny wastelands of the Costa Brava took over from the Alps, and fondue retreated to its mountain strongholds.

And there it has remained, brooding, dejected, a seasonal jest. But, joy oh joy, fondue has now regained its sense of place. It, too, has a touch of *terroir*. The poor *montagnard*, the Swiss or the Savoyard who tramped through the snow to milk his cows, who suffered so, and saw such awful dissipation of this most precious culinary jewel, now has it back.

Fondue Savoyarde

Serves 8

Ingredients
1.2kg Gruyère
600g Beaufort
600g Emmental or Abondonce
1½ bottles of dry white Savoie wine
½ glass of kirsch
1 clove of garlic
Pepper
1 *pain de campagne* or sourdough loaf, cut into cubes

Method
Heat the wine in a terracotta dish or cast-iron pan. Just as it reaches boiling point, add the cheese, which should be cut in fine slices. Stir slowly with a wooden spoon.

Just before all the cheese has melted, transfer the contents to your fondue set and place it in the middle of the table. Keep stirring. Add some pepper – freshly ground white pepper is best, since it doesn't colour the mixture. Then add the kirsch, still stirring all the while. Lower the heat when all the cheese has melted.

The fondue is now ready, and each guest should take a fork, spear some bread and dip it in the melted cheese. If anyone drops a cube of bread into the mix, then they have to pay that forfeit.

When the bottom of the pan begins to turn golden brown, you can add an egg, and stir it in. Or you can use the remains to make a *gratin de pommes de terre* by adding them to a dish lined with thinly sliced, seasoned potatoes and a little stock.

Translated and adapted by the author from *Mes Recettes Savoyardes* by Marie-Thérèse Hermann, published by Christine Bonneton, Paris, 2005.

So, to make fondue you must first find your *caquelon*. Any heavy earthenware pot should do, so long as it can be heated on an open flame without shattering into a thousand tiny pieces. Into this you will add the cheese, and allow it gently to melt.

And not just any old cheese. Although Fondue Savoyarde can be made with unpasteurized Beaufort, tradition dictates that it is better still when mixed with a little Gruyère, Emmental or Abondance. And hold that processed cheese. Not only has it been proved to be saltier than Atlantic sea water, but texturally it will be all wrong. Mere sludge. And hold the Tasmanian Cheddar, too. No cheesy aberrations, please. You will need some solid, properly ripened Swiss-type cheese. By that I mean one that is made in a thwacking weighty *meule* that weighs at least 40kg, with a solid hard-pressed texture. These forms were practical. The concave edge of Beaufort allowed it to be tied by rope to mules and donkeys for the journey over the

Alps to the markets in Switzerland and as far away as Piedmont.

If Emmental or Gruyère are not readily available, you must be living somewhere very remote indeed, so supranational have they become. However, us *terroiristes* need something finer. Beaufort, of course, which is still made according to the old ways high up in the Savoie Alps, a short drive from the toytown ski resort of Albertville. Few towns in France do so badly out of being Anglicized. Albert with a 't' wears a flat hat and a string vest. Al Bear cooks. The name has no elegance in English, very like this town that was rejuvenated for the 1992 Winter Olympics and has never looked back.

I was taken through the grid-lined streets one dark morning to visit a little-known fundamentalist group called the Syndicate for the Defence of Beaufort. I like the idea of tiny groups of passionate people fighting against the evil world of mass production. The Beaufort producers were early supporters of France's Appellation d'Origine Contrôlée, which has proved to be an effective way to preserve endangered cheeses.

The amount of cheese produced in Beaufort is pretty insignificant when compared to the millions of tonnes of Swiss cheese, so the cheesemakers have had to fight hard to survive. Cooperatives have proved essential. To the food-lover, small levels of production actually seem to be a bonus, as it is important that Beaufort retains its character and continues to be made from specific types of cattle, in a well-defined geographical area.

Beaufort is made from the milk of some particularly zen-looking cows with names to match: Abondance and Tarentaise, the first gloriously bespectacled, a professorial cow, and the second so beautiful it makes you want to curl up in bed beside it and gently stroke its warm skin. But that sort of thing is looked down upon these days. So the milk that makes this divine cheese comes not from the über cow, the Friesian, but from these doleful velvet cows that have evolved in the valleys of the Beaufortain and are deeply attached to the rhythms of the place. They have lived in the hills and mountains for hundreds of years and are used to the life here. They moo the moo, speak the language, and thrive on the unique pasturage that is, after all, the very essence of what gives a cheese its character.

The village of Beaufort is deep in snow-land. Mountain-land too, where stiff peaks have nothing to do with meringues. The night before I trekked there, I stood and gazed at Mont Blanc in moonlight, awestruck by its beauty. The mountain was luminous, a little menacing, sublime. Yup, it was thrilling to be in such penetrating cold again.

If a Savoyard has a silly longing for snow, like Smilla, he only has to wait for winter. Snow is familiar. It falls as the mountains glimmer in the moonlight. It governs how the roofs are built. Wild winds shriek and twist ice and snow into peculiar writhing shapes, but we poor fools of temperate climes, when snow falls over here, we briefly marvel then panic. The country closes down. The snow melts and that's it.

Winter has a hold on *la cuisine savoyarde* too, the lovely warming food of the Savoie, thick with fat and cheese, food that is made to that ancient rhythm of plenty and scarcity, of heat and cold, of life and death. It is food that was borne of physical demand, calorific, yes, but then mountain life called for calories to be expended just to stay warm. A snowy life was an energy-hungry life.

The appreciation of Beaufort cheese is about the subtleties of taste. The cooperative allows you to see cheesemaking, and encourages you to move on to cheese tasting, where you can happily witness how the taste of the cheese develops over time, the result of that curious process called *affinage*. As the microflora of the milk change over the season, according to the feed, so does the taste of the cheese, so that an early-summer cheese, fed on the herbs and grass of the hills, has a far more layered and complex taste to it. This is called *Beaufort d'al-page* and is sold apart. It is full of subtle flavours.

During the winter, the cattle are fed on meadow hay. No silage is used, since it alters the taste. Come the winter, the cattle are kept in stalls, under cover, but as the spring arrives and the meadow grass begins to grow, they are sent up into the pastures once more and milked by mobile dairies. Most of the milk is lugged down to the cooperatives, but some of the *alpage* cheese is set and ripens in the hills, on planks of wood that are rich in microflora and allow the cheese to breathe and develop.

Subtle, gloriously perfumed with a mild hint of hazelnut, and only slightly redolent of the udder, Beaufort sits majestically among the aristocracy of France's famously varied cheeseboard, respected, weighty, exquisite. It is one of my own very private food heroes.

So if you get to visit the little town of Beaufort, with its ding-dong aspect, its simplicity and its quietness, shut your eyes, taste the cheese and think of *terroir*. Don't get too carried away with the idea of a fondue. To be honest, a thick chunk of cheese with a piece of baguette ripped from the loaf is quite exquisite.

As I walked through the cooperative and gazed at the ancient photos of cows and poverty, I was struck by how little had changed over the years. The vast copper basins now filled with milk were, of course, beyond the peasant cheesemaker, but the idea that the cows, the feed, the air were the same appealed to me, and appeals to others too, attracted by this silly dominating vision of nostalgia.

The faux joy that things have changed so little ignores the fact that the Savoyards once travelled en masse to Paris, where they were among the poorest of the poor, and became chimney sweeps and street sellers mocked for their thick mountain accents. They migrated much as the cattle once did, but with less ceremony.

The movement of the cows from the valleys to the hills was part of that ancient rhythm of the seasons, a time for much celebration. The cows were dressed in finery. Tassels hung from their horns, and the whole community sent them on their way. Today the ceremony is still carried out, with one subtle difference. The cows are mainly trucked up to the hills, the *transhumance* or *emmontagnage* being now thoroughly modernized.

Meanwhile, I noticed that perhaps all was not quite as retro as it seemed. The cooperative had recently introduced a mechanical robot that travelled up and down the high rows of cheese, turning them with zomboid skill. This was once the job of humans. However, robots neither milk the cows nor make the cheese. The allure of the mountain still attracts with its quiet and calm, but it is now a choice rather than an obligation to work the hills. This once was the domain of the women of the household, while the men cut the hay in the valleys and stored wood for the winter.

But even now, cheesemaking is barely profitable. The cooperative battles constantly against the impression that Beaufort is too expensive for a Swiss-type cheese, and it is little known outside France. Most farmers are obliged to lead a double life, profiting from the spectacular natural beauty that brings skiers and walkers to the hills and mountains. Being a ski instructor and a farmer are no longer mutually exclusive.

So fondue has survived the gastronomic blip of a popularity that took it far from its mountain roots, and has returned in these days of *terroir* to its evolutionary heartland. Beaufort the cheese is struggling against the global power of the Emmentals and Gruyères that have become so ubiquitous. When I was there, the cooperative had come up with the brilliant wheeze of doling out chunks of cheese at the motorway exit, to give all those incomers a taste and whet their appetites. For they know only too well that these products, which are so deeply held in a gastronomic niche, need a little more security than such relatively small levels of production can afford. It is a hard life for a cheese.

29

Chocolat Chaud

THE SIREN CALL OF CHOCOLATE BROUGHT ME BACK down from the cheesy heights of Beaufort to the south-west of France again, to a city better known for its ham. But Bayonne is said to be where chocolate first crossed the border into France from Spain, and it's where you will find the Musée du Chocolat, a museum devoted to the finer arts of chocolate-making, perched over the ocean on the coast road to Biarritz.

You can swirl through the place pretty easily, accompanied by a lively commentary, and those who appreciate a little nostalgia will sigh inwardly at the Carambar and Banania tins, now icons of another age, that tell the story of the confection of sugar and chocolate brilliantly and enthusiastically.

And the grand finale of the visit is a cup of hot chocolate, of which they are rightly proud. It was the best I have ever tasted, voluptuous, not overly sweet, and truly divine.

The recipe of our merchant of Merchena

Take seven hundred cocoa nuts, a pound and a half of white sugar, two ounces of cinnamon, fourteen grains of Mexico pepper (chilli), half an ounce of cloves, three little straws of vanilla de Campeche, as much anise as will equal the weight of a shilling, of achiot a small quantity as big as a a filbeard . . . add some almonds, filbreads and the water of orange flowers.

From *A Curious Treatise of the Nature and Quality of Chocolate* by Antonio Colmenero de Ledesma, translated into English by J. Chamberlaine, 1685.

If there's anything that can provide us with a timely reminder of the global nature of foodways past and present, it must be chocolate. Its story reaches far back into distant time, and its roots are inextricably entangled with the history of Central America, and the European power that first established contact with the people who lived there: the fifteenth-century Kingdom of Spain.

The final conquest in 1492 of the Islamic Caliphates of Al Andalus, in what is present-day Spain, by the Catholic monarchs Ferdinand and Isabella heralded a radical change in society and mores. Not only was there a switch in religious dominance from Islam to Christianity, but while the old order had established a reputation for religious tolerance, this was turned on its head by the devout and unforgiving Catholic monarchs.

This was the year when an ambitious Genoan explorer by the name of Cristoforo Colon sailed across the ocean and began to reveal the extraordinary complexity of a new world to the Europeans, one which was assumed to be living proof that the theoretical westward sea route to India did actually exist. Only this wasn't India at all, it turned out, but a whole continent about which the Europeans had been entirely ignorant. Nobody in the old world knew that the Americas existed, and over the coming decades they were systematically and brutally plundered and their population permanently transformed as a result.

Gold was what the Spaniards were looking for, but even if this seemed at first to be in short supply, there was much else of interest, particularly to the band of conquistadores who had risked life and limb seeking their fortune in these strange unexpected lands about which so little was known.

And one of the most intriguing discoveries was a drink that the Mexica, the people whom we often erroneously call the Aztecs, consumed with such ritualistic pleasure that it became known as the Food of the Gods. The Mexica called it *cacahuatl*. We call it chocolate. Eventually, the closely guarded secret art of chocolate-making slipped across to Spain, and then over the border from Spain to France along with fearful *converso* émigrés. That's one theory anyway, and one that is wholeheartedly supported by Bayonne's fascinating Musée du Chocolat.

If the conquistadores seem to have been a particularly brutal bunch, then life among the Mexica was hardly a bed of roses. The native inhabitants had some pretty gruesome habits of their own. When the conquistadores first came across the Mexica in 1519, they were sipping this drink they called *cacahuatl* and nervously ripping hearts from their fellow men. The monumental clash of cultures quickly became one-sided, with the doom-laden, pessimistic Mexica unable to compete with the conquistadores' relentless brutality and their canny habit of exploiting existing rivalries between the Mexica and their neighbours.

The Mexica kept their highly controlled society in order and their gods content through daily sacrifices to the great warrior Huitzilopochtli, the terrifying, insatiable humming-bird god. It was, so they believed, the only way to keep the sun from disappearing. The only way they could survive. Ritual sacrifice was carried out with sickening regularity. The victim, honoured to be the chosen one, was fêted and entertained before being rent asunder by the obsidian knife. Priests wore the flayed skins of victims, and the pantheon of gods was constantly being appeased by blood.

There was an obligation, in other words, to sacrifice. This was not just an addiction to cruelty. Stories were no doubt exaggerated by the conquistadores, but there are extensive accounts of the Mexica culture recorded by two Franciscan missionaries and anthropologists Fray Bernardino de Sahagún and Fray Diego Duran, who were keen to counter the conquistadores' militaristic idea that these newly discovered beings were animals rather than humans, who could be exploited without a troubled conscience.

Sahagún's account, written in the native Nahuatl between 1577 and 1580 and known to us as the *Codex Florentina*, offers a mesmerizing and it is assumed largely accurate account of Mexica culture, with all its faults and all its colour. 'The physician cannot advisedly administer medicines to the patient without first knowing from which source the ailment derives,' he wrote in his introduction, justifying to the sceptical reader why he thought such attention to detail was necessary.

Among the groups he portrayed were the *pochteca*, the people from the land of the Ceiba tree, 'who travelled between the highlands and lowlands bringing in luxuries to keep the élite and the emperor fuelled'. It was they who brought in the resplendent feathers of the Quetzal bird, jaguar skins and precious amber, always under the cover of darkness. And it was they who delivered endless sacks of a strange almond-shaped bean, so precious to the Mexica that they were hoarded, traded and even used as currency. This was cacao, and the plants were grown in the tropical lowlands that the Mexica themselves had ruthlessly subjugated.

Cacahuatl was drunk in delicately gilded cups and carved gourds, but only by warriors and the élite. Supplying the Mexica imperial palace with cacao was a formidable task. Estimates reckon that over thirty-two thousand beans a day were needed to keep the emperor's dependants in chocolate, with over two thousand chocolate drinks a day being served to the soldiers of the Emperor Montezuma's guard alone.

Fray Sahagún wrote that in the markets of Tenochtitlan:

The good cacao seller sells [beans] that are developed, full, round ... firm, each kind selected, chosen. He sells; he seeks out each kind separately. Separately in one place, he sells the developed, the firm ones. Separately the shrunken, the hollow, the broken, the shattered, separately the powdered cacao, the dust; separately the small beans like chilli seeds from Tochtepec; those from Anauac, those from Guatemala, those from Xolteca; he sells those from Cacatollan separately – the whitish, the green, the varicoloured.

And he tells us how this drink was made. The beans were roasted, then ground on a stone *metate* and steeped in hot water. Then a little more water was poured from on high until foam appeared, to which a dazzling array of flavours could be added. Sugar, however, was not known, and so not among them. Occasionally ground cacao was dried into handy tablet form, and added to water when needed.

Cacahuatl was often spiced with chilli or pepper. Vanilla, another indigenous plant, was perhaps the most common flavouring, and there were more enigmatic tastes about which we know very little. The fruits and petals of the exquisite *Magnolia Delabata* were occasionally used, as were the ear-shaped flowers of a plant they called variously *teonacaztli* or *huinacaztli*. We know it as *Cymbopetalum Pendiflorum*, a type of custard apple that is still seen in modern-day Mexico. Its excessive use was not condoned, for it 'excited the testicles'.

Marigold leaves, blossom and wild honey were all part of an enormous repertoire that was not always to the taste of the European invaders. Sahagún tells us that even the bones of ancient people, fossils presumably, were ground and sprinkled on to the drink. Sometimes the brew was black, other times coloured white or pink. Achiote coloured it a deep, luscious red.

Chocolat chaud

Serves 2

Ingredients
100g best (unsweetened) cocoa powder
60g caster sugar
A pinch of cinnamon
A little freshly grated nutmeg
A turn of black pepper
½ vanilla pod split lengthways, or a drop of vanilla essence
A little chilli (optional)
Whipped cream

Method
Bring 300ml water to the boil. Take it off the heat, pour the cocoa, sugar and spices into the pan and whip it all together. Pour from on high into some decorative glasses, and top with whipped cream.

At the beginning of feasts, tobacco would be smoked. Flower-servers gave the guests bundles of exquisite blooms of orchids and huge scarlet flowers. They would eat tamales, quail and roast turkey, always followed by *cacahuatl*.

Not, you will have noticed, *chocolatl*. It seems that the 'ch' sound of chocolate was preferred by blushing Europeans for scatological reasons, the 'cack' of cacao being too similar to the popular word for shit in many of the Romance languages.

But according to Francisco Hernández, the drink that the Mexica knew as *chocolatl* was actually cacao mixed with sapote seeds and ground maize. The diminutive *chocol* came from the Yucatec word for hot, added to the Mexica ending *atl*, or water.

The Mexica also made *cacahuatl* from green, unripened pods, a drink which fermented and caused drunkenness. Not that inebriation was necessarily disapproved of. The nobles and warriors avidly took magic mushrooms, which induced a state of hallucination that they believed gave them the ability to see into the future. Culturally, many Mexica were attracted by this new drink that originated in the conquered lowlands and caused no inebriation at all, but not all were so happy. Some thought it foreign and alien to Mexica culture. You will find curious echoes of all this in eighteenth-century Europe, when coffee, tea and chocolate-drinking took the continent by storm. Tongues were loosened and rulers quaked at the reasoned discussion brought about by these non-alcoholic brews.

The Mexica had their own myths about the

origin of the drink. When their great ruler Motecuhzoma Ilhuicamina dispatched an expedition of wise men, sorcerers and wizards to look for their mythical homeland, Aztlan, they returned with tales of strange lands, habits and customs. After months of arduous travel, they had found Aztlan, an island on a lake, as was their own capital Tenochtitlan. They told the emperor of the remarkable simplicity of life in this ancestral homeland. Bearing gifts for the goddess of the hill, they began to climb the mountain, but found their footsteps became leaden, impossibly heavy, and they struggled in the heat and humidity to reach the top.

Their guide, who appeared to be a feeble old man, leapt spryly to the very summit and mocked the sweating elders. 'Why, what is wrong with you, O Mexica?' he asked. 'What do you eat in your land?'

'We eat the food that grows there, and we drink chocolate,' they answered.

'Ah!' he said. 'Such food and drink has made you heavy and that is why you find it so difficult to reach the place of your ancestors. Those foods will bring death. The wealth you have we know nothing about; we live poor and simply.'

Over the years, the Spaniards have managed to retain their fondness for drinking chocolate. Many who overindulge, and nibble or drink to excess, know to their cost that it does indeed make you heavy. And that none of us, from Mexica to Parisian, find it very easy to live simply.

So familiar has chocolate become that we have all but forgotten the unhappy fact that chocolate, coffee and even tea have particularly grim and bloody foodways, and offer us a murky glimpse of how Europe played the global game and changed the world for ever, long ago in the early sixteenth century. How thoroughly it exploited and abused indigenous American ways, and imposed its culture upon others. It was a comprehensive conquest.

30

Mousse au Chocolat

HOW HONEST ARE WE ABOUT WHAT FOODS WE REALLY like? Are we ever taken in by hype and hyperbole? Of course we are! People who are seriously serious about food can be as easily deceived as everyone else. Fads and fashion can alter the appreciation and the perception of what is good to eat. As can morals.

Horse-meat sales are now in serial decline as the French turn away from its charms, increasingly troubled by consuming a creature that is far more domesticated than the cow, pig or sheep. Parisians have never really learnt to appreciate the taste of lovely well-groomed poodles spit roasted, nor kitten pie. Except, that is, in times of particular hardship. The Paris Commune of 1871 was the last time that either cat, dog or rat was consumed en masse in France. And it was then that the horse first came to be truly appreciated for the sweetness of its flesh.

We have seen how the *hareng saur* of Boulogne is no longer so sour, and observed how stronger tastes seem to be in decline, in France as they are the world over. The extremes of particularity have no place in the twenty-first century.

So what do we make of the idea that the higher the cocoa content of the chocolate the 'better' it is? We all reach for the 70 per cent and higher still, because somewhere this idea has seeped into the culinary consciousness. You taste, and what is it that comes to mind? Tarmac and tobacco. A troubling bitterness, perhaps. Is it really a pleasant experience? It reminds me of the 'big' tannin-rich wines that wine experts become orgasmic about, and which tend to make the average lip just pucker in incomprehension. Ah, they say, you need to be educated to appreciate such things.

Anyway, chocolate. It was on the agenda, honest. On my way back to Brittany from Bayonne, after a radical piece of train juggling, I arrived at the town of Tain-l'Hermitage, better known to most for its (tannin-rich) wines than chocolate, but the base, through a curious story of happenstance, of one of France's – well, let's say the world's – most respected and successful quality-chocolate producers, a company called Valrhona, whose Willy Wonka-ish domain sits right on the River Rhône, to the south of Lyon. And it was there that I was reassured, and pampered with subtleties, and learnt that it was OK to admit to liking chocolate with as little as 64 per cent cocoa content. The relief was palpable.

One day, if you have a spare moment or two, indulge yourself with a little blind chocolate-tasting. Or perhaps chocolate blind-tasting. Buy some of this and that, and include a little of that mass-produced pap, a Hershey Bar, a Galaxy, the forbidden fruit, and nibble. And yes, why not a little chocolate from Valrhona? Strip them of all frippery, of their pretty wrappers and foil and motifs and suggestions, lay them totally naked on a plate, and contemplate. And be honest.

Look at the colour, first of all. Does it shine and glisten? Or is it a lifeless and muddy brown? Hold it a while, feel its solidity, and smell, breathe in. What do you get? A hint and a whisper, or sweet nothing? Break that chocolate. Listen. Does it part in a dull soft tap, or a crisp clean snap? The sharper the noise the better, experts say. It tells us that the chocolate-making process has been expertly carried out. But process is only part of the story. It always is.

Inevitably, perhaps, Valrhona's factory is a magical and blissful place, where try as I did, I simply could not get Willy Wonka's Oompa Loompa song out of my head. I was haunted by it while I was guided past the machines that roasted and stirred and sorted and extracted, then produced endless lines of tablets and bars, and huge slabs of *couverture*, the raw material used by *chocolatiers* and chefs, packed and stacked in a warren of rooms by eager men and women with silly hairnets and ear muffs, and all the time surrounded by the most delectable, warming and comfortingly joyous smell that is chocolate.

At one point we succumbed to temptation, tantalized and tortured by the reality of being entirely surrounded by this, the sexiest of foods. My guide, the company's charming PR lady, picked a tiny little square from the line, accidentally brushing her hand against a red alarm button that caused immediate panic. Men rushed from closed doors and scurried around frowning and tut-tutting, until order was restored and off we went with our tails between our legs to do a little tasting hidden away in a room far away from all this busyness.

And for those who like the idea, chocolate-tasting is actually a job. Yes, you can make a career out of it. There is, there has to be, perpetual analysis of the chocolate that pours through the doors at Valrhona, which involves constant testing and noting and trying new batches to make sure that they really do provide us with the best.

Valrhona's policy is to deliberately avoid playing the world's tempestuous market, snaffling up bargains through bidding wars and trickery, but to use a select few small-scale producers, who work in remote corners of the world, largely with the criollo tree that makes up but a paltry 3 per cent of the world's total cacao production. Finding quality cacao is all about *terroir* again. But far beyond the borders.

And so, back to that tablet. Broken now, you can begin the *analyse sensorielle*. Place a little in your mouth, and the aroma will hit you, or should hit you. Each and every batch has a specific profile that is noted, and not, I was told, judged too hastily, for there are different chocolates for different tastes. Which was when they told me that yes, it was a myth that higher-cocoa-content chocolates are de facto better. It is far more complicated than that.

It is about growing the beans, of course, but it is also a matter of selection. Selecting the best beans is perhaps the one job I covet more than any other. Imagine it. Travelling the world, exchanging information, learning, teaching, tweaking, and then bringing back the beans to be roasted in Tain. What a marvellous job it must be. Some of the world's greatest wine is produced around the corner – the roasted hills of the Côte Rôtie and Condrieu are not far away, the hills of Ardèche are over the river, and then there is Lyon less than an hour by road to the north. There could be worse places in the world to be enchocolated.

But to those cacao pods. There are beans and there are beans. The majority of the world's chocolate is made from the forastero bean, mass produced in Africa and South America, but Valrhona concentrates either on the criollo or the hybrid triniterio bean. But as Pierre Costet, Valrhona's head chocolate-buyer, told me, 'We are not racist! There is bad criollo just as there is good forastero. It's best to avoid characterizing the beans too much. In a way, wine and chocolate are similar. Not in the way they are produced. But just as you cannot say that all chardonnay is bad or good, so not all criollo is good, and not all forastero is bad. It is too simplistic.'

The combination of soil, light and heat, of expertise and culture seep through the very hills in the Rhône valley to produce some of the finest French wines, and the same goes for cacao, just on a wider scale. For its quality is, lest we forget, all down to the tree itself, this hugely successful New World plant, *Theobroma Cacao*.

There is one chocolate of which Valrhona are inordinately proud. It is called Pedrigal, and it comes from a plantation at the foothills of Venezuela, where, Monsieur Costet told me, the most perfect conditions for making great cacao can be found. The soil has proved to be rich and fertile, the humidity just so, the sunlight and shade ideal, and the chocolate that Valrhona produce from the cacao is simply exquisite.

But expensive. Hardly an impulse buy. It is thoughtfully and elaborately packed in baroque swirls and presented in luscious packages – a pity, I think, for it deserves to be tasted by one and all. Divine and subtle, it is significantly lacking in bitterness, and positively scintillates with its notes and indescribable flavours. Taste it and I suspect you will be forever smitten, if you are ever to be smitten at all. Back home, we all nibbled in communal bliss and cast the poor old industrial chococrap into the bin. Until we ran out of Pedrigal.

Valrhona look after their producers as a matter of course. It is very much in their interest to do so, for it is the producer who is responsible for the first key process – fermentation, carried out under his careful eye, to the standards that the buyer requires.

It was quite refreshing to see just how small scale the producers actually were. And how they thought on their feet. One would construct a wooden shelter, a hut, a grill here and there to help the fermentation along. Others would follow suit. Low-cost technology, if successful, can easily be transplanted elsewhere.

Being a tropical plant, cocoa ripens at different times, so there isn't really a season as such. Production increases in the six months following the end of the rainy season, when the pods begin to darken and redden, and the pulp inside that contains the beans – which are seeds, of course – oozes out from the pods as they are laid out to dry in the sun. They are then taken off to ferment, which takes about five days in all.

First the natural sugars turn to alcohol, then to acid. It all sounds a little brutal, but without it, or if the fermentation is too quick, too long, too hot, too anything in fact, the beans do not develop that subtlety.

So, sacks of fermented beans are shipped across the world, and when they arrive at Tain they are immediately analysed and rigorously tested. Indeed, so rigorous is the examination that it is almost an interrogation. I stumbled across one white-coated technician slicing through the beans with one of the world's last working guillotines, a delightful fierce desktop model that shot through the poor beans with a razor-sharp thud.

'We need to look at the colour, and see if they have veins running through the bean. That's a sign of good quality.' The humidity is tested, the acidity level is noted, and only then will the shipment be cleared and the beans sent off for a jolly good roasting.

So, let the roasting begin. Slowly and steadily, the beans are tumbled and turned, clattering around a great noble machine that has the solidity of age, and a suitable array of lights and alarms in case of malfunction. The noise is truly awesome.

Then on to the concassing machine, where the shells are removed and collected in bags and buckets and bins to be carted off as mulch, or fed to animals. 'The beating heart of the process,' they said. And all that are left are broken beans, the nibs, bereft of shell, but ready to be pulverized and mixed once more – with beans from elsewhere, perhaps – to make a blend. Would you still want to be a bar of chocolate?

At last you are left with something that begins to resemble that divinely unctuous substance we know as chocolate. The *grué*, as it is called, a thick, brown and deliciously scented mass that has a hint of acid, but a freshness and a clarity that is utterly beguiling. It was this that the conquistadores found being drunk by the nervous Mexica in tall foamy cups. Their love for *cacahuatl* was dangerously profound. They were institutional chocoholics.

But there was more processing to see. On to the *pétrissage*, the blending of sugar and milk in varying degrees that makes the fundamental raw material, the *pâte*. This paste will then be fiddled and fine-tuned according to infinitely precise and well-practised formulae to become the chocolate that we know and love.

So that is what happens to any lucky criollo bean that enters the domain of chocolate heaven that is Valrhona. I left laden with gifts and books and pamphlets, and set off back to Brittany to make the most spectacular *mousse au chocolat* I have ever tasted.

Mousse au chocolat

Serves 4

Ingredients
200g best bitter-sweet chocolate. Valrhona's Le Noir
Gastronomie does fabulously
4 eggs
1 soupspoon sugar
50g unsalted butter cut in dice

Method
Break the chocolate into little pieces and melt in a
bain marie, or in a bowl over hot water. Separate
the eggs, put egg whites into one bowl and the
yolks and sugar into another and work them
together. Add the butter to the melted chocolate,
and melt. Then add the yolks and sugar and mix
well. Allow to cool.

Beat the egg whites to stiff peaks and incorpo-
rate delicately into the mixture, running a spatula
from the outside of the bowl to the middle, until all
is well mixed.

Pour into individual glasses, and cool in the
fridge for three hours.

31

Caramel au Beurre Salé

FOR THIS PART OF THE JOURNEY WE ARE BACK IN Brittany. The wind is howling, as it so often does, and the waves crashing but metres away. I push open a door, and all is calm and quiet inside.

Heads look up. 'Bonjour, monsieur.'

The shop sparkles with light, as smart white-coated smiling women serenely glide around, delicately plucking the odd chocolate here, a little caramel there, their hands encased in the finest white gloves. It is part operating theatre, part plain theatre.

A man with a heavy Tropezian tan, a little dog and a pink cashmere sweater draped over his (not the dog's) shoulders hesitates, while his wrinkled and extravagantly lipsticked mother goads him to excess. Both are being expertly guided through the complexity of the lines of chocolates arranged in military precision.

'*Les ganaches sont ici, messieurs-dames.*' That lovely fusion word with which shopkeepers address any man and woman who enter.

'*Voici un petit échantillon d'une nouveauté, avec du citron vert confit à l'intérieur.*' A creation of the house. Confit of lime.

With much cajoling and teasing from his mother, he follows the pristine-gloved hands over the works of Monsieur. It is like buying diamonds in Tiffany's, only here the heavy scent is of sweetness and subtlety. Even his Yorkshire Terrier is drooling.

It is nearly a wrap when Maman, thinking perhaps how annoying it would be to have to come back from Paris within the month, says, 'Ah, we mustn't forget your *caramels au beurre salé*!' And the eyes of le Yorkshire widen. Her son smiles; and off goes Madame to pluck a few more willing sacrifices for the bag.

This everyday scene of chocolate-loving folk is set in Quiberon, famous for its bracing sea air, its oysters, and an eighteenth-century massacre of Royalist Chouans by Republicans. Sticking rather provocatively into the Breton ocean, the peninsula is pounded and thrashed by wind, seaweed and sand, as are the many enthusiasts of what the French call *thalassothérapie* who travel from the far-distant arrondissements of Paris, paying vast sums to be plastered in rejuvenating mud, slapped with seaweed, hosed down and boiled, all in the name of '*forme*' and well-being.

So popular has the town become that in summer you can spend hours stuck in a traffic jam just getting there, and then compare notes to see who has beaten the *embouteillage* record. In the town's luxurious *thalassothérapie* hotels, guests wander through the corridors looking for their *curiste* while cosseted in spectacularly white fluffy gowns, which they are no doubt tempted to pack away in their Louis Vuitton suitcases. The twenty-first-century cure may be less of a social whirl than that of the seventeenth century, but there is life after seaweed sessions, and the starved and weak-willed creep off into the town centre to write postcards home and buy chocolate.

Quiberon could be just the place for you, if when you reach the inevitable level of ennui you wish to return to the world of temptation, for the town just happens to have one of the country's finest *chocolatiers*, Henri Le Roux, or to be more exact one of the country's best *chocolatiers caraméliers*, for Monsieur Le Roux is as famous for his caramels as his chocolate.

Imagine the scene on an average day. The wind is noisily destroying the beach, and lobsters hang on grimly to the rocks. Seagulls are hurled mercilessly past the shop windows by the breeze, and the usual gaggle of Breton seaside shops tempt you with soup bowls marked Hervé and Mathilde, Gwendoline and Arthur.

A few intrepid souls, now slimline and buzzing

with health and vitality, tinged with tan and iodine, are resolute in their willingness to join the real world once more, determined to keep that healthy glow that only seaweed-thrashing creates. They immediately seek out Maison Le Roux.

This is a shop well worth a detour. I had stopped and shopped there a few times on trips from nearby Vannes, and observed their professionalism long before I was allowed behind the scenes to talk with Monsieur and nod respectfully to Madame. This morning, it was on through the doors and into the *laboratoire*, where I was ushered in to see an artisan at work. The skilled professional *chocolatier* seldom walks alone. His skills are as much in man management as in the craft, and Monsieur Le Roux was surrounded by a team of devoted white-coated *chocolatiers* and apprentices, carrying out his orders in remarkable silence.

It was a bizarre contrast to a restaurant kitchen, where clatter and pans and testosterone fly from the walls and the atmosphere is of a car almost careering out of control around the trickiest of bends. Here all was calm, and the concentration was profound while the storm raged outside.

If ever you grimace at the cost of finely crafted chocolates, be reassured there is no trickery, no greedy profiteering at Maison Le Roux. The raw materials are expensive, but it is the *main d'oeuvre*, the delicate intense labour that goes into each and every chocolate, that astonished me.

Hunched over a slowly turning belt lined with chocolates, two of his *commis* lightly touched the top of every chocolate, marking it, branding it with its own significant design. There were no machines that squidged and splodged gobs of chocolate, no hugely clinking production lines. No, this is the world of the skilled artisan.

Mass-produced chocolate-making is almost entirely mechanical, banal and boring. Since Napoleon portrayed the British as a nation of shopkeepers, British shops have been gobbled up by corporations of colossal size. Real shopkeepers live on in France. Artisans of taste, they thrive on the pursuit of excellence, men and women who practise a skill, who belong to no one other than a bank manager or two, and who are free to create, re-create and continually improve without having to consult focus groups or personnel departments.

Skills are handed on. The experts circulate among themselves and feed off the spirit of creativity. There is a long line of knowledge that is built upon and questioned, and all in the name of perfection. A nation without artisans is a dull and boring place, so may their artisanal skills live long and flourish.

Tucked into quiet corners, Le Roux's apprentices worked with their brows furrowed and hands delicately poised. And the rhythm of their work was different from that of a restaurant kitchen, too. As well as the eerie quietness, there was no sense of the diurnal climax of approaching service, when voices raise their tone and tempo, sweat drips and adrenalin rushes.

'The wonderful thing about being a *chocolatier* is that at five o'clock we can all go home,' I was told.

Henri Le Roux pulled a chocolate from the belt and slipped it over to me. As I bit, that complex combination of tastes rushed into the curious, anonymous part of my brain that deals with the world of yum. For those used only to the square caramel with its diagonal mark, the strawberry cream with its nipplish finish, let me say that the sensations were quite different.

It is a lesson for us all that, if we are to enjoy taste, then unhurried food made by hand, with care and with attention to the quality of the raw material, will rejuvenate those jaded taste buds, reawaken – awaken, even – that mysterious pleasure and the appreciation of something that truly has finesse. Be it a pastry, a chocolate or a well-hung slice of meat. Time and attention to detail cannot be replaced by deceptive packaging and adverts.

I asked Monsieur Le Roux how, after so many years, he can still be inspired, creative.

'Well, I travel. I need to be able to taste what is being done elsewhere. And to think about how we can combine spices and chocolates from all over the world. I constantly seek to be better.' A reflection of the global inevitability of good food.

Le Roux took me into his chocolatey boudoir, his dry store room, and we began a quick geographical *tour du monde*, tasting an extraordinary range of chocolate. Within minutes we had crossed from the remote African island of São Tomé right across the Atlantic to Venezuela, tasting samples from solid slabs of *couverture*. It is a salivating experience. It demands concentration, and some of the chocolate was almost too bitter to appreciate. Too much of that tarmac and tobacco. It made me recall ancient cinemas thick with smoke. I wasn't sure whether this was quite what was intended.

'Ah, but remember in here we have a thousand different tastes. This is my artist's palette, the raw material, and the combinations can be almost endless. So if you think that this tastes maybe too powerful, then I will say we will add some of this and some of that. In my head I am constantly thinking about what flavours will work together, and even then I will change, and add, and . . .'

'Tinker,' I added in English. Artisans are tinker men.

Fascinated by the alluring subtleties of spices, Le Roux uses Szechuan pepper to marvellous effect. An echo of the original Mexica way with chocolate. He combines thyme in a gentle ganache with the *citron vert*. All is delicate. Gratuitous shock is out. He even manages to make bitter almonds, one of the only foods, apart from pears, that I cannot stomach, almost edible.

But not all his inspiration comes from abroad. The grainy taste of Breton buckwheat is imaginatively harnessed, but it is what he has done to caramel that has perhaps given Le Roux his greatest claim to fame. He is credited with creating the *caramel au beurre salé*, or *le CBS*, a caramel made of salted Breton butter. It is a brilliant combination.

But, like the modest man that he is, Le Roux admits that it is perhaps wrong to say that it is purely his 'invention'. The *CBS* has leapt to fame, and is now so commonplace, so abused, that perhaps Le Roux's modesty is wise.

'Who is to say that I really invented it,' he told me. 'Maybe there was someone long ago who made *CBS*. But one thing I will tell you. I know everyone around here now makes it. You see them in all the tourist shops, but nobody knows exactly how we make them here. And that is something that I will always try and keep secret.'

Which was a pity, for I thought he might have been on the verge of telling me how they were made. But one has to respect secrecy: there will be no recipe in this chapter. I think it would be truly presumptuous to try and re-create the work of a true artisan. Get yourself to Quiberon instead. It is far easier.

32

Clafoutis

Le Temps des Cerises
Quand nous en serons au temps des cerises,
Et gai rossignol et merle moqueur
Seront tous en fête,
Les belles auront la folie en tête,
Et les amoureux du soleil au cœur.
Quand nous chanterons le temps des cerises
Sifflera bien mieux le merle moqueur.

Jean-Baptiste Clément, 1867

When cherry time comes,
And the cheerful nightingale and mocking
  blackbird
Both celebrate,
The beautiful will have happiness in their heads,
And lovers the sun in their hearts,

When we will sing of cherry time,
The mocking blackbird will sing even more
    beautifully.

IT IS CHERRY TIME. REACH INTO THE DEEP, DAPPLED shade of these ancient trees and tug a cherry gently from the branch. Still, warm and bouncing with juice. Fat, lush, glowing purple, they invite you to take a bite and await that rush of sweetness that lashes the tongue with its purity and simplicity. Ah, cherries, the most seductive of fruits!

One late afternoon in June, I was walking through the orchards of one of France's oldest biodynamic farms, the last stop in this jagged fugue, a little way from Orléans.

Only weeks away now from our wedding, I had set off to see Claire's aunt, who just happens to run this magical farm that has bitter-sweet memories for the family. So yet another train under the Channel, a fleeting trip across Paris, then a rush down through the flat and fertile land that surrounds the city of light with its very own backyard larder. The train scuds across the rich alluvial earth that has been providing Parisians with fruit and grain for millennia, before it pulls in at Orléans.

It all seemed so easy. Early morning in London, late lunch in Orléans. This time there is time for me to talk, and walk through the cherry orchard, something that I had long dreamed of but had never yet found time to do. Our visits are rare get-togethers, for family birthdays as a rule.

There is something very particular about these cherries. They are pure and happy, never once sprayed with mysterious man-made chemicals. Some were even crawling with little grubs that were merrily chomping away at the flesh. They were allowed to chomp unmolested. These were creatures that had outwitted the system. They had chosen well. Biodynamics doesn't do death and slaughter. It is far more cerebral. More, as they say in French, *raisonné*. Reasoned.

'Well, it happens. You cannot expect everything to be perfect on a biodynamic farm,' Catherine Carré told me. 'And anyway, the trees are getting old now. So maybe they will have to be replaced next year. We shall see.' She spoke in hushed tones, so as not to offend the trees.

Les Perrières has been biodynamic since 1964, and has remained so, apart from a little blip in the 1970s when they went organic, until the present day. Catherine has lived on her own since the untimely death of her husband, Michel, who in one of life's cruel ironies died of cancer in his early fifties, despite the purity of his life and beliefs. He had nurtured this farm with his very being, and lives on in the soil.

Every year, at cherry time, the phone begins to ring with real urgency, and at all hours. Cherry-pickers seeking work hear on the grapevine that the cherries are ripe, and no doubt rejoice that they are pesticide free. The pickers are mostly local students from Orléans, although Moldovans, energetic Balts and even Poles have in previous years travelled from afar to try their luck. But these latter, since becoming official Europeans, have, according to xenophobes and chauvinists anyway, now become plumbers, depriving their poor old French counterparts of their living.

So come May and June, the orchards burst into a babel of tongues and box upon box of cherries slowly fill the enormous fridge, awaiting delivery. Some are sold locally, others are sent off to Rungis, on the routine Paris run. The region has long served as a vast market garden for this most exacting of cities.

Recently an organic box scheme started in the area, helping the locals fulfil their fruit and veg quota every week. All the produce is locally grown. A few cherries go there. On Fridays, the farm opens to the public, who flock in their controlled droves to stock up on biodynamic produce for the week. And yes, that week it was cherries. But trade is becoming more diverse. Cheese is now sold in thick oozing rounds; cakes and bread made from bio-dynamic produce help fill the farm-shop shelves.

Les Perrières vibrates with *vie*. Come in blossom time and you will be utterly seduced by the rows of peach trees, the *pêches de vigne*, and amazed at the thick powerful tangling stems of the kiwi, which begin to emerge like a twisted kraken. There are hundreds of apple trees, rows of pears and quinces, as well as these most sublime cherries that explode in vigorous colour.

The cherries are the first to fruit. The earliest are the Burlat, the very variety that I had tasted in Marseilles a few weeks before. Then come Van and Durona. Sweet cherries these, exacting fruit to grow, but how lovely it is to see a true cherry orchard. There are no nets here to keep the birds away. Perhaps there is enough for all. And not a single chemical. No pesticides, no artificial fertilizers.

Cherry-picking is demanding work. You need ladders to climb to the top of some of the older trees, but this is considered far too dangerous by the Eurocrats, who have forbidden cherry-picking at any height greater than three metres. Soon we will only see dwarf trees and watch as these ancient cherry orchards are grubbed up.

But there is more than fruit on the farm. Set away from the orchards are fields with clean and serried lines of vigorous green lettuces, salads with touches of brown, and the frizzy mauve of lollo rosso, a spectacular palette of colour. The carrots with their deep-green fronds and bright-orange roots looked perfect. I bent down and pulled one from the sandy soil, and nibbled like a crazed rabbit, overwhelmed by the cleanliness of its taste.

There was carnage among the cabbages. An entire row was being quietly destroyed by a gaggle of happy caterpillars. It made me think of home, and my constant war with nature on my allotment. I have struggled for years against creatures of various hues and shapes, refusing as a matter of principle to use anything toxic. And so along come the predators. Flying ones, long-toothed ones, mice, deer, partridges. Every time I pass a vast field of cabbages I wonder why they are all so damned perfect. A conventionally grown cabbage can be sprayed up to ten times in its brief life, and fields are routinely kept clear of weeds by herbicides. Not here, though. It was in a way rather reassuring to see these touches of imperfection.

As evening approached, all seemed so serene and the last thing either Catherine or I wanted was to get into a car and eat dinner elsewhere. So we pulled up a lettuce, cut a few chives, a little parsley and some chervil, fetched some eggs, still warm, fresh and yolky, and sat down to eat under the setting sun, with the dog slumbering and slavering a little and the chickens gently clucking in the distance.

An omelette, a salad, a cherry clafoutis and a glass of biodynamic wine. Awesome.

Clafoutis

Serves 6

Ingredients
750g cherries
100g flour
75g butter

4 eggs
1 glass Eau de Vie de Kirsch
400ml milk
150g sugar
A pinch of salt

Method

Wash the cherries and leave them to marinate in the *eau de vie* for an hour.

Meanwhile, slowly melt the butter and leave it to cool a little. In a bowl mix together the flour and the salt. Add the eggs and the melted butter, and mix until smooth. Then gradually add the milk, mixing continuously.

Preheat the oven to 180°C.

Grease a shallow oven dish with the butter. Strain the cherries, reserving the marinade, and place them in the dish.

Add the marinade to the cake mixture and whip to aerate. Pour over the fruit and bake for 30 minutes.

Sprinkle with icing sugar, and serve warm.

Catherine in a sense works with a shadow beside her.

'I met Michel on the ski slopes in the Alps, and we realized that we lived only half an hour away from each other. I was still living with my parents then in the butchery at Châteaudun, so we began to see more of each other, and fell in love. Of course he had told me that he was a farmer, but I had never heard of biodynamics, so when I saw what was going on here I was fascinated. It was his father, Pierre, who started to farm this way, because he felt it was more natural. He was never happy using chemicals, and biodynamics seemed to work well. That was back in 1964. We didn't get married until the eighties so everything was working well when I came along.'

Since Michel's untimely death, life hasn't been easy for Catherine. The loss and the loneliness are hard to bear. They will never grow old together, and see their three children grow and become adult in turn. The circle has been broken.

Now Catherine juggles running the farm with her other job as *première adjointe* of her local commune of St Hilaire, which has its own demands and responsibilities. But she unquestioningly sticks to the biodynamic way with passionate enthusiasm.

Her approach seems perhaps too accepting to me at times. I come along and want to know all the answers, and pummel her with whys. In a typically British empirical way, I take the good and reject the bad. I am, in fact, a classic cherry-picker.

'You know, I cannot understand everything about how biodynamics works. I just accept that it does, without necessarily understanding it or questioning it,' she told me with steely Cartesian logic.

Often represented as a more rigorous version of

organics, biodynamic agriculture shares with it a fundamental belief in the importance of the fertility of the soil. Treat it well, and plants will grow, be productive and healthy, and able to resist disease. Abuse it, distort its natural balance, and plants become weak and prone to disease, and dependent upon the chemical crutch provided by what is called conventional agriculture. You know the one. It has been poisoning the environment for decades now.

But as farming is essentially a far from natural business, both organics and biodynamics have developed particular tools that boost productivity and fight disease. Only they are not made from synthetic chemicals. This is an important distinction. Man-made chemicals do not necessarily break down in the environment, and can be highly toxic. But that doesn't mean that chemicals are simply never used in either organics or biodynamics. Copper, for instance, is allowed. Derris is a natural insecticide and is permitted, despite being as unselective as many synthetic chemicals. Both are elemental, and as such can be absorbed and broken down by the soil. Synthetic chemicals often degrade very slowly, and can combine with each other in unpredictable ways.

Biodynamics is in a way organics plus. *Pur et dur*. It attaches great importance to the action of the moon and the stars, and accepts that our planet is part of a cosmos that has energies which can be used beneficially when producing food. Although such ideas were originally mentioned by the 'father' of biodynamics, Rudolf Steiner, they were made more concrete by Maria Thun in the twentieth century, who created a planting calendar that is absolutely crucial to biodynamic farming. It has biblical importance. Thun is a biodynamic heroine who systematized the differences in growth that she observed in plants that were sown over a succession of days, noting the results against the particular lunar and sidereal positions of the time.

And there were indeed clearly observable patterns. As the moon approached its apogee – the closest it can get to us, in other words – more energy appeared to be transmitted to the earth, favouring the germination of seeds. And as it moved towards its perigee, the furthest point from the earth, so this energy favoured leaf plants and the transplanting of seedlings.

Now if you accept that the cycle of the moon has an effect, then why not the stars? After all, we know that the sea moves with the tides, and our sanity seems to fluctuate with the moon, so it is perhaps no great leap of faith to accept that there may well be a deeply primal energy out there that could be usefully harnessed. And no, we don't understand it. Biodynamics simply systematizes it.

Although we can plot the approach of the moon quite simply, the planetary or sidereal calendar is more complicated. It has a different cycle, which relates to the time it takes for the earth to rotate to face the same point in the zodiac. To be precise, 23 hours, 56 minutes and 4 seconds.

Maria Thun's calendar does the hard mathematical bit for you, and is published neatly colour coded. So you can see when it is the best time to plant and to transplant, when to harvest and even when to pick flowers. All the complexity is removed. But there is more to biodynamics than an elaborate calendar. There are those curious preparations to grapple with, for example. Particularly preparations 500 and 501, which sound worryingly bizarre to the uninitiated. There are nine recommended biodynamic preparations that are added in minute, homoeopathic quantities, and are energized by constant stirring, either by hand or machine, in a barrel (wooden, preferably) of rainwater. The motion creates a vortex, and by creating a vortex you are again harnessing natural energy. These preparations can be ruined by using tap water, which is tainted by the addition of nasty chemicals. However, they can now be bought separately, made by others with more time. They should in theory be used quickly, within hours, sprinkled and sprayed at a density of sixty litres per hectare.

As far as what is actually in these preparations, now this becomes truly magical. Preparation 500 involves placing some fresh cow manure inside the horn of a (dead) cow – a biodynamic cow, of course – and burying it for the winter. The horn is made essentially from silicon, one of the most fundamental elements of the earth, and is said to concentrate energy. Preparation 501 is considerably less sexy than a pair of Levis. Quartz is placed inside a horn this time, and then buried through the summer.

Now I have to admit that I am smitten by the idea of producing food biodynamically, and am struggling with potions and piles of manure myself. Not quite as I write, but on the allotment. It works. And that appeals. But I do react a little vigorously to the idea that biodynamics is an invention created by a wise seer like twentieth-century free-thinker Rudolf Steiner. It seems to me that what he has really done is to popularize folk culture. Steiner learnt much from the Austrian and Slovak farmers he met in his youth, who had arrived at a system that produced ample healthy food without the need for pretty labels and nostalgic marketing.

And even if I, a fascinated outsider, find preparation 500 hard to swallow, I also have difficulty understanding telephones and televisions. Nor do I fully understand quite why nitrogen enhances plant growth. I guess I, too, just have to 'accept that it works'.

The idea that there are intrinsically powerful forces in nature was hardly new, but by the beginning of the twentieth century, agriculture had been compartmentalized as a scientific discipline, to be studied and practised by qualified experts, and it began to lose touch with indigenous knowledge, an understanding of the planet that came from thousands of years of observation. Biodynamics is essentially a world view that is in stark opposition to the dominant scientific, modern way of farming, which, using science as its tool, presumes that man can master, control, dominate and subjugate nature. Farming has become a battleground.

Ironically, some of the tools of modern farming were born from the bloodiest of conflicts. An array of mighty weapons, chemicals and fertilizers emerged from the First World War. Organophosphates became pesticides. Tanks became tractors. The nitrogen and phosphorous that were manufactured to kill were adapted to become fertilizers. They are now used to make bombs. The circle goes around.

Machines were improved. Crop rotation was more widely practised. Marshland was drained and turned to production. Cattle were bred to become over-muscled, almost immobile, but boy, did they produce. Milk squirted in profusion from the udders of the world's most ubiquitous cow, the Friesian, which began its domination of the fields and swards of Europe. But as so often, progress was not quite so simple.

There was a heavy price to be paid. Intensive agriculture has removed animals from the land and allowed a valuable resource, manure, to run off into the water system, polluting it into nitrogenous overkill. As Monsieur Madec and his oysters in Aber-

Wrac'h know to their cost. 'Conventional' agriculture then adds missing fertility in the form of chemicals.

If we need convincing about biodynamics, then we should look perhaps at viticulture and its love for *terroir*. With France so profoundly shocked by the world's incomprehensible and growing disinterest in its wine, and its distaste for fearsomely complicated, user-unfriendly wine labels and crazy over-production, French wine-producers are also seeking solace in *terroir*. It is their life raft. The one thing that is impossible to reproduce is that particularity, the character of wine, of cheese, of produce that grows with the soil and is of the soil.

Can I convince you that biodynamics actually works? We have to be clear, first of all, what 'works' actually means. That it produces crops is self-evident, as is the fact that they are produced without damaging the environment. But are, say, the biodynamic cherries produced at Les Perrières any better than conventionally produced cherries? This is a tricky area. Taste is highly subjective, so any assessment would have to be done en masse, in verifiable control groups. Same varieties, same freshness, etc.

Research is beginning to show that there may well be substantial and quantifiable differences between conventionally grown and biodynamic produce. Firstly, levels of phytochemicals – antioxidants such as flavanoids in red wine, for example – are significantly higher in biodynamic produce. But there is another area that I find particularly intriguing. At the Swiss Institute for Plant Vitality, experiments have shown that there is a clear difference in the crystal structure of fruit and vegetables that have been grown by bio-dynamic methods compared to their conventional counterparts.

The experiment goes like this. The vegetative matter is mixed with water and copper chloride under tightly controlled conditions, and crystals are allowed to form. When looked at under the microscope, the images are startling. Beautiful florid patterns of balanced and intricate design appear in the biodynamic samples, while in the conventionally produced ones there's just a mess. This imaging has been taken further, and used to compare industrially milled flour with stone-ground, and to compare artificial vitamin C from a supplement with its fresher alternative.

The only problem is in the interpretation. What does it all signify? Well, I cannot say, and nor can anyone else. But there is something in me – call it my indigenous knowledge, call it common sense – that suggests it is significant. And I for one, however cynical I may feel, am happy with that for now. We cannot have all the answers, can we?

33

Croque-en-bouche

JULY THE FIFTEENTH 2006: WEDDING DAY. CLAIRE AND I had chosen to get married the day after the great French national holiday Bastille Day, when the whole country celebrates the Revolution and the glorious threesome, *liberté*, *égalité*, *fraternité*, assuming that all the French relatives would be free. So rellies and friends had duly travelled from far and wide, and converged on time, to pepper our little Oxfordshire village with some *entente* that was really very *cordiale*, and some liquid French *esprit*.

I was back from cherry-picking, feeling exhilarated and biodynamic. I slipped off to visit my couturier, Monsieur Primark, and tried to look smart. On the day, Claire looked staggeringly beautiful, and we set off on foot through the village to get to the church on time.

The sun shone gloriously. It was to be a double whammy. Firstly, Lola was christened by a man with a booming voice and funny clothes, who sprinkled her with water. She took it all in her stride, pleased when he gave her a flaming candle, which Mummy and Daddy would never have dreamt of doing. She is now a devoted Christian.

We exchanged vows, and sang a few hymns, and felt on top of *le monde*, and set off for a day-long bilingual party just down the road in a lovely English garden.

Jean-Paul and Dany were there, of course, and chatted amiably with my madly Francophile mother, who was pleased, I think, at this late stage to have got a little closer to being French.

Régis and Fany had left the noise of cicadas behind in Provence and travelled from Bédoin, laden with *andouillettes* from Madame Jeannot, some fabulously pungent purple garlic, and a baby who was so covered with chicken pox that we were tempted to make him into a *poule au pot* for all and sundry. But rules must be respected. He was far too young.

Régis had never been to Britain before and we wondered quite what he would make of it all, especially as he, like Claire's parents, was unable to say anything really meaningful in English other than Yes, and My tailor is rich. He had lived with the Britain of his imagination all his life. A place of fog and bowler hats and politeness. I ask you! We had often talked about America. He was appalled about Bush, but then weren't we all? But America! One day, he said, he would love to see this strange and distant place. It was a dream of his.

Amazingly, he was absolutely entranced by being abroad. Amazed that the sun shone over here, and that we also knew how to eat and drink. Maybe not to cook, but early days, early days. The beef fell from the bone, it was so tender. The ham was luscious. Ah, jambon de York! It was recognizable. The bread? Well, baguettes, naturally, baked by a French bakery in Oxford. The raspberries? Picked that morning. Cream? Crème fraîche for the French, thick double cream for the others. A little cheese. A British Berkswell ewe's cheese that stunned us all, and a Montgomery's cheddar, plus a farmhouse Brie and a few Camemberts.

The one exception to all this excellence was the wedding cake, a stack of choux pastry buns piled one on top of the other and drizzled with caramel. This is known as a *croque-en-bouche*, 'a snap in the mouth' I suppose you would say if pressed to translate. In France they call it a *pièce montée*.

This surprised me. I had explained what we were going to eat, and that to give it all a French flourish we would finish with a *croque-en-bouche* . . . and no one knew what I meant. It arrived to great fanfare, looked lovely and tasted of cardboard with cream. Here was something that desperately needed the hand of an artisan, a touch of skill and lightness that comes from experience. It was the only thing that disappointed that day. Some things are untranslatable.

Now our village always seems to me to be a pretty everyday sort of place. We have a thriving sense of community, a village shop that struggles and we all worry about, and a hectically cosmopolitan array of people who come from far and wide. Icelanders, Belgians, Italians, Dutch, Finns, Turks and Americans, as well as French. Yet no one has a second home here, and it doesn't suffer from any seasonal dips, except in August when the whole world and their aunt go some-where – many to France, of course, which everyone absolutely loves. Many have second homes there. But people come here to live and work, not just to live. They are all part of the community, and do not live in ghettoized expat outposts. They assimilate.

Over dinner a few days later – our honeymoon was to follow – we had been talking about a recent poll conducted in Britain, admittedly by a French wine consortium, where a staggering 30 per cent of respondents admitted to wishing they were French. But what did they mean? What was their idea of France and the French, anyway? Was it, like mine once was and perhaps still is, a dreamland France of cheap property, swarthy smiling grannies and lovely food? Of wonderful markets and exquisite, affordable restaurants? Whooah there!!

Yes, this *was* the France that I fell in love with all

those years ago, when I sailed across the Channel, an impressionable, avid, innocent traveller, ready to be seduced by this charming, sexy country called France. Now that I had arrived at the end of this journey, this revisitation, it was time for a little synthesis. I loved the France I first saw because it allowed me to see just how dull it was to be English.

So when I take a bite of *pâté de campagne*, it takes me right back to the past and my own private France. My heart still swoons when I see a Citroën DS. Or a bar with a long, wine-stained *zinc* where everybody smoked Gitanes and waited for the phone with *jetons*.

This was the France where outsiders thought that every dog was rabid and the water was undrinkable, and marvelled as people pissed behind curious metal shields while watching the world go by. This was the France of good food, fat chefs and brilliant bread. And yes, it is a France long gone. Now but a folk memory. If I ever feel the need to top up on sentiment, I turn for the DVD and watch Jean-Luc Godard's *A Bout de Souffle* for the millionth time, and marvel at just how incredibly beautiful were Jean-Paul Belmondo and Jean Seberg, just how alluring was her French and his nonchalance. This was my France. Time has brought me closer to the antithesis, the very opposite of this dreamland France, to a country that is riven with *morosité*, depression and self-doubt. To a country that finds itself summarily removed from the head of the league of creativity, in gastronomy at least, and is a little uncertain whether to shrug its shoulders gallically or to reinvent itself as a global benchmark, the alpha male of culinary culture.

It has found some solace in the word *terroir*. *Terroir* sits as the conceptual opposite to globalization, to the standardization of wines and the dominance of particular wine styles. There is still an element in both French food and wine production that feels disdain, verging on real hatred, at the effrontery of outsiders who now dominate a market that the French once thought was theirs by right. First it was food, then wine. Add to this the gradual decline in influence of the French language, and no wonder that there is so much *morosité* in the air. No wonder so many French navels are being contemplated.

Yet the one system that respects the power of *terroir* more than any other is biodynamics. Nicolas Joly, who has become one of France's most vocal supporters of biodynamic production, creates a glorious wine at Coulée de Serrant, and in the Rhône Valley, Michel Chapoutier also produces some marvellous biodynamic wine. So it seems that producing great food and wine is far more than a matter of *terroir*. For not only is the land important, but so are the moon and the stars. The very health of the planet seems to depend upon our recognizing how we are all linked ineluctably together.

I remember how French gastronomy used to bellow its superiority, but I feel easier now that there is an element of circumspection about the way things are. In wine and food. In politics. In everyday life as well. It seems a natural progression that France should accept, be it at times reluctantly, that the world is not a place to be looked down upon and pitied in its ignorance. It has much to offer. But I fear for the future, if France continues to retreat into its shell of introspection, of *terroir*, assuming that there is something physically superior to France and French produce.

For me, the one blinding reality in all this is that it is in production that France has excelled. In the skill of the artisan, the genius of the wine-maker, the baker, the *chocolatier*, the farmer even. The culture of the market still lives on in France, and has the formidable power of tradition to help preserve it. So too does the beauty and the magic of a country that still has a passionate concern for the most beguiling of senses: taste. We can all drink (and eat) to that.

Appendix

Here are the addresses of some *Plats du Jour* favourites
– suppliers, websites and restaurants – all checked and
rigidly assessed by the *Plats* team as being suitable locations for any devoted *terroiriste*.

Brittany

Vannes
Markets on Wednesday and Saturday.

Seafood
Le Chantier
13 Chemin du Passeur
56470 Saint-Philibert

Oysters
Yvon Madec
Prat-Ar-Coum

29870 Lannilis BP9
Tel: 00 33 (0)2 98 04 00 12
Fax: 00 33 (0)2 98 04 49 79

Onions
Maison des Johnnies
48 rue Brizeux
29680 Roscoff (near the station)
Tel: 00 33 (0)2 98 61 25 48
Fax: 00 33 (0)2 98 61 19 38
Email: maisondesjohnnies@wanadoo.fr
Website: www.roscoff-tourisme.com

Chocolate
Chocolatier-Caramélier Le Roux
18 rue de Port-Maria
F-56170 Quiberon
Tel: 00 33 (0)2 97 50 06 83
Fax: 00 33 (0)2 97 30 57 94
Email: info@chocolatleroux.com
Websites: www.chocolatleroux.com,
www.chocolat-leroux.com, www.lerouxquiberon.com,
www.caramelier.com

Normandy

La Mère Poulard
Grande Rue BP 18
50116 Mont-St-Michel
France
Tel: 00 33 (0)2 33 89 68 68
www.mere-poulard.fr

The North

Le Châtillon
6 rue Tellier
62200 Boulogne-sur-Mer
Tel: 00 33 (0)3 21 31 43 95
Fax: 00 33 (0)3 21 87 56 50

Paris

Pierre Gagnaire's Gaya Rive Gauche
44 rue du Bac
75007 Paris
Tel: 00 33 (0)1 45 44 73 73
www.pierre-gagnaire.com

Génération C
Gilles Choukroun can be found behind the stoves at
L'Angl'Opéra, which is part of the prestigious
Hôtel Edouard VII, at:
39 avenue de l'Opéra
75002 Paris
Tel : 00 33 (0)1 42 61 86 25
Fax: 00 33 (0)1 42 61 47 73
www.anglopera.com

Yves Camdeborde runs Le Comptoir/Hôtel Relais
Saint Germain, at:
9 carrefour de l'Odéon
75006 Paris
Tel: 00 33 (0)1 44 27 07 97
Fax: 00 33 (0)1 46 33 45 30
Email: hotelrsg@wanadoo.fr

L'Omnivore
L'Omnivore work closely with Génération C. They can be contacted through their website: www.omnivore.fr

Le Fooding
Check them out at www.lefooding.com

Restaurants
Restaurant du Palais Royal
Jardins du Palais-Royal
110 Galerie Valois
75001 Paris
Tel: 00 33 (0)1 40 20 00 27

Restaurant des Quatre Frères
127 Boulevard de Ménilmontant
75011 Paris
(Metro stop: Ménilmontant)
Tel: 00 33 (0)8 99 78 27 39

Centre

Les Perrières
45160 St Hilaire/ St Mesmin
Orléans
Tel: 00 33 (0)2 38 76 32 66

The South-West

Markets
Markets in the Gers start at ten a.m. in the following places:

Monday: Samatan
Tuesday: Fleurance
Wednesday: Gimont and Condom
Thursday: Eauze
Friday: Seissan
Saturday: day off
Sunday: Gimont

Pierre Accoceberry
SARL Accoceberry
64250 Espelette
Tel: 00 33 (0)5 59 93 86 49
www.accoceberry.fr

Chocolate
Le Musée du Chocolat
14 avenue Beau Rivage
64200 Biarritz
www.lemuseeduchocolat.com

Restaurants
La Tupina
6 rue Porte de la Monnaie
33800 Bordeaux
Tel: 00 33 (0)5 56 91 56 37
Fax: 00 33 (0)5 56 31 92 11
Email: latupina@latupina.com

O Gascon
13 rue du Château
64000 Pau
Tel: 00 33 (0)5 59 27 64 74
Email: ogascon@ipvset.com

Cheese
Go to Aste Béon, and ask for Patrick. They know him at:
L'Etape du Berger
Bourg de Béon
Tel: 00 33 (0)5 59 82 65 58

Estofinado

Restaurant Carrier
Courbies
12300 Almont les Junies
Tel: 00 33 (0)5 65 64 10 41

Musée de la Mine Lucien Mazars
12100 Aubin
Tel: 00 33 (0)5 65 43 58 00

Lyon and the Alps

Restaurants
Chez Paul
11 rue Major Martin
69001 Lyon
www.chezpaul.fr

Carnegie Hall
253 rue Marcel Mérieux
69007 Lyon
Tel: 00 33 (0)8 26 10 11 07

Cheese
La Mère Richard

Halles de Lyon
102 cours Lafayette
69003 Lyon
Tel: 00 33 (0)4 78 62 30 78
At Beaufort itself you are welcome to buy and taste
Beaufort cheese, and even watch it being made at the
Cooperative. Le Syndicat de Défense du Beaufort can
be contacted at:
www.fromage-beaufort.com

Chocolate
Valrhona
Quai du Général de Gaulle
26600 Tain l'Hermitage
Tel: 00 33 (0)4 75 07 90 90
www.valrhona.fr

The South

Le Lunch
Calanque de Sormiou
13009 Marseilles
Tel: 00 33 (0)4 91 25 05 37

Index

INDEX

INDEX

AL DENTE
By William Black

'AL DENTE IS TO ITALIAN FOOD WHAT A MAP IS TO ITALIAN ROADS – ESSENTIAL READING. I LOVED IT!'
Giorgio Locatelli

In *Al Dente*, William Black travels the length and breadth of Italy to get to the roots of Italian food. His dedication to his task knows alarmingly few bounds and he eats whatever gets in his way: cheese enriched with maggots; pasta with donkey sauce; risotto made with seagull broth . . .

His quest for the most delicious and authentic cooking and the very finest ingredients takes him to wonderfully familiar places and hidden delights: he drinks great coffee in Turin, and views the *mattanza*, the annual tuna catch, off the coast of Sardinia. William scoffs eel *brodetto*, and waxes lyrical about frog stew. And as he eats his way to the country's culinary heart, he unearths the fascinating story of his own family's role in Italian history.

'I COULDN'T PUT IT DOWN. THEY HAD TO CALL ME FROM THE KITCHEN. WHEN I WAS READING IT I FELT I WAS ALMOST THERE. IT BROUGHT A TEAR TO MY EYE!'
Gennaro Contaldo

'FOR ANYONE WHO ENJOYS GOOD FOOD, AL DENTE IS A MUST' *Financial Times*

'AL DENTE IS FUNNY, AT TIMES POETIC, AND MOST USEFUL' *Daily Mail*

'A DELICIOUS MIXTURE THAT EVOKES ITALY, BOTH PAST AND PRESENT' *Woman and Home*

'THIS VIBRANT AND WITTY ACCOUNT OF HIS GASTRONOMIC TRAVELS THROUGH ITALY COMBINES MOUTH-WATERING DESCRIPTIONS OF DISHES AND FOODSTUFFS, SIMPLE AUTHENTIC RECIPES AND A TRAVELOGUE THAT IS AS RICHLY OBSERVED AS IT IS FASCINATING'
Economist

9780552999984

CORGI BOOKS

THE FRENCH KITCHEN:
A COOKBOOK
Joanne Harris and Fran Warde

Anouchka, Madame Douazan, Great-Aunt Simone . . .
These are not characters from one of Joanne Harris's
novels, they are the inspiration for a mouth-watering
celebration of French cuisine. For, like Framboise, the
heroine of *Five Quarters of the Orange*, Joanne Harris
has family recipes that have been passed down through
the generations, and she shares them with us now.
From Grandmothers' Festival Loaf to traditional French
classics like Moules Mariniere or Daube of Beef,
The French Kitchen is a tantalizing collection
of casseroles, soups, roasts, salads, tarts and sweets.

A collaboration between a writer who loves food
and a former chef who loves writing about food,
The French Kitchen gathers together simple yet stylish
recipes from the heart of a French family.

9780385604765

Doubleday

SEASONAL COOKING
By Claire Macdonald of Macdonald

'WHOLESOME AND IMAGINATIVE COOKERY'
House & Garden

On the Isle of Skye, Claire Macdonald, with her husband, is famous for her cooking at Kinloch Lodge where the Macdonalds entertain their family, friends and guests. This book is a distillation of Claire's years of cooking on Skye, and the two hundred recipes are a combination of family food and gourmet dishes which blend the use of seasonal ingredients with her own special talent for serving delicious fare.

There are homely soups, pot roasts, pies and puddings juxtaposed with tempting specialities like Chicken and Broccoli in Mayonnaise Cream Sauce, Mushroom, Cheese and Garlic Soufflé and sensational desserts such as Raspberries with Cinnamon Ice Cream or Plum and Port Mousse.

Seasonal Cooking is an irresistible invitation to enjoy fresh country flavours, and a first-class source for every cook who, like Claire, is fascinated by food and loves to eat.

'INSPIRES CONFIDENCE WHILE WHETTING THE TASTE BUDS'
Jocasta Innes, *Sunday Times*

9780552992169

CORGI BOOKS

THE LAND THAT THYME FORGOT
By William Black

Singing Hinnies, tripe, solomongundy, Hindle wakes,
Sussex Pond pudding and flummery. Great names, but
who on earth still eats, let alone cooks, them?
William Black talks to producers and restaurateurs,
visits the great and the awful, and seeks out the country's
disappearing specialities – searching for the heart and
soul of Britain through the food we eat, reclaiming
our very rich culinary tradition.

William goes in search of lobscouse in Liverpool,
finds salmon in the Severn and cheddar in, well, Cheddar.
This journey through the lost traditions of British cuisine is
never less than fascinating. Prepare to be amazed . . .

'WILLIAM BLACK'S BOOK CONFIRMS MY LONG-HELD
BELIEF THAT BRITISH FOOD HAS A HISTORY TO MATCH
ANY OTHER CUISINE IN THE WORLD'
Antony Worrall Thompson

'A FASCINATING TOUR ROUND OUR
FOOD ROOTS . . . I LOVED IT AND SO WILL YOU'
Clarissa Dickson Wright

9780552152099

CORGI BOOKS